HISTORICIZING LIFESTYLE

Historicizing Lifestyle

Mediating Taste, Consumption and Identity from the
1900s to 1970s

Edited by
DAVID BELL
Manchester Metropolitan University, UK
JOANNE HOLLOWS
Nottingham Trent University, UK

ASHGATE

Published by
Ashgate Publishing Limited
Gower House
Croft Road
Aldershot
Hampshire GU11 3HR
England

Ashgate Publishing Company
Suite 420
101 Cherry Street
Burlington, VT 05401-4405
USA

Ashgate website: http://www.ashgate.com

British Library Cataloguing in Publication Data
Historicizing lifestyle : mediating taste, consumption and
    identity from the 1900s to 1970s
    1. Lifestyles - History - 20th century 2. Popular culture -
    History - 20th century 3. Lifestyles in literature
    4. Consumption (Economics) - History - 20th century
    I. Bell, David, 1965 Feb. 12- II. Hollows, Joanne
    306'.0904

Library of Congress Cataloging-in-Publication Data
Historicizing lifestyle : mediating taste, consumption and identity from the 1900s to
1970s / edited by David Bell and Joanne Hollows.
        p.cm.
    Includes bibliographical references and index.
    ISBN 0-7546-4441-3
    1. Lifestyles--Cross-cultural studies. 2. Lifestyles--History--20th century. I.
    Bell, David. II. Hollows, Joanne.

    HQ2042.H57 2006
    306.09182'10904--dc22

                                                                        2005029880
ISBN 0 7546 4441 3

Printed and bound in Great Britain by MPG Books Ltd. Bodmin, Cornwall.

Contents

Acknowledgements   *vii*
List of Figures   *viii*
Notes on Contributors   *ix*

1   Towards a History of Lifestyle   1
    David Bell and Joanne Hollows

2   Science and Spells: Cooking, Lifestyle and Domestic Femininities
    in British *Good Housekeeping* in the Inter-war Period   21
    Joanne Hollows

3   The Restaurant Guide as Romance: From Raymond Postgate   41
    to Florence White
    Janet Floyd

4   Presenting the Black Middle Class: John H. Johnson   54
    and *Ebony* Magazine, 1945-1974
    Jason Chambers

5   The Politics of *Playboy*: Lifestyle, Sexuality   70
    and Non-conformity in American Cold War Culture
    Mark Jancovich

6   Rapture of the Deep: Leisure, Lifestyle and the Lure of
    Sixties Scuba   88
    Bill Osgerby

7   Lifestyle Print Culture and the Mediation of Everyday Life: 108
    From Dispersing Images to Caring Texts
    Sam Binkley

8   Depression and Recovery: Self-Help and America in the 1930s   131
    Sue Currell

9   Pushing Pneus: Michelin's Advertising of Lifestyle   145
    in Pre-World War I France
    Stephen L. Harp

10   Creating 'Modern Tendencies': The Symbolic   156
      Economics of Furnishing
      Tracey Potts

Index   *173*

Acknowledgements

We would like to thank the contributors for their hard work and their patience, and Zhang Pinggong and Malcolm Henson for their work on the index. David would like to thank Joanne for being such a fabulous co-editor, and Mark, Jon, Daisy and Ruth, as ever. Joanne would like to thank everyone at NTU who made her 'admin relief' possible and to thank Ben, who ended up doing more than his fair share of office hours on the food module while the book got completed. Thanks, as usual, to Mark. I am VERY grateful for David's willingness to do the 'techie stuff' on the book – without this, it's quite likely it wouldn't exist!

We would also like to thank those individuals and organizations who gave permission to use copyright material. Every effort has been made to trace copyright holders and to obtain their permission to publish copyright material; the editors and publishers will gladly receive any information enabling them to rectify any error or omission in subsequent editions.

List of Figures

6.1 'Skin Diver Action!': theatre poster for *Underwater!*, 1955   99
6.2 'The Sociables Prefer Pepsi – They Do Lively Things With
     Lively People': advertisement for Pepsi-Cola, 1960   101
6.3 'Nemrod Treasure Hunt Adventure': advertisement for Nemrod
     diving equipment, 1969   103
7.1 Cover of *Living on the Earth* by Alicia Bay Laurel   120
7.2 Cover of *Tassajara Bread Book* by Edward Espe Brown   122
7.3 Cover of *Getting Clear* by Anne Kent Rush   124

Notes on Contributors

David Bell teaches Cultural Studies at Manchester Metropolitan University. His research interests include consumption and lifestyle, science and technology, and urban and rural cultures. His recent books include *Ordinary Lifestyles*, co-edited with Joanne Hollows, and *Science, Technology and Culture*.

Sam Binkley is assistant professor of Sociology at Emerson College, Boston. His forthcoming book, *Consuming Aquarius: Style of Life in the Crisis Decade* (Duke University Press) examines the lifestyle literature of 1970s' counterculture from the perspective of theories of narrative identity and a Foucauldian notion of the ethics of the self. He has also published in the *Journal of Consumer Culture*, *Journal of Material Culture*, *Cultural Studies–Critical Methodologies* and *Consumption, Markets and Culture*. He lives in New York City.

Jason Chambers is an assistant professor in the Department of Advertising at the University of Illinois at Urbana-Champaign. He is currently completing a book examining the contributions of African-Americans to the advertising industry, tentatively entitled *The Black Mirror Makers*.

Sue Currell is lecturer in American Literature at the University of Sussex. She is currently editing a collection of essays on eugenics and popular culture in the 1930s and a biography of self-improvement writer Walter B. Pitkin called *Streamlining the Self: A Cultural Biography of Walter B. Pitkin*. She is author of *The March of Spare Time: The Problem and Promise of Leisure During the 1930s* (University of Pennsylvania Press, 2005).

Janet Floyd is lecturer in American Studies at King's College London. Her research interests lie in the writing of the domestic and in the American West. She has co-edited *Domestic Space* (Manchester University Press, 1999, with Inga Bryden) and *The Recipe Reader* (Ashgate, 2003, with Laurel Forster), and has published a monograph on the writing of the domestic in North American emigrant autobiography, *Writing the Pioneer Women* (Missouri University Press, 2001).

Stephen L. Harp, professor of History at the University of Akron, is currently writing a global cultural history of rubber. His publications include *Marketing Michelin: Advertising and Cultural Identity in Twentieth-Century France* (Johns Hopkins University Press, 2001) and *Learning to Be Loyal: Primary Schooling as Nation Building in Alsace and Lorraine, 1850-1940* (Northern Illinois University Press, 1998).

Joanne Hollows is principal lecturer in Media and Cultural Studies at Nottingham Trent University. She is the author of *Feminism, Femininity and Popular Culture* (Manchester University Press, 2000), co-author of *Food and Cultural Studies* (Routledge, 2004), and co-editor of *Approaches to Popular Film* (Manchester University Press, 1995), *The Film Studies Reader* (Arnold, 2000), *Ordinary Lifestyles* (Open University Press, 2005) and *Feminism in Popular Culture* (Berg, 2006).

Mark Jancovich is professor of Film and Television Studies at the University of East Anglia. He is the author of *Horror* (Batsford, 1992), *The Cultural Politics of the New Criticism* (Cambridge University Press, 1993), *Rational Fears: American Horror in the 1950s* (Manchester University Press, 1996) and *The Place of the Audience: Cultural Geographies of Film Consumption* (with Lucy Faire and Sarah Stubbings, BFI, 2003). He is also the editor of several edited collections, the most recent of which are *Quality Popular Television: Cult TV, the Industry and Fans* (with James Lyons, BFI, 2003) and *Defining Cult Movies: The Cultural Politics of Oppositional Taste* (with Antonio Lazaro-Reboll, Julian Stringer and Andrew Willis, Manchester University Press, 2003).

Bill Osgerby is reader in Media, Culture and Communications at London Metropolitan University. His books include *Youth in Britain Since 1945* (Blackwell, 1998), *Playboys in Paradise: Masculinity Youth and Leisure-Style in Modern America* (Berg, 2001), *Action TV: Tough-Guys, Smooth Operators and Foxy Chicks* (Routledge, 2001), and *Youth Media* (Routledge, 2004).

Tracey Potts is lecturer in Critical Theory and Cultural Studies at Nottingham University. She works on issues of taste, class and material culture, focusing in particular on pathologized taste formations, and is the author of *Critical Thinkers: Bourdieu* (Routledge, forthcoming) and *Kitsch: A Cultural Politics of Taste*, with Ruth Holliday (Manchester University Press, forthcoming).

Chapter 1

Towards a History of Lifestyle

David Bell and Joanne Hollows

Since the 1980s, it has increasingly been claimed that there has been an explosion of lifestyle media across a range of forms such as magazines and television (see Bell and Hollows, 2005). During the same period, the concept of lifestyle has become central to debates about transformations in consumer culture and cultural identities, frequently articulated in relation to shifts identified with post-Fordism and/or postmodernism. Both these trends work to emphasize the extent to which lifestyle media, and practices of lifestylization in everyday life, are largely new phenomena that are the product of recent social, economic and cultural processes.

For example, Mike Featherstone argues that the contemporary preoccupation with the construction of individual lifestyles is a product of a postmodern culture in which there has been an aestheticization of everyday life. 'Rather than unreflexively adopting a lifestyle, through tradition or habit', he argues, 'the new heroes of consumer culture make lifestyle a life project and display their individuality and sense of style in the particularity of the assemblage of goods, clothes, practices, experiences, appearance and bodily dispositions they design together into a lifestyle' (1991: 86). For Featherstone, this seems to imply a radical break with life in the 1950s, a period characterized by 'grey conformism' and '*mass* consumption' (p. 83).

Featherstone is not alone in thinking that the contemporary preoccupation with lifestyle constitutes something radically new. A series of critics have highlighted how recent transformations in consumer culture invite us to play with our identities. It is claimed that identities are no longer fixed and ascribed; instead, consumer culture now offers us the resources to 'play' with identity, developing individual lifestyle projects. For example, Bocock (1993) argues that, in postmodern culture, work is no longer central to identity but instead we construct our identities through consumption and 'leisure-work' (Bell, 2002). Similar arguments can be found in Chaney (2001). For some critics, including Featherstone, this emphasis on lifestyle does not necessarily mean the end of class identities, but rather the heightened importance of consumption in the construction of class identities through lifestyle choices (we return to these issues later in this chapter). However, as Warde (2002) notes, for critics such as Beck, Giddens and Bauman, consumer culture now appears to present us with endless choices of who to be. For example, Giddens argues that late modernity has accentuated a process of 'detraditionalization' so that increasingly 'lifestyle concerns the very core of identity, its making and remaking' (1991: 8).

Similar themes emerge across a range of critics, who also tend to share the idea that there is something radically new going on that constitutes a break with past ways of living. For some, such as Giddens, these changes represent an intensification of the logic of modernity. For others, they are the product of a postmodern culture in which, following Baudrillard, consumer goods now only possess a 'sign value' rather than any intrinsic 'use value', so consumption is opened up as a realm for us to play with identity in a world that has lost any 'real' meaning. Other critics see the contemporary concern with lifestyle which privileges consumption as a response to changes in production. This is the result of a shift from the mass production of mass commodities addressed to the 'mass consumer' associated with Fordist production methods, to a form of flexible and specialized production associated with post-Fordism that highlights the stylistic differences between commodities addressed to niche markets. However, what these critics share is a sense that lifestyle is now central to the organization and experience of everyday life. Lifestyle becomes a way of drawing together 'a range of concepts such as taste, income, health, status, diet, aspiration, subculture and leisure in order to represent everyday life in advanced capitalist cultures as an accretion of *personal style achieved primarily through consumption*' (Jagose, 2003: 109; original emphasis).

However, this preoccupation with the novelty of contemporary lifestyle practices tends to obscure the extent to which processes of lifestylization have a longer history. Just as Don Slater (1997) has charted a long history of commentary on the 'newness' of consumer culture, so the current preoccupation with the newness of lifestyle also has a history (see also Glennie, 1995). Indeed, Jukka Gronow (1997: 32) traces concerns about the increasing emphasis on lifestyle and status in consumer culture back through the work of Vance Packard in the 1950s to Thorstein Veblen at the turn of the twentieth century. Our aim in putting together this book has been to show how the preoccupation with the novelty of lifestyle limits the possibilities for thinking through the continuities, as well as the discontinuities, in people's consumption and lifestyle practices. As Frank Mort (2000: 8) argues

> Understanding the historical processes whereby older hierarchies were transformed and newer ones created by the impact of the commercial domain remains an underdeveloped project for historians of Western Europe [and elsewhere] in the ... twentieth century. ... [A] single unified chronology, which focuses exclusively on the post-war decades, is unhelpful in this respect.

The level of abstraction at which many of the debates about the novelty of lifestyle has operated masks a more complex historical picture (Trentmann, 2004) by working to suggest a radical rupture or 'big bang' in which lifestyle suddenly became important.

Therefore, *Historicizing Lifestyle* seeks to show how 'lifestyle' as a concept and as a set of practices has evolved over time, progressively over-writing 'tradition'. In too many accounts, lifestyle explodes onto the social scene, either in the 1950s or 1960s as a result of mass consumption or in the 1970s or 1980s as a result of post-Fordism. But these decades do not mark grand historical ruptures; they are the culmination of processes with a much longer historical reach. The chapters that follow maintain a dialogue with theories of modernity and postmodernity but also offer a concrete analysis of the specific ways in which ideas about lifestyle have been mediated at particular moments in specific contexts. As Mort (2000: 7-8) argues, there is a need to move 'away from historical generality and towards specificity' and to investigate 'the impact of the expanding world of goods on historically specific aspects of social identity and subjective experience'. In the process, some of the chapters highlight how abstract theories of lifestyle have been blind to forms of difference. For example, in chapter four, Jason Chambers demonstrates how middle-class African Americans were excluded from constructions of the middle-class 'mass consumer' in the 1950s. Likewise, in chapter two, Joanne Hollows problematizes the idea that 'traditional' identities were based on paid work, showing how this produces a gender-blindness in many conceptualizations of lifestyle. Frequently, theories of lifestyle have highlighted the construction of identity through consumption practices, 'leisure-work' and domestic space as something distinctly new. However, this ignores a longer history of women's participation in the construction of classed and gendered lifestyles through both domestic labour and 'leisure-work' in the private sphere.

Furthermore, the history of cultural policy shows how concerns about the uses of non-work-time placed emphasis on productive leisure, for example through the idea of rational recreation, where cultural institutions such as museums and parks were established to provide 'improving' experiences for working people (Thompson, 1997; Rojek, 2000). In Britain in the second half of the nineteenth century, non-work practices became made over as 'leisure work' – in opposition to 'idle leisure' (Bell, 2002) – marking the colonization of non-work time by the logic of production. At the same time, leisure also became colonized by the logic of consumption, as Victorian commodity culture developed. As Thomas Richards (1990) shows, events such as the 1851 Great Exhibition consolidated the central role of commodities as culturally communicative, by exhibiting national cultures through material objects. At the same time, advertising was expanding to find new ways of mediating consumerism, based increasingly on the sign value of goods. The connections between consumer culture and rational recreation during this period gave birth to the very idea of lifestyle, in terms of ways of living that utilize the sign value of commodities and connect this with evaluative judgements of, or distinctions between, different socio-economic groups. As we shall see later, however, this does not mean that lifestyle is wholly tied to consumerism; while it has been progressively expressed through commodities, there have also been other important 'sites' for the fostering of lifestyles, such as the sphere of education (Gunn, 2005).

Mediating Lifestyle

If lifestyle has been seen to have a new significance in contemporary culture, then the rapid growth of lifestyle media has been understood as a response to this. In a world in which there is allegedly an overwhelming array of choices to be made in our everyday lives, lifestyle media can be understood as guides to what and how to consume, and select from, a vast array not only of goods but also of services and experiences. Lifestyle media offer the opportunity to 'make over' our lives and our selves (Moseley, 2000), demonstrating how we can both morally and aesthetically *improve* ourselves. While this emphasis on improvement has been linked to the increasing aestheticization of everyday life, it also has clear links back to earlier forms of rational recreation mentioned above (Holliday, 2005).

    While there has been a relative academic neglect of lifestyle media – perhaps because, as Frances Bonner (2003) suggests, they are just *too ordinary* – there is now an emergent body of work on contemporary lifestyle media (see, for example, Bell and Hollows 2005; Brunsdon *et al.*, 2001; Palmer, 2004; Strange, 1998; Taylor, 2002). The preoccupation with the novelty of lifestyle media has meant that a longer history of lifestyle formats has been overlooked (O'Sullivan, 2005). However, critics such as Charlotte Brunsdon (2004) have begun to explore generic shifts over time within lifestyle media. For example, she identifies the differences between contemporary DIY television shows and those shown in postwar Britain, noting how the earlier shows were marked by a 'realist aesthetic' and unfolded in 'real-time', demonstrating the investment of time, skill and labour demanded by DIY projects. There has been a clear shift from the emphasis on the acquisition of skills in postwar television programming (Brunsdon, 2001) to the range of forms and types, not to mention quantity, of lifestyle television today (see Bell and Hollows, 2005). While there has been work on historical shifts in forms such as women's magazines (for example, Winship, 1987) and cookery writing (for example, Jones and Taylor, 2001; Mennell, 1996), there has been less attention paid to continuities and discontinuities between these forms as lifestyle media. Therefore, this collection seeks to demonstrate not only how lifestyle has a history, but also how lifestyle media have a history. The chapters that follow discuss how ideas about lifestyle are mediated across a range of forms, from magazines and 'whole-earth' cookbooks, to self-help manuals and restaurant guides. Other chapters also consider the more specific role of advertising and marketing in mediating ideas about lifestyle and educating their audiences in specific dispositions towards consumption.

    Anthony Giddens' work offers one way of understanding why lifestyle media become crucial guides to living within, and with, modernity. For Giddens, the processes of detraditionalization associated with modernity mean that people increasingly come to rely on forms of expert knowledge and guidance in constructing projects of the self – a self increasingly constructed through consumption practices (Slater, 1997). While Giddens believes that these processes are amplified in late modernity, he acknowledges a longer history in which forms such as self-help books and conduct manuals not only offer advice on how to construct the self, but also contribute to changing ideas about the self (Johnson and

Lloyd, 2004). Many of the chapters in this collection can be understood in this context. For example, in chapter eight, Sue Currell's analysis of self-help books in the interwar period clearly demonstrates how the self was constructed as malleable and capable of being made over in 'projects of the self': self-help literature presents us with a freedom to choose how we want to produce ourselves in a world free from traditional constraints on identity. In different ways, the chapters by Chambers on *Ebony*, Jancovich on *Playboy* and Binkley on countercultural publishing also consider how these forms not only mediate and produce ideas about lifestyle but also link consumption to a wider project for creating forms of self-identity.

However, these chapters also raise questions about whether lifestyle projects are necessarily divorced from more traditional forms of identity. Both Jancovich and Binkley demonstrate that while the forms they discuss are concerned with the production of new forms of identity through lifestyle, the identities that are produced are classed. The construction of lifestyles, then, cannot simply be thought about in terms of processes of detraditionalization; it also needs to be understood in terms of transformations in, and movements within, the social space of class relations. Chambers' chapter demonstrates how *Ebony* magazine constructed lifestyles through consumption, but that these were also sites for mediating, and rendering visible, the lifestyles of a black middle class. Therefore, while all these forms can be seen to encourage forms of reflexivity about identity, this does not necessarily mean that lifestyle projects are individualized projects. Processes of detraditionalization do not necessarily lead to the end of ascribed identities based on class, 'race' and gender, but instead the reformulation and resignification of these identities.

Indeed, the importance of lifestyle media is not simply that they both produce and reproduce ideas about the significance of lifestyle; they also create the basis for making distinctive lifestyles legible. While clearly all consumption practices are not primarily about communication (Campbell, 1995) or distinction (Warde, 1997), lifestyle media do highlight the communicative potential of consumption practices. By creating recognizable lifestyle practices, lifestyle media play a part in creating visibility and legibility that might also offer grounds for legitimization. If the concept of lifestyle emphasizes the importance of choice but also the legibility of our choices to others (Jagose, 2003), then lifestyle media offer a means of 'writing status'.

Historical Contexts

In order to place lifestyle in a fuller historical context, we also need to account for the development of practices and ideas that are later incorporated within the term. This includes understanding how consumer culture has developed, how consumer goods have come to take on communicative and symbolic roles, how ideas of taste have become tied to notions of status and social standing, and so on. It is beyond the scope of this chapter to map a full history of these developments: as Glennie (1995) argues, various 'revolutions' in consumption have been identified as occurring from the sixteenth century onwards. However, what follows identifies some moments in the emergence of lifestyle, primarily in the UK. There is clearly a need to differentiate between different uses of the concept of lifestyle: for example, Weber's (1968) discussion of 'styles of life' which link to the ways of life of distinctive status groups differs in some key ways from contemporary uses of the term (Featherstone, 1991; Jagose, 2003). Crucially, while the concept has a long history in terms of describing the ways of life of specific groups, more recent uses of the term suggest that lifestyles are no longer tied to ascribed social groupings, and that putting together a lifestyle is now an active process that involves choice.

Nonetheless, the different elements that comprise contemporary understandings of lifestyle did not emerge overnight; they have a history. In this section, we chart one of the ways in which this history has been narrated; a way that focuses on the role of fashion in producing new dispositions towards consumption and the self. This narrative tends to emphasize the role of emulation and imitation, indicating how ideas about what and how to consume 'trickle down' social hierarchies and become diffused from elite groups to wider populations. However, as Slater (1997: 157) argues, the idea of emulation has some key problems, as it reduces the meaning of consumption to competitions over status, and 'reduces social motivation almost exclusively to a desire to "ape one's betters"'. Furthermore, by emphasizing how ideas 'trickle down' social hierarchies, it ignores the ways in which 'class competition can involve the very opposite of lifestyle emulation' (p. 158). These alternative understanding of consumption are developed in the next section, on the work of Pierre Bourdieu.

Grant McCracken (1988) identifies one moment in this history in the Elizabethan royal court where, in the last quarter of the sixteenth century, there was a kind of consumer boom. Queen Elizabeth I used taste and status as a way to consolidate her royal standing and centralize her realm. The nobility were increasingly expected to make pilgrimages to the royal court in London, which operated as an emblem of the queen's majesty, the site of ceremony and spectacle, and a way of making the queen's stature visible. Because the nobles also wanted to gain the queen's favour, and wanted to be noticed at court, they now had to spend money on their appearance and on gifts for the queen that demonstrated their devotion to her. In competition with other noblemen coming to court, their status in the social hierarchy had to be enacted and embodied: the nobleman was 'drawn into a riot of consumption' (McCracken 1988: 12), buying fancy clothes, giving huge feasts and bringing lavish gifts. This new system also had a significant impact back in the noble's country seat. Where there had previously been a well-established system of noblesse oblige through which commodities were given as gifts by the nobility to the wider community, the expensive demands of the London court meant that 'this warbling brook of wealth was now blocked' (Corrigan, 1997: 4). This worked to create new distinctions between the consumption patterns of different socio-economic groups.

Queen Elizabeth's political use of consumption had broader impacts, too. For one thing, it transformed the meaning of consumption, and its relation to time. Prior to this new system, goods were purchased with a long-term view to inheritance: goods would be passed down through generations and this was encapsulated in the idea of patina, that things accrued a valuable veneer over time, through use. Old things were more valued as they signified longevity and lineage: having old things marked your family as having long-term stability and status over time, and was one of the key ways of policing boundaries between social groups (others include manners, codes of conduct, etiquette and so on.) The new necessity of spending in the context of the court led to a decline in the old kind of family-oriented consumption, and an emphasis instead on newness and on an individualized consumption which might reap instant social rewards. McCracken (1988) sees this as the birth of fashion. Fashion disrupts the value of lineage and blurs previously stable class distinctions, as both 'old' and 'new' money are equally useful in buying new things. Fashion also leads to imitation, as the 'codes' that govern it are more transparent. Unlike patina, fashions could be copied and the new system became subject to increasing acceleration, as the newly fashion-conscious nobility attempted to outdo each other. So begins that 'dance of distinction', the on-going struggle by different class groups to define their tastes in relation to – or in opposition to – those above or below them in the social order. As Corrigan (1997: 7) puts it: 'lower-class imitation led the upper classes to differentiate themselves again, only to be imitated again, and then differentiate themselves once more, then be imitated again, then yet again differentiate themselves – and so on without any apparent limit'.

By the late eighteenth century, economic prosperity in England was driving the now-established consumer society and worked to modernize consumption (McKendrick *et al.*, 1982). With increasing class mobility, acquiring consumer goods as a way of marking social standing was now also increasingly commonplace, facilitating 'the growth of emulative consumer expenditure' (Corrigan, 1997: 8). McKendrick *et al.* (1982: 23) note the growth of 'home products' in this period, partly attributed to the rise in female employment: 'with women having command of earnings of their own and access to a greater total family income, one would expect a greater demand for goods dominated by female consumer choice – clothes, curtains, linens, pottery, cutlery, furniture, brass and copper for the home; buckles, buttons and fashion accessories for the person'. Hence whole new worlds of goods opened up, and these too became subject to the rules of imitation and differentiation. Manufacturers picked up on this, giving birth to marketing and advertising as ways of 'adding value' (sign value, that is) to products through fashion. In England, the pottery manufacturer Josiah Wedgwood is credited as a pioneer of this, using newspaper adverts and showrooms to sell ceramics as fashionable rather than purely utilitarian commodities. Wedgwood also pioneered what we would now see as niche marketing, product differentiation, and even lifestylization, producing ranges of ware that were consciously made and sold as markers of distinction. However, there is considerable debate about the extent to which consumption in this period is best characterized by emulation – where ideas about consumption 'trickled-down' the social hierarchy – or differentiation, as consumption practices were given different meanings within distinctive class cultures (Glennie, 1995).

As we move into the nineteenth century, the full consolidation of the industrial revolution and the factory system enabled mass production of a growing range and variety of goods, creating conditions for wider participation in consumer culture by the expanding industrial working class. Other structural transformations around this time had an important impact on the history of lifestyle, too. The mass migration of people to cities changed the format of social relations irrevocably. Urban living threatened to break down the traditional social structure – the city was a teeming mass of strangers, and people who don't know you don't know where you stand in the social order. It therefore becomes much more pressing to make social position visible, and positional goods therefore take on an even greater role. Lifestyles and embodied practices marking out status become vital tools in the communication of social location (Simmel, 1904/1957). Manufacturers and the developing professions of marketing and advertising were able to capitalize on these concerns.

The fact that manufacturers and marketers could knowingly exploit this new consumer culture also meant, of course, that these kinds of people began to get very rich. And new ways of getting rich meant that the wealthy had to develop a distinct lifestyle to prove their wealth, now things like patina had all-but vanished. The tension between old and new money here resurfaces, as the old rich retreated to their ancestral homes and their ancestral ways of life as a way of maintaining their superiority from the newly moneyed. The secret codes of the old rich become more important, and they closed ranks to prevent the new rich from entering the very upper echelons of society. Veblen (1899/1970) examines this process in the USA, showing how the new rich had little option but to try to emulate the old rich, in order to pass into high society. They did this, Veblen argues, through adopting two visible markers of a moneyed lifestyle: conspicuous consumption and conspicuous leisure. The first involved patterns of expenditure centred on visible ostentation, via very high status positional goods – big country houses and manicured estates, lavish parties, armies of servants and so on. Embodied symbols of excess were also in vogue, such as gout. Conspicuous leisure was about making invisible the labour that generated the wealth – it was vulgar to be seen to be working hard. Both of these were embodied in the figure of the upper-class woman: 'the more expensive and the more obviously unproductive' she was, the more status a family had (Veblen, 1970: 126). For Veblen, then, 'the conspicuous wasting of both time and things comes together in … the cultivation of the aesthetic faculty for making endless discriminations of taste' (Slater, 1997: 155).

As Corrigan notes, an important part of the broader lifestyling of domestic space in the nineteenth century was to 'nullify all associations with work', achieved through particular modes of domestic design that produce home as the space of 'not-work'. So the consumption of 'home products' takes another lifestyle turn, and the idea of styling the home's interior and its contents gains hold. Of course, as we have already suggested, this separation is in fact breached by the idea of productive 'leisure-work' (as well as feminine domestic labour within the home), and through the growing emphasis on the need to 'work at' self-improvement through lifestyle. But this does not contradict the broader argument made by Corrigan, about the ways in which the home, and the commodities collected within it, have come to be 'curated' by homemakers, so that the 'ensemble' can be used to narrate and perform an appropriate and coherent lifestyle that is also legible for others to read (see also Rybczynski, 1986; McKellar and Sparke, 2004).

Outside the home, the department store, frequently given a pivotal place in histories of consumption, came during this time to operate as a key site for not only offering a spectacular range of consumer goods but also educating consumers about the appropriate use of these goods. Between the 1860s and 1920s, during what is commonly termed 'the golden age' of the department store, these shops offered female consumers the visual pleasure of looking at spectacular displays, variously described as luxurious 'fantasy palaces and 'magnificent stage sets' (Nava, 1997; for more work on department stores see, for example, Chaney, 1983, Lancaster, 1995, Laermans, 1993, Rappaport, 2001; Wilson, 1985). Moreover, shopping itself was reworked as a leisure practice, and department stores offered safe urban public space to middle-class women, against a backdrop of concerns about women's presence in urban public space more generally (sales staff were often women, too). Department stores changed the practice of shopping, for example by making browsing possible, so luxury became available for all to see, if not buy – what Sennett (1976) calls the 'democratization of luxury'. By putting goods on display, and by showing connections and arrangements of goods assembled in a coherent whole, department stores further the lifestylization project by teaching shoppers how to furnish not only their homes, but also their lives (Potts, this volume). In this way, the history of retailing, alongside wider histories of marketing and advertising, also offers important insights into the histories of lifestyles.

Class, Taste and Lifestyle

If ideas about emulation shape some of the ways in which some histories of consumption have been constructed, the work of Pierre Bourdieu (1984) offers a very different way of understanding the relationships between class and lifestyle. Rather than imitating the classes above them, Bourdieu argues, subordinate classes have their own distinctive tastes that they often fiercely defend. Therefore, from Bourdieu's perspective, ideas about lifestyle do not simply trickle down class hierarchies, because the tastes and lifestyles of different classes arise from the distinctive life experiences of classes that are placed in antagonistic relations to each other.

Bourdieu argues that the differences between consumption practices are linked to the different amounts and types of capital that people possess. As well as the conventional economic capital (money, property, etc.) there is cultural capital, whereby 'wealth' is expressed through taste (he also discussed symbolic and social capitals). Cultural capital refers to the dispositions we bring to our everyday practices, demonstrated by, for example, the goods we choose to consume. Those who are rich in cultural capital not only legitimate their own dispositions as *the* legitimate dispositions (they have the power to do so because they possess symbolic capital), but also pass on these cultural resources to their children. While we can acquire forms of cultural capital through education or through on-going works of self-improvement, it is primarily inherited during our upbringing in our families, through what Bourdieu calls the habitus. The codification of rules of behaviour and social interaction becomes embodied in the habitus: ways of talking, moving, acting and thinking that appear sedimented and naturalized are in fact learnt. Therefore taste is carried by the body, which helps explain the emphasis on body discipline and bodily transformation in contemporary lifestyle discourses and practices.

Although the family is the key site for the transmission of cultural capital, cultural capital is also evaluated and legitimated through the education system: qualifications are the reward for demonstrating the 'right' kind of dispositions. Those who acquire 'legitimate' cultural capital rather than inherit it – either through formal education or informal guides such as lifestyle media – always, however, risk feeling anxious. Judgements of taste must appear effortless and natural – too much obvious effort appears to be fake.

Bourdieu maps the relationship between social class and consumption to demonstrate the relationship between what he calls the space of social positions and the space of lifestyles. A superimposition of these two spaces shows the relative 'position' of different occupational categories graphed against axes showing 'capital volume' and the relative balance of economic and cultural capital (Bourdieu, 1984: 128-9). So, for example, at the time of Bourdieu's study of French society in the 1960s, teachers in higher education are shown to have relatively high overall capital volume, but much more cultural than economic capital – they may not be paid that well, but they have 'excellent' taste. Engineers, by contrast, have high overall amounts of capital, but more of this is economic than cultural. Farm labourers occupy the lowliest position, with low overall capital volume and more economic than cultural capital, and so on. Overlaying these social positions are a whole set of commodities and 'taste practices' – so, for example, we can see that higher education teachers like chess, read *Le Monde*, like modern art, and can speak foreign languages. Engineers prefer sailing, Scrabble, Knoll furniture and *Le Figaro*. Pernod, petanque, accordion music, the Renault 4 and Brigitte Bardot, mark farm labourers' tastes. In this way, Bourdieu argues, we reveal something of ourselves to be read by others through what we consume, but we equally reveal something about our tastes through the way we read other people's tastes.

Clearly, the positioning of these goods isn't fixed over time, and such maps of lifestyle will be place- as well as time-specific. The spaces of social positions and lifestyles are not static, and nor are the positional goods used to demarcate these spaces. One of the reasons for the 'movement' of individual things around on Bourdieu's maps is the possibility of imitation. This is one of the central paradoxes of taste and of the work of cultural intermediaries, the taste-makers Bourdieu highlights as having a central role to play in processes of distinction; they seek to produce distinction by making judgements about taste, but in making those judgements public they also produce democratization, by making these very ideas about good and bad taste available to other people. This leads inevitably to the devaluing of some things, and the revaluing of others and here again, the work of cultural intermediaries is very important. As Featherstone (1991) shows, new cultural intermediaries are engaged in an unending quest, to stay 'ahead of the game': once something becomes too popular, the taste-makers must jettison it in favour of something new, something undiscovered (or rediscovered). An important part of any project to historicize lifestyle must be to track these movements, and to thereby map the histories of taste formations; as Simon Gunn (2005: 62) writes, it is important 'to identify historical changes in the forms and definitions of cultural capital'. However, a key reason that changing tastes for particular things does little to disturb the wider social system is that, for Bourdieu, the key markers of lifestyles are not simply *what* goods we consume, but *how* we consume them. As we have already suggested, our class habitus not only shapes our preferences for certain goods; it also shapes whether, for example, we are interested in the form of goods, or their function.

Bourdieu's work has been criticized for offering only a static picture of lifestyle, a 'snapshot' of classed taste formations at a particular historical moment (see, for example, Mennell, 1996; Gronow, 1997). For this reason, it has been argued that he is unable to account for fashion and for the dynamics of historical change in consumption over time. While these criticisms suggest that Bourdieu is only able to offer a model of cultural reproduction, his emphasis on class trajectories – the movements of classes within social space – does offer opportunities for understanding historical changes, because he enables us to understand how different classes have different opportunities to *capitalize* on their assets at particular historical moments. The key movement within social space at the time of his study in France in the 1960s was the rise of new middle classes, the new bourgeoisie and new petite bourgeoisie. The product of expanding higher education and new types of middle-class jobs (for example, in marketing, the media and the caring professions), these new middle classes use the capital they have at their disposal in an to attempt to legitimate new dispositions towards everyday life and to present a challenge to 'old' bourgeois legitimacy. In particular, these new classes are characterized by an aesthetic that emphasizes hedonistic pleasure, in contrast to the emphasis on restraint and sobriety that characterizes the established middle classes. It is the new bourgeoisie in their role as 'cultural intermediaries', or taste-makers, who are, moreover, best placed to legitimate their lifestyle, given their occupations: 'Through their slyly imperative advice and the example of their consciously "model" lifestyle, the new taste-makers propose a morality which boils down to an art of consuming, spending and enjoying' (Bourdieu, 1984: 311). If the new bourgeoisie seek to legitimate their lifestyle, presenting their taste as *the* taste, then the new petite bourgeoisie also invests heavily in the art of everyday life, playing 'a vanguard role in the struggles over everything concerned with the art of living, in particular, domestic life and consumption, relations between the sexes and generations, the reproduction of the family and its values' (pp. 366-7). While other class formations have lifestyles, therefore, these new middle classes invest in making lifestyle into an art form.

In this way, Bourdieu's emphasis on transformations in the space of class relations does offer a way of historicizing struggles over lifestyle. Nonetheless, the *use* of Bourdieu's work has often produced an inflexible history of class and lifestyle. Because the new middle classes emerged during a similar period to that identified with processes of postmodernization, there has been a tendency, following Featherstone (1991), to map the two together at an abstract theoretical level. However, despite the value of these arguments, this works to fix our understanding of the history of lifestyles and can mask the extent to which the details were far more messy and uneven in practice. In particular, the chapters here by Jancovich, Osgerby and Binkley all address these issues in relation to the US, demonstrating that there is a more complex history of both the emergence and nature of the new middle classes to be written. Likewise, in Britain for example, the so-called 'swinging meritocracy' of new professions in the 1960s was clearly the product of transformations spanning the whole postwar period (Hewison, 1997): the cultural intermediaries working in the expanding media and arts insititutions were benefiting from the culture of political consensus that made (new) middle-class values ascendant, while providing expanding opportunities for social and geographical mobility.

But there are longer histories to tell, too; the histories of taste and cultural capital stretch back beyond the twentieth century, as we have already seen in our sketch of the histories of fashion and shopping. Simon Gunn (2005) has recently explored the history of cultural capital in the middle classes in nineteenth-century England, in an attempt to provide 'a corrective to more familiar depictions of the twentieth century as a continuous series of social breaks' (p. 62). He shows how the middle classes sought to classify and colonize cultural activities, which were 'transformed into public rites for the well-to-do' (p. 52), placing increased emphasis on the public display of cultural consumption as a marker of status. As he sums this up, 'For much of the nineteenth and the twentieth century, "culture" was understood to be a significant – if not indispensable – part of what it meant to be "middle class"' (p. 54). Gunn also discusses the importance of the expanding space of the suburbs in the later nineteenth century, as the site for a new form of 'home-centred consumerism' (p. 53); so private space also became an important element in the display of taste, as already noted. Given the gendering of domesticity, Gunn argues that this means that women had an important but neglected role to play in the transmission of taste, as homemakers and as mothers. They did this in large part 'by embodying [cultural competence] in their own person, their dress, deportment and behaviour'; women became, he says, 'the bearers of class' (p. 55). The importance of the relationship between gender, class and lifestyle is underdeveloped in Bourdieu's work, but these themes are taken up in chapters here by Hollows, Jancovich and Osgerby.

Moreover, while this book also seeks to contribute to constructing a longer history of the work of cultural intermediaries – and this is significantly developed in Binkley's chapter – there are still many histories yet to be written here. While stress has been placed on a rapid expansion of the occupational sectors associated with taste making in the second half of the twentieth century, there are longer histories to consider. There is work to be done on the ways in which the professions of economics and advertising sought to understand, but also shape, what Mort (2000: 9) calls the 'consuming personality' (see also Nixon, 2000a;

questions about the role of advertising in mediating ideas of lifestyle are taken up by Chambers, Harp and Potts in this volume). Furthermore, women's magazines have been sharing with their readers ideas about taste and style since the turn of the eighteenth century at least (Corrigan, 1997), while Elias's history of manners returns to the Middle Ages, and Michel Foucault's (1986) discussion of self-improvement stretches back to classical times. Varieties of what we might now label 'lifestyle writing' have therefore been produced by 'lifestyle gurus' and 'cultural intermediaries' since long before the coming of the modern mass media. The chapters assembled in *Historicizing Lifestyle* begin some of these tasks, and we want to move now to present an outline of the remainder of the book.

Historicizing Lifestyle

The contributors to *Historicizing Lifestyle* pursue a series of the themes that we have identified so far. While our focus in primarily on the 1920s to 1970s, it should be clear that we are not suggesting that this period is a definitive one in the history of lifestyle. Our emphasis on these years reflects our original conception of the book, to show that processes and practices that are frequently seen as late twentieth-century phenomena in fact have a much longer and more complex history. As we have shown above, this stretches back way before the 1900s, and also way beyond the reach of a single volume.

The first three chapters demonstrate how ideas about gender, nation and 'race' problematize some of the taken-for-granted assumptions about lifestyle. In the first of these, Joanne Hollows examines domestic cultures, considering how forms of feminine leisure and labour have frequently been excluded from contemporary debates about lifestyle. Hollows focuses on how class tensions in inter-war Britain were negotiated in the pages of *Good Housekeeping* magazine in a historical context in which there was a shift in the meaning of middle-class domestic femininity as the use of domestic servants declined. She explores how the values of novelty, economy and health were employed to give meaning to middle-class women's 'feeding work' (DeVault, 1991). Although there is clearly a 'scientificization' of housework in the magazine, the appliance of science is not unequivocally endorsed: domestic life is also treated as an 'art'. Ultimately, Hollows' chapter is about struggles to redefine 'proper' middle-class domestic femininity, and about how *Good Housekeeping* inserted itself into these struggles, ambivalently producing democratization and distinction. *Good Housekeeping* is thus shown to evidence a struggle over the legitimation of different forms of cultural capital in an uncertain period of detraditionalization.

The emphasis on novelty in *Good Housekeeping* contrasts with the emphasis on tradition in discourses surrounding commercial dining in the same period. Janet Floyd discusses two British restaurant guides, the annual *Good Food Guide*, conceived by Raymond Postgate, and published since the early 1950s, and Florence White's *Good Food Registers* from the 1930s. Both guides are concerned with reviewing the experiences of eating out, and thereby provide commentary on national (and regional and local) culinary culture, reflecting different stances towards British food: White sees cookery as a folk art under threat from modernity, whereas Postgate sees British cooking as an impoverished experience when compared with France. However, these guides are also about the practices of *writing about* food and eating out: the restaurant review is a particular form of lifestyle text, partly a guide to making 'safe' future choices and partly a guide to trends in taste, read to stay 'in the know'. Both White and Postgate emphasize a particular figure of the consumer, marked by their mobility. The capacity to move through the nation, stopping off to search out places to eat, makes the restaurant guide a kind of social cartography of taste, a map of centres and margins, metropolis and province. How these different locations are valued helps us understand how the nation as a whole is imagined, and the cultural work that food and eating do in that imaginary. Both guides help us understand what we might call the Englishness of eating out, and the eating out of Englishness – the former meaning how taste judgements about 'good food' are franked with national sensibilities, in part of course propagated by the guides; the latter meaning how the guides assemble their maps of what good and bad English food is. As Floyd points out, one of the interesting things overshadowing the *Good Food Guide* is anxiety – the anxiety of making a bad choice, of ending up sitting in front of a plate of bad food. This is about more than the possibility of going hungry or getting indigestion, of course: it reflects the public nature of eating out, and so the anxieties of *being seen* eating bad food. This reminds us of the centrality of anxiety to much lifestyle work, and of the concomitant need for constant reassurance and update; hence, for the *Good Food Guide* at least, the 'hurried snapshot' and annual revisions that mark the ephemerality of food venues, but also over a longer period map the changing taste formations around 'good food' (Warde, 2003).

If Hollows and Floyd consider how questions about gender and nation impact on debates about lifestyle, then Jason Chambers focuses on the birth and subsequent development of *Ebony* magazine in the USA, and the ways in which it addressed a black middle class. In the process, the magazine not only sought to construct and negotiate an idea of a distinctive black middle-class lifestyle, but also made the black middle class visible and legitimated their 'rights' as consumers. As we noted earlier, his argument challenges ideas about the 1950s as a period of mass consumption by demonstrating how African-American consumers were excluded from the ways in which the 'mass consumer' was envisaged. Furthermore, Chambers suggests that *Ebony*'s attempts to gain recognition for the black middle class as consumers cannot be divorced from wider struggles by African Americans to gain recognition and win equal rights as citizens. In this way, he argues, *Ebony* 'politicized' consumption by encouraging the black middle class 'to press for equality as consumers'. *Ebony*'s founder John Johnson's success in securing advertising for mass consumer goods is significant within this process. Chambers identifies how pride, consumption, and individual and group aspiration were the central components of the African-American middle-class lifestyle constructed by the magazine. In the process, he demonstrates how *Ebony* needs to be read within the wider politicization of consumption during a period in which the right to sit at a lunch counter acted as a metaphor for wider struggles over civil rights.

The chapters by Jancovich, Osgerby and Binkley all concentrate on questions about the new middle classes in the US. Like Chambers on *Ebony*, Mark Jancovich's chapter on *Playboy* magazine also questions the idea that the 1950s in the US was an era of mass consumption that promoted conformism, identifying how the construction of lifestyle in the magazine also challenged ideas of conservatism. Drawing on Bourdieu, Jancovich writes that, far from promoting white middle-class lifestyle as a homogeneous and one-dimensional way of life constructed through the consumption of mass-produced goods, the *Playboy* reader was constructed as someone distinguished from 'the masses' through his consumption. In this way, Jancovich suggests, *Playboy* politicized consumption by using 'cold war rhetoric to challenge aspects of American society and culture'. However, he also identifies how the dispositions towards consumption promoted by the magazine share remarkable similarities with the characteristics of lifestyle that are usually attributed to the rise of postmodern culture. Indeed, the ways in which Hugh Hefner constructed the *Playboy* lifestyle are remarkably similar to the ways Featherstone envisages the postmodern 'heroes' of consumer culture. Furthermore, Jancovich argues, *Playboy* not only articulated masculinity and consumption in ways more commonly associated with developments in the 1980s, but also articulated dispositions towards consumption frequently associated with the new middle classes in later formations of consumer culture. In this way, his chapter seeks to challenge the ways in which debates about class, gender and lifestyle have frequently been historicized.

Bill Osgerby's chapter on scuba diving in the 1960s also draws on Bourdieu's ideas about the new middle classes. Indeed, he identifies how *Playboy* was a key site for popularizing ideas about scuba as a lifestyle pursuit. Drawing on the work of scholars such as Belinda Wheaton, Osgerby argues that scuba is best understood as a 'lifestyle sport' that offers opportunities to mark out a distinctive cultural identity through the consumption of specific signifiers of that lifestyle. While lifestyle sports are frequently understood in terms of postmodern consumer culture, Osgerby demonstrates that the ways in which the scuba lifestyle was mediated in films, magazines and television during the 1960s problematizes such a straightforward periodization. In the process, he not only shows how lifestyle has a history, but also how lifestyle sports have a history. Furthermore, Osgerby argues, the scuba lifestyle was not only constructed through the consumption of specific commodities, but also privileged particular dispositions towards consumption that closely resemble those Bourdieu associates with the new petite bourgeoisie. In this way, he says, the scuba phenomenon needs to be understood in terms of an emergent new petit bourgeois taste formation in the US in the 1960s that invested in the art of lifestyle – a lifestyle based around an ethic of fun and pleasure.

Sam Binkley's chapter on the 'countercultural lifestyle print discourse' that developed in grassroots West Coast publishing in the late 1960s and early 1970s also examines transformations in class-based lifestyle politics. As Binkley makes clear, this period is frequently identified as the point where there is a shift from modern to postmodern culture. Yet while abstract debates about postmodernity have privileged the realm of the visual as central to a postmodern culture that fragments identity, his chapter demonstrates how a closer inspection of the ways in which ideas about lifestyle were mediated in the period reveals a more complex picture. Binkley analyzes how the counterculture produced a whole raft of publications centred on how to transform or improve your life (style), covering topics from food and relationships to sex and spirituality. The writers and publishers of these lifestyle guides, he argues, need to be understood as new cultural intermediaries promoting new forms of middle-class lifestyles and dispositions towards the self. However, the chapter shows how the 'fun' ethic identified with the new middle classes 'reveals not only a comprehensive technique of self-cultivation and care, but also a concerted effort to sustain and consolidate clear public and personal identities'. In the process, by tracing transformations in these middle-class lifestyles, Binkley questions any straightforward connection between postmodern consumer culture and fragmented identities, demonstrating instead how lifestyle media were used to promote a *unified* idea of identity by promoting an idea of 'individual authenticity'.

While Binkley looks at how countercultural lifestyle manuals promoted particular dispositions towards the self as a form of self-improvement, Sue Currell examines some overlapping themes in her discussion of the development of self-help literature in the US in the 1930s. As we noted earlier, Giddens highlights how the forms of detraditionalization associated with modernity means that expert guidance has become increasingly important in managing the self. The rise of self-help literature that offers lifestyle guidance must be understood in this context. However, Currell argues, self-help needs to be understood historically, and she identifies particular characteristics of the boom in lifestyle advice following the Great Depression in the USA. These books offered advice on how to respond to detraditionalization and create an improved self who could adjust to new economic conditions, and offered an alternative philosophy to those promoted by religion: rather than believing in an afterlife, the reader was encouraged to think that 'life can be better on Earth through changes made to the physical and psychological self'. Nonetheless, Currell argues that despite their promises of liberation, self-help manuals of the 1930s contributed instead to 'a culture of conformity and self-surveillance'.

The final two chapters are concerned in different contexts with the role of advertising and marketing in mediating ideas about lifestyle. While self-help media offer us opportunities to engage in work that will improve the self, advertising frequently works to show particular commodities will 'magically' improve our lifestyle. Stephen Harp demonstrates how Michelin's 'lifestyle-orientated advertising' in the early twentieth century marked a shift in how manufacturers used adverts to depict not only products, but also lifestyles and identities. Bibendum, the tyre-bodied Michelin man, became a metonymic transmitter of the values and status of the Michelin-buying car driver. Class, 'race' and gender are all used to reinforce the superiority of the product, and then to re-reflect that superiority back onto the consumer. Close reading of selected poster ads shows how the idea of the 'man about town' or *mondain* was figured as a new aspirational lifestyle, and how Michelin tyres worked as positional goods in the pursuit of this lifestyle. The tyres emphasized mobility as part of this new lifestyle – others are fixed, but Bibendum is on the move (literally, and also in terms of class mobility).

Michelin advertising connoted an aristocratic life, of fine food and drink, leisure, mastery of inferiors, etc., all embodied in Bibendum, himself the literal embodiment of Michelin tyres. Bibendum also operated as a figure for emulation, and acted as a bridge to an ideal world: 'In buying Michelin tyres, one might fashion oneself as a strong, rich, bourgeois superman of sorts, resembling Bibendum'. In short, Harp shows how Michelin used branding to connect a product – pneumatic tyres – with an entire lifestyle. As other historical studies of advertising have shown, this emerging profession has come to play a paramount role in matters of taste, status and distinction, with its mastery of the semiotic arts conjuring entire lifestyles from single products (Nixon, 2000b). Locating its craft historically presents us with a richer understanding of these lifestyle-makers.

Tracy Potts also examines the role that particular companies can take (and have taken) in mediating, and helping to redefine, ideas about lifestyle and taste. Her chapter analyzes marketing materials and plans from Heal's furniture store in London in the inter-war period, demonstrating how *design* became a tradable symbolic currency in the context of home furnishings. Potts shows how design came to operate as a key 'regime of value' (Appadurai, 1986) in the way Heal's promoted its products (predating the current slew of products sold through appeals to design discourses and specific designers) – yet in order to do so it also had to 're-educate' its customers. In order to make its goods distinctive, the store drew on discourses from the elite world of art and aesthetics: Heal's created a gallery in its shop, offered invitations to 'private views', and tried to inculcate an art-like appreciation, or connoisseurship, of its commodities. Potts' close reading of this shows the many sleights of hand used by the retailer to resignify and revalue mass-produced home furnishings. Whereas today we are more likely to find a shop in a gallery, as cultural consumption becomes ever more commodified, Heal's Mansard Gallery inverts this connection in order to appeal to a particular fraction of consumers, which it constructs as 'in the know', as connoisseurs of precisely the symbolic value it is attempting to accrete to its wares. This is achieved through denying or obscuring the commodity status of the things on display, and cultivating a disinterested, aesthetic appreciation of its furniture by 'adventurers' (who, of course, it also wants to be shoppers, though without naming them as such, since shopping is too vulgar). By utilizing the 'exhibitionary complex' (Dicks, 2004) to *sell-by-not-selling*, or to *advertise-by-not-advertising*, Heal's achieved that elusive goal of contemporary lifestyle discourse: to promote something as exclusive without that very promotion diminishing its exclusivity. As we have become more savvy spectators of advertising, even if dressed as advertorial or infomercial, such strategies might no longer be possible (Goldman and Papson, 1996). Nevertheless, the story Potts tells in her chapter very clearly illustrates the lineage of what we might now consider niche marketing, in the service of lifestylization, working to produce particular forms of value which concomitantly legitimate certain taste formations.

References

Appadurai, A. (1986) *The Social Life of Things: Commodities in Cultural Perspective*, Cambridge: Cambridge University Press.

Bell, D. (2002) 'From Writing at the Kitchen Table to TV Dinners: Food Media, Lifestylization and European Eating', paper presented at the Eat Drink and Be Merry? Cultural Meanings of Food in the 21st Century Conference, Amsterdam, June.

Bell, D. and J. Hollows (eds) (2005) *Ordinary Lifestyles: Popular Media, Consumption and Taste*, Milton Keynes: Open University Press.

Bocock, R. (1993) *Consumption*, London: Routledge.

Bonner, F. (2003) *Ordinary Television: Analyzing Popular TV*, London: Sage.

Bourdieu, P. (1984) *Distinction: A Social Critique of the Judgement of Taste*, Trans. R. Nice, London: Routledge.

Brunsdon, C. (2004) 'Taste and Time on Television', *Screen*, Vol. 45(2), pp. 115-129.

Brunsdon, C., Johnson, C., Moseley, R. and Wheatley, H. (2001) 'Factual Entertainment on British Television: the Midlands TV Research Group's "8-9 Project"', *European Journal of Cultural Studies*, Vol. 4(1), pp. 29-62.

Campbell, C. (1995) 'The Sociology of Consumption', in D. Miller (ed.) *Acknowledging Consumption*, London: Routledge.

Chaney, D. (1983) 'The Department Store as Cultural Form', *Theory Culture and Society*, Vol. 1(3), pp. 22-31.

Chaney, D. (1996) *Lifestyles*, London: Routledge.

Chaney, D. (2001) 'From Ways of Life to Lifestyle: Rethinking Culture as Ideology and Sensibility', in J. Lull (ed.) *Culture in the Communication Age*, London: Routledge.

Corrigan, P. (1997) *The Sociology of Consumption*, London: Sage.

DeVault, M. (1991) *Feeding the Family: The Social Organization of Caring as Gendered Work*, Chicago: University of Chicago Press.

Dicks, B. (2004) *Culture on Display: The Production of Contemporary Visitability*, Buckingham: Open University Press.

Elias, N. (1939/1994) *The Civilizing Process*, Oxford: Blackwell.

Featherstone, M. (1991) *Consumer Culture and Postmodernism*, London: Sage.

Foucault, M. (1986) *The History of Sexuality Vol. III: The Care of the Self*, trans. R. Hurley, New York: Vintage.

Giddens, A. (1991) *Modernity and Self-identity: Self and Society in the Late-modern Age*, Cambridge: Polity.

Glennie, P. (1995) 'Consumption within Historical Studies', in D. Miller (ed.) *Acknowledging Consumption*, London: Routledge.

Goldman, R. and S. Papson (1996) *Sign Wars: The Cluttered Landscape of Advertising*, London: Guilford.

Gronow, J. (1997) *The Sociology of Taste*, London: Routledge.

Gunn, S. (2005) 'Translating Bourdieu: Cultural Capital and the English Middle Class in Historical Perspective', *British Journal of Sociology*, Vol. 56(1), pp. 49-64.

Hewison, R. (1997) *Culture and Consensus: England, Art and Politics since 1940*, London: Mehuen.

Holliday, R. (2005) 'Home Truths', in D. Bell and J. Hollows (eds) *Ordinary Lifestyles: Popular Media, Consumption and Taste*, Milton Keynes: Open University Press.

Jagose, A. (2003) 'The Invention of Lifestyle', in F. Martin (ed.) *Interpreting Everyday Culture*, London: Arnold.

Johnson, L. and J. Lloyd (2004) *Sentenced to Everyday Life: Feminism and the Housewife*, Oxford: Berg.

Jones, S. and B. Taylor (2001) 'Food Writing and Food Cultures: the Case of Elizabeth David and Jane Grigson', *European Journal of Cultural Studies*, Vol. 4(2), pp. 171-88.

Laermans, R. (1993) 'Learning to Consume', *Theory Culture and Society*, Vol. 10(4), pp. 79-102.

Lancaster, B. (1995) *The Department Store: A Social History*, Leicester: Leicester University Press.

Lury, C. (1996) *Consumer Culture*, Cambridge: Polity.

McCracken, G. (1988) *Culture and Consumption: New Approaches to the Symbolic Character of Consumer Goods and Activities*, Bloomington: Indiana University Press.

McKellar, S. and P. Sparke (eds) (2004) *Interior Design and Identity*, Manchester: Manchester University Press.

McKendrick, N., Brewer, J. and Plumb, J. (1982) *The Birth of a Consumer Society: The Commercialization of Eighteenth-Century England*, London: Europa.

Mennell, S. (1996) *All Manners of Food: Eating and Taste in England and France from the Middle Ages to the Present*, Urbana and Chicago: University of Illinois Press.

Mort, F. (2000) 'Paths to Mass Consumption: historical perspectives', in P. Jackson, M. Lowe, D. Miller and F. Mort (eds) *Commercial Cultures: Economies, Practices, Spaces*, Oxford: Berg.

Moseley, R. (2000) 'Makeover Takeover on British Television', *Screen*, Vol. 41(3), pp. 299-314.

Nava, M. (1997) 'Modernity's Disavowal', in P Falk and C Campbell (eds) *The Shopping Experience*, London: Sage.

Nixon, S. (2000a) 'In Pursuit of the Professional Ideal: Advertising and the Construction of Commercial Expertise in Britain 1953-64', in P. Jackson, M. Lowe, D. Miller and F. Mort (eds) *Commercial Cultures: Economies, Practices, Spaces*, Oxford: Berg.

Nixon, S. (2000b) *Advertising Cultures*, London: Sage.

O'Sullivan, T. (2005) 'From Television Lifestyle to Lifestyle Television', in D. Bell and J. Hollows (eds) *Ordinary Lifestyles: Popular Media, Consumption and Taste*, Milton Keynes: Open University Press.

Palmer, G. (2004) 'The New You: Class and Transformation in Lifestyle Television', in S. Holmes and D. Jermyn (eds) *Understanding Reality Television*, London: Routledge.

Rappaport, E. (2000) *Shopping for Pleasure: Gender and Public Life in London's West End, 1860-1914*, Princeton, NJ: Princeton University Press.

Richards, T. (1990) *The Commodity Culture of Victorian England: Advertising and Spectacle, 1851-1914*, London: Verso.

Rojek, C. (2000) *Leisure and Culture*, Basingstoke: Macmillan.

Rybczynski, W. (1986) *Home: A Short History of an Idea*, London: Pocket Books.

Sennett, R. (1976) *The Fall of Public Man: On the Social Psychology of Capitalism*, New York: Vintage.

Simmel, G. (1904/1957) 'Fashion', *American Journal of Sociology*, Vol. 62(6), pp. 541-58.

Slater, D. (1997) *Consumer Culture and Modernity*, Cambridge: Polity.

Strange, N. (1998) 'Perform, Educate, Entertain: Ingredients of the Cookery Programme Genre', in C. Geraghty and D. Lusted (eds) *The Television Studies Book*, London: Arnold.

Taylor, L. (2002) 'From Ways of Life to Lifestyle: the 'Ordinari-ization' of British Gardening Lifestyle Television', *European Journal of Communication*, Vol. 17(4), pp. 479-493.

Thompson, K. (1997) 'Regulation, De-regulation and Re-regulation', in K. Thompson (ed.) *Media and Cultural Regulation*, London: Sage.

Trentmann, F. (2004) 'Beyond Consumerism: New Historical Perspectives on Consumption', *Journal of Contemporary History*, Vol. 39(3), pp. 373-401.

Veblen, T. (1899/1970) *The Theory of the Leisure Class*, London: Unwin.

Warde, A. (1997) *Consumption, Food and Taste: Culinary Antinomies and Commodity Culture*, London: Sage.

Warde, A. (2002) 'Setting the Scene: Changing Conceptions of Consumption', in S. Miles, A. Anderson and K. Meethan (eds) *The Changing Consumer: Markets and Meanings*, London: Routledge.

Warde, A. (2003) 'Continuity and Change in British Restaurants, 1951-2001: Evidence from the Good Food Guide', in M. Jacobs and P. Scholliers (eds) *Eating Out in Europe: Picnics, Gourmet Dining and Snacks since the Late Eighteenth Century*, Oxford: Berg.

Weber, M. (1966) *Theory of Social and Economic Organization*, New York: Free Press.

Wilson, E. (1985) *Adorned in Dreams*, London: Virago.

Winship, J. (1987) *Inside Women's Magazines*, London: Pandora.

Chapter 2

Science and Spells: Cooking, Lifestyle and Domestic Femininities in British *Good Housekeeping* in the Inter-war Period

Joanne Hollows

As the introduction to this book makes clear, the explosion of lifestyle media has frequently been associated with the changes brought about by post-Fordism and postmodernity. The terms of these debates have led to a concentration on what is new and novel about lifestyle media and, in the process, marginalized questions about how lifestyle media have a *history* (although see Brunsdon, 2004; O'Sullivan, 2005). This focus on how lifestyle media are a response to profound changes in social, economic and cultural life tends to explain them in terms of an epochal shift which precludes the possibilities of looking at continuities and discontinuities within a wider history of lifestyle.

For theorists of postmodernity such as Featherstone, 'Rather than unreflexively adopting a lifestyle through tradition or habit, the new heroes of consumer culture make lifestyle a life project' (1991: 86). Leaving aside for the moment the problematic gendering of this claim, his argument also begs the question of when, and by whom, were lifestyles merely adopted through 'tradition or habit'. By concentrating on processes of transformation within the middle classes in the UK in the inter-war period, and struggles for legitimacy between these classes, this chapter explores how modern lifestyles cannot simply be thought of in terms of tradition or habit, but were in the process of active, and often reflexive, formation and reformation.

The chapter focuses on *Good Housekeeping* magazine, which was launched in the UK in 1922 – a launch frequently seen as a key intervention in the women's magazine market during the inter-war years – and which is frequently seen as offering an education in, and a shop window for, the new consumer goods associated with Fordist mass production and consumption. From the mid-nineteenth century, there had been a series of new publications addressed to middle-class women concerning domestic arrangements which, like Isabella Beeton's books on household management, 'simultaneously addressed, and sought to bring into being, the middle-class domestic woman' (Beetham, 2003: 20). While

Good Housekeeping has been primarily understood in terms of its articulation of a vision of 'modern femininity' for the middle classes (Giles, 1995: 5) – in particular, by championing a more scientific and professional approach to homemaking that incorporated the use of new 'labour-saving' technologies – the magazine is in fact a more contradictory space than is often acknowledged. As Mennell notes, in *Good Housekeeping* there was sometimes a conflict between 'a spirit of social improvement and a pursuit of the new' (1996: 245; see also Giles, 2004). In this way, while the appliance of science offered to ensure reproducibility between culinary efforts, on occasion this was tempered by wider moral and aesthetic considerations in the ways in which cooking was represented. The magazine did not simply reproduce middle-class lifestyles, but created a space for the production of, and negotiations and struggles between, *different forms of* middle-class lifestyle.

Writing on the British middle classes during this period highlights how this group was in a process of expansion, change and fragmentation. The expansion in the size of the middle class has been linked with changes in the composition of that class. The nineteenth century had seen an expansion of the professional middle class, and the redefinition of occupations such as medicine and engineering (as they became increasingly professionalized and linked to formal education) was mirrored in the redefinition of domestic knowledge (Beetham, 2003: 22). From 1900 onwards, there was a rise of the managerial middle class (Savage *et al.*, 1992) followed by an expansion of technological-scientific professions in the 1930s (McKibbin, 1998). For McKibbin, from the 1930s onwards, the middle class increasingly became 'a technical-scientific-commercial-managerial class' who were 'self-consciously modern' (1998: 48-9). Nonetheless, while the middle class shared many 'cultural and social priorities' and were becoming 'a national class', McKibbin argues that there remained divisions within the middle class that make it difficult to speak of a singular middle class rather than multiple middle *classes*. For example, while the established professions and the emergent scientific-technical professions were dependent on 'cultural assets' reproduced or acquired through education, the managerial middle class was far more dependent on the 'organizational assets' which were less transferable and secured through investment in a particular employer (Savage *et al.*, 1992).

My chapter analyzes and contextualizes the representation of cooking and lifestyle in British *Good Housekeeping* during this inter-war period, arguing that the way in which the magazine addressed its readers needs to be understood in the context of struggles between these different class fractions who had different forms and amounts of capital at their disposal. As Alison Light argues, being 'middle class' in the inter-war period 'depends on an extremely anxious production of endless discriminations between people who are constantly assessing each other's standing' (1991: 13). Indeed, *Good Housekeeping* itself overtly contributed to this anxiety and fascination with a series of articles contributed by readers called 'How Others Live'. This suggests that the production of class cultures and identities in this period cannot simply be related to (male) occupation, but that the work of femininity in the private sphere made a strong contribution to ideas about 'standing'. Indeed, critiques of the suburban lower middle classes frequently denigrate their 'standing' by portraying them as a domesticated (and hence feminized) class primarily characterized by their consumption practices. Domestic production and consumption are therefore key sites for the production of articulated classed and gendered identities. Moreover, as Davidoff and Hall (2002) suggest, class formation is always gendered.

This chapter, therefore, focuses on lifestyle in the context of what Giles calls 'domestic modernity', which she characterizes as 'the ways in which women negotiated and understood experience and identities in terms of the complex changes that modernization provoked in the so-called private sphere' (2004: 6). For critics such as Giles, and Felski (2000), a consideration of domestic life has been marginalized from accounts of modernity because these accounts have emphasized modernity as a masculine experience located in the public sphere. In theories of modernity, it is the public sphere that is the realm of action, production and identity formation while the private sphere is a realm of reproduction, of a mundane and repetitive 'everyday life'. In Featherstone's terms, this domestic realm of everyday life is 'the sphere of women, reproduction and care' and is opposed to the 'heroic life' (cited in Felski, 2000: 80). However, Felski argues that

> Home is not always linked to tradition and opposed to autonomy and self-definition: on the contrary, it has been central to many women's experience of modernity. A feminist theory of everyday life might question the assumption that being modern requires an irrevocable sundering from home, and simultaneously explicate the modern dimensions of everyday experiences of home. (2000: 89)

My discussion draws on Giles and Felski to explore how modern domestic lifestyles involved a break from tradition for many women and an active process of reformulating class identities. By concentrating on the inter-war period, my analysis of cooking focuses on a time in which middle-class domesticity was profoundly shaped by the idea of a 'servant crisis', and as middle-class femininity was increasingly organized around the figure of the modern homemaker rather than the mistress of servants. In the process, middle-class femininity could no longer simply be displayed through a distance from domestic labour, and became increasingly portrayed through bringing distinctive dispositions *towards* domestic labour that enabled the demonstration of cultural and symbolic capital. The chapter then moves on to focus on the practice of cooking as something that constituted a distinctively new and modern practice for many middle-class women. Put another way, this chapter is concerned with how *Good Housekeeping* negotiated the figure of the middle-class cook and how cooking, as part of a wider process of housekeeping, was part of a broader struggle over classed and gendered identities. In the process, I challenge not only the idea that home cultures can be simply understood in terms of tradition and reproduction, but also feminist portraits of the inter-war period that understand femininities during this time as profoundly conservative (see, for example, Beddoe, 1989; for other critiques, see, for example, Giles, 1995 and 2004; Light, 1991). At the end, I return to the question of 'lifestylization', suggesting that modern middle-class femininities were produced through aestheticized lifestyle practices that are more often seen as a product of postmodernity or late modernity.

Making Middle-class Cooks

This chapter forms part of a larger project on the relationships between cookery and middle-class femininity. The inter-war period provides an appropriate point of departure for this project as it is seen to mark a key transformation in middle-class feminine identities from the figure of the 'mistress of the house' to that of 'ordinary housewife' (Giles, 1995). This transformation is frequently linked to the decline of domestic service and the professionalization of housework through which 'modern' ideas of science and rational planning were applied to private sphere. Nicola Humble links these shifts in middle-class feminine identity with changes in, and the expansion of, the cookery book and women's magazine markets. Crucially, this involved a shift from the construction of the middle-class woman as domestic manager found in Mrs. Beeton's *Household Management* to the servantless middle-class woman as cook: 'because the middle-class woman now had to cook, decorate and serve her guests herself, these activities were suddenly declared to be stylish' (Humble, 1996: 15).

However, while this period can be equated with the reconciliation of cooking with middle-class femininity, the evidence about the extent to which middle-class women actually *cooked* is far more hazy, and there remains considerable debate about the true extent of the decline of domestic service. For example, Taylor (1979) has argued that live-in domestic service persisted during the inter-war period, and suggests that the expanding lower-middle classes demanded servants to symbolize their 'middle-classness'. At the other end of the spectrum, critics such as Sparke (1995) largely portray the inter-war period as one where the appliance of science and rational household engineering had already constructed the modern housewife. Moreover, writers such as Glucksmann (1990) have suggested that there was a decline in the number of domestic servants (and, in particular, live-in servants). Furthermore, Glucksmann argues that the 'new' lower-middle classes were rarely in a financial situation to employ live-in servants. Indeed, the lower-middle classes of the period are frequently imagined as living in the smaller new suburban houses which were the product of the inter-war housing boom, and where housing design tended to presume 'a servantless house', or at least the absence of live-in domestic help (Oliver *et al.*, 1994). What is clear, as Giles (1995: 134) suggests, is that the idea of a 'servant problem', and the 'cultural narratives' through which the importance of domestic service were understood, undoubtedly framed the construction and experience of middle-class femininity during a period in which domesticity was in this 'state of flux'. Furthermore, despite the considerable debate over whether domestic service was in decline, the evidence does suggest that middle-class women's experience during the period was fragmented, and that middle-class women were constructed simultaneously as home-managers and mistresses of servants *and* as 'modern housewives' without servants.

Indeed, the middle-class audience addressed by *Good Housekeeping* is one whose experience is anticipated to be fragmented (and the title of the magazine neatly encompasses the dual roles of household manager and homemaker/housewife). Advertisers in the magazine in the 1920s addressed new 'labour-saving' devices both at middle-class women as employers of domestic servants (the Polliwashup machine is for 'considerate housewives' seeking ways for 'lightening the maid's duties') and as users of these appliances (where the Goblin vacuum cleaner offers to 'banish household drudgery' and 'gives you time to spare') (Braithwaite and Walsh, 1992: 14, 84). Likewise, while one article on 'The Ideal Home' assumes that in a substantial house 'the kitchen will be the servants' living-room' (Welch, 1922/1992: 20), another offers a more efficient model for 'The Servantless House' which can 'solve the problem of costly living' (Moore, 1923/1992: 28). The magazine anticipates that readers may either have a number of live-in servants, or that they may rely on the services of a live-in 'general maid' or a live-out 'daily maid', or that they may be servantless. Likewise, advice is given to single working women living in bed-sitters as well as married women running family homes. While Horwood (1997) identifies a shift in *Good Housekeeping* during the 1920s and 1930s from a situation in which middle-class women were imagined as 'mistresses of the house' (where domestic servants are assumed) to the image of largely servantless 'housewife', evidence also suggests that this narrative was never straightforward.

The debates about domestic service in the inter-war period rarely have anything specific to say about cookery. However, some information about dispositions towards cooking in the period is offered by Crawford and Broadley's large-scale survey, published in 1938 as *The People's Food*. The conceptualization of class position in this study is crude by more recent standards, with class determined by income yet also characterized by Crawford (who worked in advertising) in terms of marketing-inspired lifestyle profiles. Nonetheless, their results confirm a portrait of Britain in the 1930s in which there was an expansion of the cookbook market and a small 'revival of home cooking', partly attributed to the influence of the Women's Institute and Townswomen's Guilds (for more on the Women's Institute during this period, see Andrews, 1997). This is linked to evidence of an increase in the amount of home cooking women were undertaking and to relatively high levels of interest in cooking (Crawford, 1938: 110-11). The use of cookery books was, perhaps unsurprisingly, closely related to class, with between 37 and 50 per cent of women across the middle classes claiming they used them, compared to between around 15 to 27 per cent across the working classes. Among the cookbooks used, Mrs Beeton remained a strong favourite (although Crawford pauses to speculate how many copies of Beeton were ever removed from the shelf), while among more recent publications, the most popular author was Elizabeth Craig and the most popular cookbooks those linked to appliances such as gas ovens and products such as flour (pp. 112-15). Compared to cookery books, Crawford reports a relative lack of interest in magazine and newspaper articles on food: only between a quarter and a third of women across the middle classes declared an interest in them. While some women's primary interest in these articles was information about slimming and diet, 'It was the more practical side of devising and preparing meals which appealed most to those who declared they were interested in newspaper and magazine articles on food' (Crawford, 1938: 86).

While Crawford's research is useful in demonstrating the extent to which there was an interest in cooking and the expanding cookery book market, it tells us little about the extent to which they were used by middle-class women in the cooking process or for menu planning. The ways in which *Good Housekeeping* addresses its readers is equally ambiguous. Single women tend to be addressed as if they will be performing their own cooking on very limited cooking apparatus in 'rooms'. While in 1922, the pleasure of the practice of cooking is measured by the end result in 'food that is not only tasty, but has some cheer and comfort as well' (Anon., 1922a/1990: 15), by 1932 the cooking process itself is also presented as a potential source of pleasure that might be understood as leisure in contrast to paid labour ('a pleasant change from office work') and as a skill that many women might need to set out to acquire (Peck, 1932/1990: 130).

However, in the cookery columns with a more general address, *Good Housekeeping* presents recipes frequently centred around an ingredient which might be addressed to the home cook ('Good Things from the Egg Basket', 'A Word in Praise of Mushrooms') with menu plans which include recipes centred around events ('Catering for a Dance') which might be more difficult for the solo home-cook to pull off. Many of the columns achieve a delicate balancing act, leaving space for the reader to be addressed as cook or as manager of a cook. However, in other places, the reader is more directly addressed as responsible for cooking: Good Housekeeping Institute cookery courses were almost exclusively aimed at the middle-class cook and rarely took on the training of servants. Likewise, an advertisement for a 1926 edition of the *Good Housekeeping Cookery Book* claims that 'Thousands of the women who read "Good Housekeeping" would tell you that they are good cooks' (advertisement from 1926, in Braithwaite and Walsh, 1992: 55).

Therefore, while evidence from the period is too sketchy to conclude that middle-class women had now been wholly transformed into cooks, cooking increasingly needed to be reconciled with middle-class femininity. Upwardly mobile women, new to middle-class status, are unlikely to have had experience of servants and would be more likely to have experienced cooking as an expected part of their role as housewife and mother. However, this doesn't necessarily mean that such women were experienced cooks, and changing class status involved some changing culinary expectations. Middle-class women who grew up accustomed to domestic servants were also unlikely to have had the opportunity to acquire culinary skills: one reader of *Good Housekeeping* who decided to give up her 'cook-general' in order to invest in her son's private education admitted to 'no practical experience' of cooking (Anon., 1934/1992: 126). E. M. Delafield's Provincial Lady also notes an 'unsuccessful endeavour to learn cooking by correspondence in twelve lessons' (1984: 200). While elementary school education did provide a schooling in domestic subjects for girls from the late nineteenth century, with cookery established as a separate subject in 1882, the curriculum avoided as much 'hands-on' experience as possible, as it was thought to cost too much (Attar, 1990).

The overall decline in the number of homes having domestic servants, and a decline in the number of live-in servants within the middle-class household, combined with the expansion of the middle classes, meant that the middle-class cook was clearly an emergent figure during this period. Furthermore, Giles suggests that those women who found themselves with a reduced amount of domestic help would be more likely to take on 'worthy' domestic tasks such as cooking (a task which had high status within the hierarchy of domestic service) than the less pleasant and 'unworthy' aspects of domestic labour:

> Women's magazines focused on personal care, cooking, sewing, interior design and childcare rather than on how to whiten steps or scrub a scullery floor. Thus those tasks which were potentially creative ... were highlighted as acceptable and indeed fulfilling activities, while 'the rough' remained unspoken – degrading work, hidden and suppressed in these respectable and 'modern' conceptions of housework. (Giles, 1995: 151)

Indeed, there are some striking similarities here to the recent uses of elements of domesticity by the 'new' middle classes, who also concentrate on the more 'pleasant' and 'creative' elements of domestic life which make a more significant contribution to maintaining distinctive and distinguished lifestyles (Bell, 2002; Gregson and Lowe, 1995; Hollows, 2003). In this way, the creation of the middle-class cook was part of a wider shift in which class differences were less clearly signified by one's relationship to domestic labour (as employer or employee), and instead signified through one's relationship to specific forms of domestic labour and the dispositions that were brought to these tasks (see Glucksmann, 1990).

However, in a period in which middle-class femininity was still strongly associated with the figure of 'the mistress of the house', the extent to which middle-class women sought to make their participation in the more 'worthy' aspects of domestic labour visible is still subject to some debate. While the Women's Institute and associated organizations undoubtedly promoted skills such as jam making through which women could demonstrate their culinary expertise, and while producing an 'interesting' meal could be used to signify 'modern femininity', many women may also have chosen to make their culinary practices 'invisible' as a means of masking the extent of their 'servantless' existence. For example, Oliver *et al.* (1994: 91) note how housing design in the inter-war suburbs positioned the kitchen to enable 'the housewife to cook meals without the embarrassment of being seen at work by visitors'. Nonetheless, in this period, class differences were increasingly articulated through domestic labour as 'the meanings attributed to housework, rather than "servant-keeping" itself, became key signifiers of social identity' (Giles, 2004: 90). This provides a context for understanding the meaning of cooking – amid other elements of domesticity – as part of the lifestylization of domestic labour.

The Value of Cooking in *Good Housekeeping*

Women's magazines have proved a useful resource for critics working on historical changes in culinary tastes and cultures. Although Crawford's comments noted above suggest the need for caution in generalizing from representations of cooking to lived food practices, Mennell (1996: 233) suggests that from the late-nineteenth century, 'There is a high degree of correlation between the food found in cookery columns and cookery books on the one hand, descriptions of domestic food in contemporary literature, memoirs and journalism'. Furthermore, and central to the analysis developed below, Warde (1997: 44) suggests that cookery columns offer 'an implicit set of answers to the questions "what and how shall we eat?"' In what follows, I expand Warde's questions to show that women's magazines also propose some answers to the question, 'How and what shall we cook?' In this way, women's magazines need to be understood as providing guidance on the more widespread activities involved in what DeVault (1991) calls 'feeding work', which incorporates not only planning and shopping for meals and cooking them, but also scheduling meals to create the *experience* of family life. For DeVault, feeding work is primarily about caring, the 'undefined, unacknowledged activity central to women's identity' (1991: 4). While *Good Housekeeping* addressed an audience who may or may not have been involved in the activity of cooking, it nonetheless addressed an audience who were united in their overall responsibility for feeding work.

Mennell (1996) argues that the representation of food in *Good Housekeeping* in the 1920s and 1930s not only emphasized a new spirit of modernity in relation to cookery but was also underpinned by two key values, economy and anti-monotony. This argument is certainly supported by my analysis below, although health emerges as a key third value. The analysis that follows also draws on the culinary antinomies identified by Warde which, despite being deployed in different ways in different contexts as 'principles of recommendation' (1997: 47), act as 'values which legitimize choice between foodstuffs' (p. 55). These oppositions are: novelty and tradition, health and indulgence, economy and extravagance, and care and convenience. These antinomies not only provide a useful basis for understanding the representation of dispositions towards cooking in the inter-war period; they also provide the basis for analyzing how the meanings of cooking are related to the construction of classed and gendered dispositions.

A clear stance against monotony, with a corresponding emphasis on novelty, acts as a guiding 'principle of recommendation' in *Good Housekeeping* in the inter-war period. As the magazine claims, 'When "Good Housekeeping" comes in the at the door, monotony in diet flies out of the window' (Anon., 1923a/1990: 25). Novelty can be added through the use of different ingredients – for example, mushrooms add 'variety' (Anon. 1923b/1990: 27) – and through techniques of cooking and presentation that offer 'uncommon' ways with rice (Edwards, 1925/1990: 46) or suggest that 'scalloped tomato surprise is particularly novel' (Anon., 1922b/1990: 12). Over the period, international influences also offer a means of adding novelty (see, for example Laverty, 1932 and van Blokland, 1932), although this can be simply reduced to a process of renaming so that Brussels sprouts become the more exotic 'choux de bruxelles' in 1928's Christmas menu (Cottington Taylor, 1928/1990: 86). By the late 1930s, anti-monotony had becomes something of a mantra: 'monotony should always be avoided in cooking' (Anon., 1939/1990: 172). New ways of combining ingredients – or the addition of sauces to offer new tastes – not only combated monotony but were a means for the homemaker to demonstrate her 'ingenuity' (Anon., 1922b/1990: 12) and 'individuality' by, for example, adding a dressing to a plain salad (Anon., 1926/1990: 61). In this way, the magazine creates a correspondence between novelty and creativity.

The relationship between science and novelty is more ambivalent in the magazine. While *Good Housekeeping* clearly embraced the use of new technologies, they were not necessarily presented in terms of their novelty value. However, this does appear in advertising, where science is harnessed to the war on monotony. For example, the Parkinson New Suburbia Gas Cooker in 1929 was recommended because it made the same foods taste different (advert in Braithwaite and Walsh, 1990: 96). The relative lack of attention to the novelty value of new convenience foods and appliances in editorial content can be related to the magazine's emphasis on individuality and creativity as a means of demonstrating difference from the conformity associated with the suburban lower-middle class who were identified with new convenience foods: 'preparing and cooking fresh foods was a signifier of a certain "cultural capital" even though such work had more often than not been performed by a cook or general servant' (Giles, 2004: 116). This recalls Mennell's observation that in *Good Housekeeping* there was sometimes a conflict between 'a spirit of social improvement and a pursuit of the new' (1996: 245): the magazine did not simply negotiate a mode of middle-class domestic femininity but was also concerned with making discriminations between different *modes* of domestic femininity based on different forms of capital.

If the antinomy between novelty and tradition demonstrated some anxieties about class, it also reflected 'the ambivalence of modernity, the tension between the excitement associated with new experience and the familiarity of that to which one had become accustomed' (Warde, 1997: 67). On occasion, *Good Housekeeping* addresses this ambivalence, and a recommendation to try 'something a little out of the common to please the men-folk' is tempered by the assurance that the recipes 'ought to please the most fastidious' (Anon., 1923a/1990: 25). In this way, the pursuit of novelty is incorporated within the wider demands of women's 'feeding work'. This does not mean that tradition is neglected: a 1935 article on 'The Fascination of Old English County Cookery' notes 'a great revival of interest in good English cookery' and suggests that 'it is surprising how easy it is in the rush of modern life to lose touch with old English customs, pursuits and foods' (Cottington Taylor, 1935/1990: 148).

However, the embrace of 'lost' traditions remains consistent with the fight against monotony and, in such instances, the values of tradition and novelty are reconciled. Indeed, a similar note in struck in Florence White's *Good Things in England* (1932/99). White's work with the English Folk Cookery Association spearheaded the revival of traditional English cookery that *Good Housekeeping* notes (see Floyd, this volume). For White, 'lost' traditions were not about monotony of diet but discovering novelty in England's past: traditional regional foods 'had once more come into their own and were now "the vogue"' (1932/99: 9). Likewise, foreign traditions could add novelty: 'The Dutch housewife avoids monotony with vegetables by stewing Brussels sprouts and chestnuts in butter and water.' (van Blokland, 1932: 82). Exotic traditions could also blend culture and novelty: 'novel' ways with fish are offered by the 'influence of the Moors' which offers 'good cooking that has been brought to a fine art' (Laverty, 1932: 82). A similar, if more developed, theme, is found in a contemporary cookbook, *Good Food from Italy*, in which Countess Morphy, a key influence on Elizabeth David, recommends Italian food on the basis of its rich living cultural tradition in which gastronomy is as important as 'the arts and letters' (1937: xxiii). In this way, novelty and tradition are not only combined, but being modern is also reconciled with being cultured while maintaining a distance from the convenience foods that represented 'mass culture'.

The recommendation of novelty in *Good Housekeeping* is also articulated with its emphasis on the importance of health: for example, piquant sauces are a means of adding novelty that helps to 'stimulate the appetite and therefore aids digestion' (Anon., 1923d/1990: 31). This contributed to a wider discourse on the importance of combating monotony to improve health during the period: for example, in *The People's Food*, Crawford (1938: 77) claimed that 'variety was the spice of diet' and monotony in meals made their 'digestion and assimilation more of a task for the system'. In this way, the modern woman's willingness to be adventurous in the kitchen was reconciled with her role as domestic medical expert, part of the growing responsibilities associated with both motherhood and feeding work (Sparke, 1995).

However, the importance of health was also invoked through scientific discourses and so needs to be understood within wider concerns about cleanliness and hygiene during the period that were linked to the popularity of 'germ theory' (Forty, 1986; Martens and Scott, 2005). If scientific rationality offered to create a modern home which was more able to resist the threats posed by dirt and germs, then science also offered to liberate people from superstitious attitudes to food. Just as science and technology provided jobs for many men of the expanding middle classes, the *Good Housekeeping* reader is addressed as an educated and intelligent modern woman who embraces scientific knowledge in the home and wishes to make informed decisions. Indeed, in 'Cookery as a Career for Women', Florence Jack attempts to legitimate feminine domestic practice as equal to scientific professions: cooking 'should stand on an equal footing with medicine. To prevent a body becoming diseased by feeding it properly is surely as advantageous to mankind as curing it with drugs' (Jack, 1924/1990: 38). However, on other occasions, scientific experts are called in to address the reader. In 'The Truth about Canned Food', a response to a food scare of the 1920s, William G. Savage aims to 'set out the scientific facts of the case, so that the reader may be able to form a reliable opinion of the subject' (1923/1990: 20).

Health was also a key means of recommendation in advertising. In response to a food scare about preservatives, an advert for the Kelvinator fridge warns that 'no housewife will choose to feed her family on adulterated products containing benzoic acid or other metallic poisons' (advertisement from 1927 in Braithwaite and Walsh, 1990: 67). Text-heavy advertising for the 'natural' food, 'Allinson unadulterated *whole*meal bread', also mobilizes an array of scientists and nutritional 'facts' to warn of 'the dangers of that apparently harmless article of diet, white bread' (Advertisement from 1924 in Braithwaite and Walsh, 1990: 43). As well as the familiar attention to digestion and constipation that characterizes the inter-war years, 'scientific knowledge' about diet is intertwined with moral appeals to the health of the nation: white bread will 'turn us into a C3 nation'. Another advertisement for the same product reiterates the medicalization of feeding the family: 'Good Housekeeping is something more than the efficient management of your home, or the balancing of the family budget. Far more important than these is the maintenance of the health, vigour and physical fitness of the whole family' (advertisement from 1926 in Braithwaite and Walsh, 1990: 63). Likewise, the Grape Nuts Company, in its appeal to 'thinking mothers', confidently states that 'The modern mother – above all people – is the family health specialist' (advertisement from 1928 in Braithwaite and Walsh, 1990: 80-1). Horlick's goes for a more emotional appeal to readers, combining the backing of the medical profession for the drink with the suggestion this 'energy-food' can also assist with mental health, fighting such problems as fretfulness, being 'a bit backward' and having 'a whole bad term in school' (advertisement from 1932 in Braithwaite and Walsh, 1990: 123).

If these appeals to health addressed the reader as an intelligent family scientist and medical expert, they also need to be understood within wider concerns about healthy eating in the period. First, diet had become a question of the 'national health' when the recruitment of the forces during World War I revealed high levels of under-nourishment. In the post-war period, a country 'fit for heroes' became identified with a country in which there was 'nutritional adequacy' (Burnett, 1968: 283). Second, appeals to 'healthy eating' became a key mechanism for advertising some forms of branded goods. In particular, the British breakfast was being reconstructed during the period, with companies like Kellogg's promoting 'American-style' cereals. In *Good Housekeeping*, these cereals were recommended because they offered variety, were convenient, and aided digestion (Garbutt, 1932/1990: 121), forming part of a wider trend towards 'lighter eating' identified by Mennell (1996). Finally, this was linked to the increasing importance of nutritional science, which situated feeding work squarely within scientific discourses. For example, in 'What Should a *Woman* Eat?', Dr. Cecil Webb-Johnson (1924/1990: 41) not only includes a table in which foods are ranked in terms of the length of time they take to digest, but the reader is also encouraged to see their food choices in nutritional terms. The reader is warned about the medical dangers of over-indulgence in 'flesh foods' while reminded that some meat it necessary for energy (thus avoiding the 'bitter' and 'acrimonious' ways of vegetarians). Likewise, the doctor advises, 'The green vegetables … are not particularly nutritious, but contain the useful vitamines [*sic*].' In this way, 'food values' become a key principle of recommendation, and a key component of the practice of menu planning. Furthermore, despite Webb-Johnson's jibes, there are a surprising number of features on meat-less and vegetarian meals, especially during the early 1930s, that clearly articulate health with another key value, economy.

If the emphasis on health over indulgence emphasizes a sense of moderation and restraint that distinguishes the morality of the middle class from the concupiscence associated with a non-modern aristocratic class, then so does *Good Housekeeping*'s obsessive concern with economy. This is not unique to the magazine: Mennell identifies a long-standing concern with economy in British domestic cookery and, within the inter-war period, highlights the importance of economy in *Woman's Life* and *Woman's Own*, magazines he associates with the lower-middle and affluent working classes. Definitions of 'good housekeeping' in *Good Housekeeping* usually include the importance of good budgeting. For example, 'The Business of Good Housekeeping' (1922) makes analogies between domestic budgeting and middle-class occupations, advising readers on spending money 'wisely and scientifically', running the household as a 'business', and knowing when it is appropriate to be more extravagant or more economical (Wooler and Wooler, 1922/1990: 9). This concern with economy, and an abhorrence of waste, is manifest in repeated advice about the use of leftovers in recipes, with some columns (such as 1923's 'The Humble Crumb Disguised') entirely devoted to the topic (Anon., 1923c: 29). Advice is also given on making the most of inexpensive ingredients such as eggs, and the use of extravagant cuts of meat is claimed to be a sign of ignorance that, moreover, also leads to monotony (Anon., 1927/1990: 68-9). Indeed, the importance of economy is demonstrated through the ways in which it is made to cohere with the other values espoused by *Good Housekeeping*. In particular, economy is not only shown to be a means of applying the science of budgeting to the practice of feeding the family, but is also linked to an ability to demonstrate creativity. Feminine creativity is not simply based on traditional arts and crafts but embraces the spirit of modern scientific adventure. For example, in 'Home-made Liqueurs' (1931), Ann Benshaw (1931/1990: 117) claims, 'Man, conservative ever may scoff at home-made concoctions ... but woman, adventurous, likes to experiment in search of novelty and economy'.

The significance of the concern with economy cannot simply be explained by the material position of the middle classes in the inter-war period. The period 1918-23 has been linked to a sense of 'crisis' among the British middle classes, with the threat of 'pauperization' experienced as real by many members of the class (McKibbin 1998: 52). However, McKibbin suggests that in the period 1923-38, the middle classes experienced relative economic stability, and frequently economic gain, although middle-class cultures were still shaped by the threat of instability and crisis. While this threat, and the spectre of pauperization, may partly explain the importance of economy in the pages of *Good Housekeeping*, the pursuit of (appropriately-judged and scientifically-based) economy was also a means of distinguishing the responsible figure of the middle-class woman from other figures of femininity such as the pleasure-seeking 'gad-abouts and the fools' (Sidgwick, 1924/1986: 29-30). By giving the middle-class homemaker a sense of vocation, and making her responsible for professionalized work that enable her to demonstrate her educational capital, she is not only distinguished from the idle rich 'expensive parasite' (Bonham-Carter, 1924/1986: 34) but also from the lower-middle-class or working-class domestic drudge, 'those who toil and moil to no purpose' (Sidgwick, 1924/1986: 29). By emphasizing the potential for individuality and creativity in the practices of cooking, *Good Housekeeping* articulates domestic labour and middle-class femininity, creating a modern figure distinguished from what Vera Brittain described as 'the socially irresponsible woman who doesn't want to use her mind or to take any part in disinterested service' (cited in Giles, 2004: 43).

Science and Spells

It is in this context that the representation of new 'labour-saving' technologies in *Good Housekeeping* needs to be understood. It would be easy to read the increasing entry of forms of scientific management into the home, along with the increasing mechanization of the cooking process through appliances such as electric cookers, as part of a process of culinary deskilling. Such transformations have certainly been read this way by feminist critics who express a form of 'culinary Luddism' (Laudan, 1999). Luce Giard (1998) and Mary Drake McFeeley (2001), for example, both argue that capitalist rationalization has destroyed a 'living tradition' of feminine culinary culture. However, not only is it problematic to see 'technological innovation in the home as expression of a conspiracy towards a devaluation of essentially womanly activities' (Silva, 2000: 626) but this also ignores the ways in which entry of new technologies into the private sphere cannot simply be understood as colonization as it ignores the multiple ways in which 'the modern becomes real at the most intimate and mundane levels of experience and interaction' (Felski, 2000: 66; see also Hollows, forthcoming). Furthermore, in a context in which many middle-class women in the period had little in the way of culinary skills in the first place, the introduction of new technologies cannot really be thought of in terms of deskilling but more in terms of reskilling, or, indeed, simply skilling.

On one hand, then, *Good Housekeeping*'s incorporation of science and technology into cookery can be seen as part of the process of constructing the housewife, a middle-class figure who is a product of modernity. Its embrace of science virtually took the form of a manifesto in its first edition:

> in the offices of GOOD HOUSEKEEPING, a modern and properly equipped kitchen has been installed, and there every recipe before being printed will be tested, and only those recipes which have passed the test of a widely known practical cookery expert, skilled in the knowledge of what a family welcomes, will be given. These dishes, old and new, will be closely described, and there will be nothing casual about the choice of the explanations. They will be well-worth keeping in the note-book that will always be found on the good housekeeper's kitchen shelf.' (Anon., 1922c/1986: 11)

The magazine offered advice on buying new appliances such as fridges and incorporating them into the home, commenting on details such as the scientific principles underpinning them, the suitability of different types, their advantages in terms of family health, their appearance and their cost to run (Garbutt, 1932). The 'scientific' approach to housework was also incorporated within the recipes which, it claimed, were 'tried and tested' and, therefore, ensured the reproducibility and reliability of results 'if the directions are followed completely' (Jack, 1922/1990: 10).[1] Indeed, such an approach is still evident in the magazine's food columns today.

On the other hand, despite the magazine's association with a scientific approach to housework, cooking is not simply reduced to a science. This needs to be understood in terms of critiques of mass culture during the period that saw technology, industrialization and scientific rationality as responsible for a process of decline in which culture was divorced from a living tradition and became mass produced, in turn producing a homogeneous mass of conformist consumers. Narratives of culinary decline as cultural decline were also circulating in the period. For example, in *The People's Food*, Crawford claimed it is crucial to encourage 'home-cooking' because 'in a modern civilization we are in danger of losing our hold on the art and crafts of life. Our requirements are machine-made and machine-satisfied. A free democracy can ultimately be preserved only on the basis of individuals expressing their individuality' (1938: 17).

Good Housekeeping occupied a difficult position in relation to these discourses. It was the (lower) middle class suburb that was most frequently located as the home of mass culture and the middle-class female consumer, the target audience for new mass-produced appliances, who was seen as synonymous with mass culture. Therefore, Giles argues, the magazine needed to address its readers with 'a version of femininity in which "common sense" and robust reason were highlighted rather than the promiscuous passivity inscribed in the figure of the irrational female consumer or the "neuroticism" of the suburban housewife' (2004: 123). Given its importance to middle-class housing patterns, the magazine does address the characteristics and practicalities of suburban living across a range of articles. However, there is still scope for dialogue within its pages. For example, Lady Violet Bonham-Carter identified the suburbs as an 'unsatisfactory compromise' between the metropolis and the country, where 'villas grow like weeds' and where there 'can never be atmosphere or romance' as 'they have no soil, no key or colour of their own' (1926/1992: 52).

The stress on individuality and creativity in cooking needs to be understood in this context, offering scope to wed the application of modern scientific dispositions with more 'artistic' and traditionally 'cultured' modes of cultural capital. However, this also creates space for the struggle between different *forms* of capital. This is best summed up in another feature by Bonham-Carter, 'Are you a Good Housekeeper?', in which she argued that

> We find that the prescribed proportions do not really vitally matter. It is
> the spell one mutters over them. Some people come into the world

knowing the spell, others die without having learnt it ... in the main
good housekeepers are born and not made. (1928/1995: 73)

In the process, while much of *Good Housekeeping* seems to democratize
knowledge about household management for the 'intelligent reader', Bonham-
Carter reminds (or reassures) the reader that there are perhaps limits to a modern
lifestyle education, suggesting that the inherited cultural capital of the established
professional middle classes still forms the basis for the most legitimate
dispositions. The 'spells' which magic up good housekeeping are cultured rather
than scientific: she tells us 'how food can be treated lyrically' and advocates that it
is artistry that can be conjured up in the fine details of everyday life:

> Oysters, caviare [sic] and *foie gras* are treats of course, once in a way,
> but they are not things it occurs to us to miss from the menu of our daily
> lives. It is humiliating to reflect that it is not to want of money but to
> want of skill, taste, intelligence and resource that we owe our nasty and
> our dreary fare. We are food-bores, food-Philistines, where we might be
> food-wits, food-artists, food-poets. (p. 74)

In this way, the reader is reminded that, while managerial and scientific
dispositions towards housekeeping might be part of the process of creating *a*
middle-class housewife who is part of an expanding middle-class, the differential
distribution of more legitimate forms of cultural capital still marks forms of
distinction *between* fractions of the middle class and between different modes of
middle-class domestic femininity. A 'modern' scientific approach to cooking might
distinguish middle-class femininities, but 'spells' gesture towards inherited class
dispositions that distinguish between new and established middle classes.

Good Housekeeping can therefore be seen as a form of lifestyle media,
with its contributors acting as cultural intermediaries both educating its readers
about new forms of 'modern' living and interpreting the significance of these ways
of living. In the magazine the tension between democratization and distinction
identified by Bell (2002) in contemporary lifestyle media is resolved *across* its
pages: while the broad sweep of the magazine is to democratize knowledge in
keeping with its modern image, distinction is nonetheless maintained through
appeals to tradition. Although both Bennett (2002) and Giles (2004) correctly
identify this struggle between the modern and the traditional in terms of different
conceptions of the meaning of 'home', it also needs to be understood as an
overlapping struggle between different forms of cultural capital.

This chapter has situated the domestic at the heart of transformations
associated with modernity. Drawing on Felski, my discussion has problematized
the idea that domestic life can be simply equated with tradition and cultural
reproduction, and demonstrates how domestic life contributes to the experience of
modernity. In this way, this chapter seeks to contribute to a feminist understanding
of home that challenges any simple opposition between modernity and domesticity.
However, Felksi's observations also signal how a consideration of gender
problematizes theories of lifestyle as a primarily postmodern or late-modern
phenomenon. If critics such as Featherstone have highlighted how an emphasis on

lifestyle characterizes the dispositions of the new middle classes from the 1960s and 1970s onwards, there is a longer history of class struggle through lifestyle waged between earlier waves of 'new' and 'old' middle classes (see Gunn, 2005). *Good Housekeeping* thus highlights how lifestyle was used in the inter-war period as part of a wider struggle in social space over both classed and gendered identities. Far from home simply operating as a site of reproduction and stasis, therefore, it operates as a site of on-going class production, reproduction and negotiation which is also about a dynamic struggle over the meanings of femininity.

Note

1   However, while some recipes advocated the use of an oven thermometer to achieve precise temperatures, this is frequently supplemented – or replaced – by less precise terms such as 'hot', 'moderate' and 'cool'. The magazine did not presume the reader had access to a regulo-controlled gas oven, and electric cookers with thermostatic controls that measured temperature in Fahrenheit were not introduced until 1933 (and then only on expensive models). For more, see Forty (1986) and Silva (2000).

References

Anon. (1922a/1990) 'For the Bachelor Woman: A Quickly Made Meal at the End of a Busy Day', in B. Braithwaite and N. Walsh (eds) *Food Glorious Food: Eating and Drinking with Good Housekeeping, 1922-42*, London: Random House.

Anon. (1922b/1990) 'Vegetable Dishes for Lent', in B. Braithwaite and N. Walsh (eds) *Food Glorious Food: Eating and Drinking with Good Housekeeping, 1922-42*, London: Random House.

Anon. (1922c/1986) 'The Reason for Good Housekeeping', in B. Braithwaite, N. Walsh and G. Davies (eds) *From Ragtime to Wartime: the Best of Good Housekeeping, 1922-1939*, London: Random House.

Anon. (1923a/1990) 'To Please the Men', in B. Braithwaite and N. Walsh (eds) *Food Glorious Food: Eating and Drinking with Good Housekeeping, 1922-42*, London: Random House.

Anon. (1923b/1990) 'A Word in Praise of Mushrooms', in B. Braithwaite and N. Walsh (eds) *Food Glorious Food: Eating and Drinking with Good Housekeeping, 1922-42*, London: Random House.

Anon. (1923c/1990) 'The Humble Crumb Disguised', in B. Braithwaite and N. Walsh (eds) *Food Glorious Food: Eating and Drinking with Good Housekeeping, 1922-42*, London: Random House.

Anon. (1923d/1990) 'When the Cupboard is Bare', in B. Braithwaite and N. Walsh (eds) *Food Glorious Food: Eating and Drinking with Good Housekeeping, 1922-42*, London: Random House.

Anon. (1926/1990) 'Piquant Salad Dressings', in B. Braithwaite and N. Walsh (eds) *Food Glorious Food: Eating and Drinking with Good Housekeeping, 1922-42*, London: Random House.

Anon. (1927/1990) 'The Bride's Primer of Cookery: Selecting and Purchasing Beef', in B. Braithwaite and N. Walsh (eds) *Food Glorious Food: Eating and Drinking with Good Housekeeping, 1922-42*, London: Random House.

Anon. (1934/1992) 'How Others Live VII: A Fifteen-Roomed House and an Income of £376', in B. Braithwaite and N. Walsh (eds) *Home Sweet Home: the Best of Good Housekeeping, 1922-39*, London: Random House.

Anon. (1939/1990) 'Seasoning is a Subtle Art', in B. Braithwaite and N. Walsh (eds) *Food Glorious Food: Eating and Drinking with Good Housekeeping, 1922-42*, London: Random House.

Andrews, M. (1997) *The Acceptable Face of Feminism: the Women's Institute as Social Movement*, London: Lawrence and Wishart.

Attar, D. (1990) *Wasting Girls' Time: The History and Politics of Home Economics*, London: Virago.

Beddoe, D. (1989) *Back to Home and Duty: Women Between the Wars, 1918-1939*, London: Pandora.

Beetham, M. (2003) 'Of Recipe Books and Reading in the Nineteenth Century: Mrs Beeton and her Cultural Consequences', in J. Floyd and L. Forster (eds) *The Recipe Reader: Narratives – Contexts – Traditions*, Aldershot: Ashgate.

Bell, D. (2002) 'From Writing at the Kitchen Table to TV Dinners: Food Media, Lifestylization and European Eating', paper presented at the Eat Drink and Be Merry? Cultural Meanings of Food in the 21st Century Conference, Amsterdam, June.

Bennett, T. (2002) 'Home and Everyday Life', in T. Bennett and D. Watson (eds) *Understanding Everyday Life*, Oxford: Blackwell.

Benshaw, A. (1931/1990) 'Home-Made Liqueurs', in B. Braithwaite and N. Walsh (eds) *Food Glorious Food: Eating and Drinking with Good Housekeeping, 1922-42*, London: Random House.

Bonham-Carter, Lady V. (1924/1986) 'Should Wives Have Wages?', in B. Braithwaite, N. Walsh and G. Davies (eds) *From Ragtime to Wartime: the Best of Good Housekeeping, 1922-1939*, London: Random House.

Bonham-Carter, Lady V. (1926/1992) 'A Home in London or in the Country', in B. Braithwaite and N. Walsh (eds) *Home Sweet Home: the Best of Good Housekeeping, 1922-39*, London: Random House.

Bonham-Carter, Lady V. (1928/1992) 'Are You a Good Housekeeper?', in B. Braithwaite and N. Walsh (eds) *Home Sweet Home: the Best of Good Housekeeping, 1922-39*, London: Random House.

Braithwaite, B. and N. Walsh (eds) (1990) *Food Glorious Food: Eating and Drinking with Good Housekeeping, 1922-42*, London: Random House.

Braithwaite, B. and N. Walsh (eds) (1992) *Home Sweet Home: the Best of Good Housekeeping, 1922-39*, London: Random House.

Braithwaite, B., N. Walsh and G. Davies (eds) (1986), *From Ragtime to Wartime: the Best of Good Housekeeping, 1922-1939*, London: Random House.

Brunsdon, C. (2004) 'Taste and Time on Television', *Screen*, Vol. 45(2), pp. 115-29.

Burnett, J. (1968) *Plenty and Want: A Social History of Diet in England from 1815 to the Present Day*, Harmondsworth: Penguin.

Cottington Taylor, D.D. (1928/1990) 'A Christmas Dinner Planned by the Chef of the Good Housekeeping Restaurant', in B. Braithwaite and N. Walsh (eds) *Food Glorious Food: Eating and Drinking with Good Housekeeping, 1922-42*, London: Random House.

Cottington Taylor, D.D. (1935/1990) 'The Fascination of Old English Country Cookery', in B. Braithwaite and N. Walsh (eds) *Food Glorious Food: Eating and Drinking with Good Housekeeping, 1922-42*, London: Random House.

Crawford, Sir W. (with H. Broadley) (1938) *The People's Food*, London: Heinemann.

Davidoff, E. and Hall, C. (2002) *Family Fortunes: Men and Women of the English Middle Class 1780-1850*, revised edition, London: Routledge.

Delafield, E.M. (1984) *The Diary of a Provincial Lady*, London: Virago.

DeVault, M. (1991), *Feeding the Family: The Social Organization of Caring as Gendered Work*, Chicago: University of Chicago Press.

Edwards, E. (1925/1990) 'Uncommon Ways of Serving Rice' in B. Braithwaite and N. Walsh (eds) *Food Glorious Food: Eating and Drinking with Good Housekeeping, 1922-42*, London: Random House.

Featherstone, M. (1991) *Consumer Culture and Postmodernism*, London: Sage.

Felski, R. (2000) *Doing Time: Feminist Theory and Postmodern Culture*, New York: New York University Press.

Forty, A. (1986) *Objects of Desire: Design and Society, 1750-1980*, London: Thames & Hudson.

Garbutt, P.L. (1932) Selecting a Household Refrigerator', *Good Housekeeping*, Vol. XXI(4), pp. 48-9, 138, 140.

Garbutt, P.L. (1932/1990) 'The First Meal of the Day: the Values of Cereals as a Breakfast Food', in B. Braithwaite and N. Walsh (eds) *Food Glorious Food: Eating and Drinking with Good Housekeeping, 1922-42*, London: Random House.

Giard, L. (1998), 'Doing-Cooking', in M. De Certeau, L. Giard and P. Mayol, *The Practice of Everyday Life: Volume 2: Living and Cooking*, Minneapolis, University of Minnesota Press.

Giles, J. (1995) *Women, Identity and Private Life, 1990-1950*, Basingstoke: Macmillan.

Giles, J. (2004) *The Parlour and the Suburb: Domestic Identities, Class, Femininity and Modernity*, Oxford: Berg.

Glucksmann, M. (1990) *Women Assemble: Women Workers and the New Industries in the Interwar Years*, London: Routledge.

Gregson, N. and Lowe, M. (1995) '"Too Much Work": Class, Gender and the Reconstitution of Middle Class Domestic Labour', in T. Butler and M. Savage (eds) *Social Change and the Middle Class*, London: UCL Press.

Gunn, S. (2005) 'Translating Bourdieu: Cultural Capital and the English Middle Class in Historical Perspective', *British Journal of Sociology*, Vol. 56(1), pp. 49-64.

Horwood, C. (1997) 'Housewives' Choice: Women as Consumers Between the Wars', *History Today*, Vol. 47(3), pp. 23-8.

Hollows, J. (2003) 'Feeling Like a Domestic Goddess: Post-Feminism and Cooking', *European Journal of Cultural Studies*, Vol. 6(2), pp. 179-202.

Hollows, J. (forthcoming) 'The Feminist and the Cook: Betty Friedan, Julia Child and Domestic Femininity', in E. Casey and L. Martens (eds) *Gender and Domestic Consumption*, Aldershot: Ashgate.

Humble, N. (1996) 'A Touch of Boheme', *Times Literary Supplement*, June 14, pp. 15-16.

Jack, F. (1922/1990) 'A Seasonable Lunch', in B. Braithwaite and N. Walsh (eds) *Food Glorious Food: Eating and Drinking with Good Housekeeping, 1922-42*, London: Random House.

Jack, F. (1924/1990) 'Cookery as a Career for Women', in B. Braithwaite and N. Walsh (eds) *Food Glorious Food: Eating and Drinking with Good Housekeeping, 1922-42*, London: Random House.

Laudan, R. (1999) 'A World of Inauthentic Cuisine', proceedings of the Conference, *Cultural and Historical Aspects of Food: Yesterday, Today, Tomorrow*, Oregon State University, April 9-11, pp. 146-65.

Laverty, M (1932), 'Spanish Ways with Fish', *Good Housekeeping,* Vol. XXI (3), p. 82.

Light, A. (1991) *Forever England: Femininity, Literature and Conservatism Between the Wars*, London: Routledge.

McFeeley, M. Drake (2001*) Can She Bake a Cherry Pie? American Women and the Kitchen in the Twentieth Century*, Amherst: University of Massachusetts Press.

Martens, L. and Scott, S. (2005) 'The Unbearable Lightness of Cleaning: Representations of Domestic Practice and Products in *Good Housekeeping* Magazine (UK) 1951-2001', *Consumers, Markets and Culture*, Vol. 8(3), forthcoming.

McKibbin, R. (1998) *Classes and Cultures: England 1918-51*, Oxford: Oxford University Press.

Mennell, S. (1995), *All Manners of Food: Eating and Taste in England and France from the Middle Ages to the Present*, 2nd edition, Chicago: University of Illinois Press.

Moore, D.J. (1923/1992) 'The Servantless House', in B. Braithwaite and N. Walsh (eds) *Home Sweet Home: the Best of Good Housekeeping, 1922-39*, London: Random House.

Morphy, Countess (1937) *Good Food From Italy: A Receipt Book*, London: Chatto and Windus.

Oliver, P., I. David and I. Bentley (1994) *Dunroamin: the Suburban Semi and its Enemies*, London: Pimlico.

O'Sullivan, T. (2005) 'From Television Lifestyle to Lifestyle Television', in D. Bell and J. Hollows (eds) *Ordinary Lifestyles: Popular Media, Consumption and Taste*, Milton Keynes: Open University Press.

Peck, P. (1932/1990) 'Meals for the Business Girl', in B. Braithwaite and N. Walsh (eds) *Food Glorious Food: Eating and Drinking with Good Housekeeping, 1922-42*, London: Random House.

Savage, M., J. Barlow, P. Dickens and T. Fielding (1992) *Property, Bureaucracy and Culture: Middle-class Formation in Contemporary Britain*, London: Routledge.

Savage, W.G. (1923/1990) 'The Truth about Canned Foods', in B. Braithwaite and N. Walsh (eds) *Food Glorious Food: Eating and Drinking with Good Housekeeping, 1922-42*, London: Random House.

Sidgwick, A. (1924/1986) 'Should Married Women Work?', in B. Braithwaite, N. Walsh and G. Davies (eds) *From Ragtime to Wartime: the Best of Good Housekeeping, 1922-1939*, London: Random House.

Silva, E. (2000), 'The Cook, The Cooker and the Gendering of the Kitchen', *Sociological Review*, Vol. 48(4), pp. 612-28.

Sparke, P. (1995) *As Long as its Pink: the Sexual Politics of Taste*, London: Pandora.

Taylor, P. (1979) 'Daughters and Mothers – Maids and Mistresses: Domestic Service Between the Wars', in J. Clarke, C. Critcher and R. Johnson (eds) *Working Class Culture: Studies in History and Theory*, London: Hutchinson.

Van Blokland, C.B. (1932) 'Recipes from Holland', *Good Housekeeping*, Vol. XXI(2), pp. 82-3.

Warde, A. (1997) *Consumption Food and Taste: Culinary Antinomies and Commodity Culture*, London, Sage.

Webb-Johnson, C. (1924/1990) 'What Should a Woman Eat?', in B. Braithwaite and N. Walsh (eds) *Food Glorious Food: Eating and Drinking with Good Housekeeping, 1922-42*, London: Random House.

Welch, H.A. (1922/1992) 'The Ideal Home: Part IV', in B. Braithwaite and N. Walsh, eds, *Home Sweet Home: the Best of Good Housekeeping, 1922-39*, London: Random House.

White, F. (1932/1999) *Good Things in England: A Practical Cookery Book for Everyday Use*, London: Persephone Books.

Wooler, M. and F. Wooler (1922/1990) 'The Business of Housekeeping: Making a Budget', in B. Braithwaite and N. Walsh (eds) *Food Glorious Food: Eating and Drinking with Good Housekeeping, 1922-42*, London: Random House.

Chapter 3

The Restaurant Guide as Romance: From Raymond Postgate to Florence White

Janet Floyd

> Varied menus bring diversity to the meals, which take in lobster ravioli, terrine of ham with roast parsnips, and roast rabbit with tarragon and wild mushrooms. Not all ingredients are top notch, but, despite a few inconsistencies in timing and seasoning, the cooking shows much promise. … Cheeses are served with good prune bread, and a well-executed pear Tatin has made a fine finish, accompanied by a creamy vanilla ice cream and a pool of sweet caramel sauce. Champagne is a big story on the wine list. (Ainsworth, *The Good Food Guide 2003*: 367)

No publication, it would seem, more perfectly accords with a view of lifestyle in which elaborate distinctions are enforced on the eager consumer's consciousness than the restaurant guide: this is a publication that tells the reader where to consume and what to ingest. From the newspaper review of the new restaurant to the annually issued guides to gastronomy, the reader may be inducted into or reconfirmed in the abstruse but absolute judgement of the food connoisseur on the current 'big story'. The assertion of the quality of the cultural capital to be gained through the appreciation of a fine meal could hardly evoke a more thoroughgoing confidence: the quotation from *The Good Food Guide 2003* above is full of echoes of high cultural activity (the 'well-executed' tart) and elegant forms (the 'finish'), as well as references to high status ('top notch' ingredients), and to 'diversity' tamed. This kind of commentary has the ring of truths universally acknowledged – and handed down – by a privileged group of which the reader becomes a member simply by grasping the codes to which these reviews refer. The restaurant guide addresses itself to a tiny proportion of the mass of restaurants (and even those included are subject to the most rigorous and unforgiving judgement); most catering establishments and the vast majority of experiences of 'eating out' are ignored. Rather, the judgements made in these reviews suggest a practice of dining that forms part of an expansive lifestyle, and a lifestyle characterized by unfettered choice and leisured consumption.

Traditionally, of course, gastronomy has been the province of the independent (socially privileged) male traveller who need take little notice of the petty restrictions of the restaurant. And indeed the restaurant guide does tend to convert the regions under discussion to spaces to be 'explored' according to the lifestyle of the socially disengaged traveller. The *Rough Guide to London*

Restaurants 2004 discusses the metropolis as 'really a series of villages' and (rather unconvincingly) Highgate and Shepherd's Bush as 'far-off lands' to the inhabitants of Clapham (Campion, 2004: x). The gastronomic traveller tells his readers of places more exotic than home, and celebrates the survival of a pre-industrial food culture elsewhere, where food is prepared without recourse to the systems characteristic of mass catering and the modern technologies of production with which his readers must grapple. A review of the elaborate offerings at the Old Bridge Hotel in Huntingdon in *The Good Food Guide 2003* demonstrates how firmly the restaurant guide still stands on the familiar ground of the gastronomic traveller with his love of the 'rustic' (gnocchi, pasta, beans, roast food, game) and his nostalgic (and, of course, highly misleading) association between 'peasant' foods and qualities of plenitude, tenderness and warmth:

> A starter of spinach and ricotta gnudi (like gnocchi) comes with sage butter, Parmesan and oil, while a large raviolo of Portland crab may be spiced with ginger, lemon-grass and coriander bisque. A perfectly cooked roast salmon steak with flageolet beans and braised fennel may follow, or a rustic seared breast of tender wood pigeon with garlic polenta, spinach and red wine sauce. There may be delicately flavoured cherry and camomile compote with lemon mousse to finish, or perhaps macaroons with warm apricots and coconut ice cream. (Ainsworth, 2003: 367)

Of course, Pierre Bourdieu (1984: 185) has traced the link between 'traditional cuisine' and the professional classes' 'taste for rare aristocratic foods'. The well-heeled would-be gastronome is encouraged to look backward for perfection, following the traveller of fine taste and independent means: the same edition of the *Guide* exhorts us, in its introduction, to visit our local restaurants in order to help (re)generate local traditions (Ainsworth, 2003: 30), and goes on to write lyrically of Hunstrete House Restaurant: a 'mellow golden-stone building with deer grazing outside the windows', where 'the menu appears not to change very often, but materials are sound' (p. 366).

However, even as the guide provides a highly-elaborated set of criteria to enable the reader to discern 'good' food and thus to participate in a particular range of activity, it does at the same time promote a sense of the dangers of dissatisfaction. If the guide's impulse is apparently to prevent unpredictable and unsatisfactory experiences by showing the consumer where to go, nonetheless, the possibility of 'bad' experiences looms. Traditionalism (or what is imagined as traditional), with its associations of simplicity and transparency in the preparation and appearance of familiar dishes, is reassuring as well as satisfying. Thus, from the first 1951-2 edition of the bible of British gastronomy, the *Good Food Guide,* the editor, Raymond Postgate uses the terms 'solid' and 'good plain cooking' to describe good food; while, in the 2003 edition, David Kenning still calls for food that has not been 'mucked about' (Postgate, 1951: 16, 22; Ainsworth, 2003: 31). The *Egon Ronay Guide* (1963) takes the focus on what 'you' can see in another direction, warning still, though, of the possibility of deception: 'You enter into soft pink lights, décor and furniture of subdued elegance, and are impressed by the convivial bustle. ...The menu and, to some extent, the selection of wines are impressive and you wonder whether it will all be as good as it reads' (Ronay, 1963: 280). Joanne Finkelstein (1989: 17) has drawn to our attention the 'controlled mutual scrutiny that characterises the restaurant', but perhaps the greatest scrutiny, as far as the restaurant guide is concerned, needs to be given to the goodness of the food diners must put in their mouths.

The serving of the food offers a further challenge for, somehow, the diner must put in a convincing performance as a discerning and deserving subject. Postgate, in the 1951-2 edition of the *Good Food Guide*, focuses on the class relations of 'service' and how the behaviour of male and female diners should be nuanced in the face of difficulty. He exhorts the reader to think of himself as at war with the restaurant staff: 'If the enemy hears one of you say: "I'll have whatever you do, dear," he immediately decides that he has no serious foes to encounter'. Postgate explains to the (assumed) female member of the party that her 'escort is engaged in delicate and dangerous warfare'. 'You are the reserve battalions; you must give him steady and calm support' (Postgate, 1951: 19-20). As Bourdieu argues, dining is always associated with gender and 'the whole conception of the domestic economy' (1984: 185), and indeed with understandings of the gendered body. Yet it is mildly surprising to find the twenty-first-century *Guide* still using terms of embattlement and indeed assertions of what are now outmoded norms of masculinity to describe the fight to eat 'organic' food. This 'fight', the editor argues, is not to be understood, 'as some detractors would argue', as 'some airy-fairy, namby-pamby "lifestyle" consideration on the part of "townies"'(Ainsworth, 2003: 18). The task of asserting food preferences is not a mere matter of 'townie' style nor the mere exercise of choice nuanced by a 'namby-pamby' élite, but an issue that may be understood in terms of gender and sexuality, identity and space.

Thus does the restaurant guide exemplify much that sociology and cultural studies have helped us to understand about dining out and its relationship to the definition and confirmation of class and gender. And yet, the work that the restaurant guide performs – and the conceptions of identity that it brings into play – may not necessarily as easily grasped or as firmly situated as is suggested by such terms as definition and confirmation. It is not only that this kind of text deals with that most uncertain and potentially troubling of substances, food, and with an activity, travel, that may be as disorienting as it is empowering;[1] the restaurant guide is almost invariably directed towards the reading of place, local, regional and national. And although most restaurant guides restrict themselves to the task of representing regional and metropolitan areas, the minority that undertake the task of surveying the nation must grapple with (and somehow put convincingly to rest) a range of debates about its identity.

David Chaney (1996: 35) has defined lifestyle as a 'way-of-being-in-the-world', but discussions of lifestyle characteristically evoke the predicament or the liberation of the individual in a situation in which cultural boundaries are of little significance. Indeed Chaney argues, as do others, that lifestyles 'undermine nation-state narratives' (p. 159). The guide to good food, however, loaded as it is with the task of delineating goodness and mapping where it may be found, is caught up in the work of describing how behaviour is to be achieved within, and in relation to, a national landscape. The qualities of that landscape must, inevitably, inflect the pursuit of satisfaction.

The two examples with which I am concerned here, Postgate's *Good Food Guide* and Florence White's *Where Shall We Eat Or Put Up?*, take contrasting approaches to the challenge of evoking what it is to pursue good food in England. Postgate's text may represent the very pattern of 'formulaic', 'highly circumscribed' class and gender behaviour described by Finkelstein (1989: 11, 179) but his work is dominated by the sense of the elusiveness of goodness and the relentless need to accept what is less than, perhaps merely reminiscent of, good. Florence White's proto-*Good Food Guide*, the 'Good Food Register', meanwhile, which she produced between 1934 and 1936, offers a much more utopian vision of finding an English identity through choosing and consuming food, and attempts to synthesize the finding of good food with the achievement of a satisfying national life. We can fruitfully attribute this contrast to the historical contexts of post-war disillusionment and the sense of Britain's waning powers experienced by Postgate's generation; and, in White's case, to the idealizing of rural tradition in the late 1920s and 1930s at a time when 'the total bankruptcy of the capitalist system shouted aloud for some sort of quick, rational, simple alternative' (Klugmann, 1979: 15). But I want to argue here that the differences between Postgate's and White's guides rest on the very different ways in which they understand the meaning of 'eating out' in England and their sense of what the activity of searching for good food can deliver in terms of an 'English' sense of self.

Raymond Postgate's *Good Food Guide*

Histories of British gastronomy offer considerable consensus in their view of Raymond Postgate's intervention in the scene of post-war eating in the late 1940s and early 1950s. The two best informed discussions of his work, those of Christopher Driver (1983) and Stephen Mennell (1996), differ in their sense of the context in which Postgate's *Good Food Guide* appeared; Driver is at pains to describe the rationing policy of the Labour Government in the period after World War Two as inimical to good food. Both, however, see Postgate as an important figure in regenerating British food, and as a gastronome of substance. And both are at pains to position Postgate as a man laden with cultural capital – an Oxford man, a classicist, a well-connected amateur historian and journalist, a lover of good wine – and yet not complacently privileged: we are told that he was a conscientious objector, left-leaning in his politics, an individualist.

The inception of the *Guide* lay in Postgate's article, 'Society for the Prevention of Cruelty to Food' published in 1949 in the short-lived *Leader Magazine*. Driver describes the process by which the 'Good Food Club' was launched in May 1950 by means of a membership form that readers could use to report on restaurants that they visited (1983: 48-52). The response provided the raw material for the first *Guide*, produced in Postgate's home and published in 1951.

Postgate starts from a position on British food in which he explains what the consumer desires through describing its absence. He sounds a predictable note in the first edition of the *Guide* when he follows the English tradition of assuming that the British cannot hope to emulate French cuisine; writing in 1951, his faint praise of restaurants in Britain extends only so far as to pointing out that 'There are even – though this is not France and cannot be – really individual dishes that one is anxious to taste' (Postgate, 1951: 25).[2] (And still, interestingly, the 2003 *Guide*, warns that despite the 'cult of the celebrity chef and saturation coverage of glitzy new restaurant openings', 'we' are not 'doing as well as France and Italy' (Ainsworth, 2003: 29).) Accordingly, of the categories of judgement of restaurant cookery generated by Postgate, only the second best is used to describe 'the man who is a real artist – who has dishes and specialities of his own'. The highest accolade available goes not to creativity, but to 'the real all-embracing Hotel Magnifique programme', that is, a *French* gastronomic experience (Postgate, 1951: 11).

Thus, from the start, Postgate is writing a guide to rarely attainable experiences, and describing a scene on the cusp of further deterioration. While poor British food is identified as a tradition stretching back to the mid-eighteenth century (Postgate, 1951: 16), the 'the last great war lowered standards even more … it remains worse only because public discontent is unorganised and (it must be admitted) sometimes also ignorant' (pp. 7-8). Certainly complaints about food and restaurants became a kind of *locus classicus* for élite anxieties about state control and mass culture in Britain during this post-war period of rationing and food legislation; and nostalgia for the quasi-feudal relations recalled by 'traditional' English or indeed French cuisine was commonly expressed by the privileged classes. But Postgate goes further than this kind of delineation of the baleful influence of mass taste and interests over the 'national' life; he is questioning the vitality of values driving those whom Inglis (2002) calls the 'eating out classes'.

Diners in Postgate's and other guides to dining of the period find themselves at a loss 'out there'. They face an uncertain sense of reality when they venture out to eat. For example, W. Bentley Capper, in *Dining Out?*, writes of the post-war diner 'bewildered by the changes brought by war-time, by "blitz" and by social "revolution"' (1950: 2). Capper makes no bones about the reasons: 'It had become less a matter of what one wanted than of what was left, and beyond that, what one was allowed to have; allowed not by the restaurant management but by dubious new powers like the Ministry of Food' (1950: 3). Postgate, however, is not so much interested in the political and legislative context in which degeneration has occurred, as in the more unnerving problem of how to situate oneself as a diner. It is characteristic of him to imagine his reader 'in a strange town', as he does in the first *Guide*, or to identify a type of restaurant as 'a place where any respectable woman can go for her lunch', leaving the reader with a sense of how far a woman might be compromised by going unknowingly to the *wrong* restaurant (Postgate, 1951: 15); to write of how 'nothing, however repellent' is 'what it should be' (p. 12); to recommend 'eternal vigilance' (p. 14). The effect is to evoke situations and moments of choice in which there is a danger of encroachment on the sense of self and limited means of self-preservation in the face of what one might have mistakenly chosen to eat. A kind of social chaos is threatened by the failure of readers to make correct choices themselves.

Postgate is grappling with a range of spatial dimensions, with the question of the context of our consumption. Post-war food writing is strongly, perhaps especially, shaped by the contested issue of international relations in a post-war Europe and, in particular, the problem how Britain should ally herself (either to Europe or to the United States) for best advantage.[3] There is no doubt that France dominates the gastronomic arena. There is also the United States, though, with its dark and uncontrollable forces of attraction and influence. In both contexts, Britain – the space in which Postgate's readers must somehow position themselves as men of taste – seems vulnerable.

The nation itself is difficult to map. As Patricia Yaeger (1996: 25) points out, we may expect space to be 'negotiable or continuous', but of course it is 'actually peppered with chasms of economic and cultural disjunctions'. Postgate struggles to plot London – teeming with restaurants – within the same space as the rest of the country. 'Out there' are the regional and the local: potentially the site of vibrant traditionalism, actually (as Postgate later recalled it in the 1969-70 *Guide*) a 'great grey plain of desolation' (p. vi). Some of the problems of drawing together the local, regional and metropolitan are expressed in Postgate's category, Class B. Flanked by Class A, 'Good Plain Cooking', and Class C, which is the work of the individual chef, lies Class B, 'Imaginative Local and National Cooking', which, interestingly, is illustrated by regional foods (haggis), local food (fish) and 'Chinese, Greek and Italian' cooking. The term 'imaginative' seems inappropriate to food that is apparently traditional (haggis) or simply locally available (fish); the point seems to be that this food, though 'good', is difficult to situate in relation to other categories of worth. Thus, while Postgate's references to himself as 'mapping an unexplored country' appear to recall the (post)colonial certainties of a writer like Elizabeth David (who follows the early twentieth-century gastronomic tradition in opposing 'peasant' food in Europe to the British culinary ineptitude), he actually sets himself a far greater challenge in attempting to project, for his readers, qualities of 'goodness' onto a nation that has little claim to (culinary) goodness traditionally, and which, in any case, seems to defy summary.

The judgements printed in the *Guide* had – still have – a peculiar claim to reliability: they are not the verdict of anonymous perfectionists, nor are they generated, in Postgate's words, by 'an earnest government official or a trade organization'; rather they are 'the quiet judgement of the consumers themselves' (Postgate, 1951: 2, 8). From the start, diners sent their views – using a little form at the back of the *Guide* – to the editor who checked verdicts by the use of anonymous inspectors. Fred Inglis (2002: 28), writing for the fiftieth anniversary of the *Guide*, describes the 'faint, agreeable air of secret service with which members went to work … a future Chancellor of the Exchequer, three world famous English conductors, a great painter, a socialist bishop, and … the most famous military historian … and the most famous cricket commentator … of the 50 years of the *GFG*'s longevity'. But, while Inglis envisions the *Guide* as the work of the ruling classes drawn together in a common project, Postgate is less willing to link gastronomic discrimination to class solidarity. The club, as Postgate explains in each edition, is made up of people who will never see one another and who are constituted as members only by their use of the pages at the back of the *Guide*. Postgate describes his centreless club with a negative catalogue: 'It is a curious organisation ... It has no club premises or meeting place, no subscription, no funds, no list of members, practically no officers, and no staff at all' (1951: 3). How is the understanding of 'goodness' to be confirmed and refined using a scattering of experiences reported by those merely believing themselves to be of a like mind?

The implicit comparison made later by Postgate (1951: 11) between the *Guide* and the Mass Observation project of the late 1930s suggests thoroughness and reliability of observation rather than a compendium of good practices. And actually Postgate is emphatic about the shortcomings of a guide to so transient a scene as the restaurant. He begins his second edition of the *Guide* by telling his readers that last year's is 'out of date and as useless as last year's calendar' (p. 10): 'This book is something like a gigantic snapshot of a huge number of people. Nearly all will "come out" clearly, but some are certain to have moved. By next year, quite a number of them will have; and some will have gone away altogether' (p. 26). The image is an interesting one, for it suggests a protean scene that photography cannot be expected to represent with clarity. And indeed, the reviews of restaurants given in the *Guide* have themselves the quality of a hurried snapshot:

> BRIGHTON OLD   SHIP HOTEL   Tel. 203
> High reputation for a long time; most courteous staff; a 6/- dinner consisted of three courses with an ample portion of very tender roast duck (8/6 for four courses). À la carte main dishes, 4/- to 5/6. (*Recommended: J. O. C. Dalton; Phyllis Phillips*). (Postgate, 1951: 48)

Not surprisingly, not only is the state of the nation's restaurants – and the national context in which they operate – difficult to grasp or describe in detail, but the restaurants are themselves sites of obscure and unpredictable relations. Studies of eating out have examined both the possibilities and the constraints of a 'framework of prefigured actions' (Finkelstein 1989: 5). Postgate, in the satiric mode of the ex-classicist, likes, at times, to evoke a sense of the embattled middle-class diner trying to ward off entrapment by unscrupulous restaurants: 'On sitting down at your table, polish the glasses and cutlery with your napkin. ... You wish to give the impression not that you are angry with this particular restaurant, but that you are suspicious, after a lifetime of suffering' (1951: 19).

But he also conveys a scene where the sullen demeanour of 'staff' is matched by the sullenness of customers. There is little conviviality to be found in the *Guide*, much less of the transformative power of the journey rewarded with the physical pleasures of food. Only rarely do we catch a reference to food's comforts: 'satisfying' is almost the only word that Postgate uses to describe a good meal – 'Liberal helpings and satisfying meal' (1951: 48). Warde and Martens (2000: 195), discussing the range of pleasure to be gained from eating out, define 'satisfaction' as 'a term describing the acceptability of a particular exchange or service'. Postgate's use of the term evokes the pleasure of fullness in an era of rationing, but never the delights of anticipated luxury or satisfied desire, never the confirmations of conviviality, never the therapeutic sense of expectation fulfilled.

Florence White and the Good Food Register

When Raymond Postgate was preparing his *Guide*, he was shown Florence White's 'Good Food Register', presumably as a model, since the third and most substantial edition, *Where Shall We Eat Or Put Up?*, took a quite similar form to the prospective *Guide*:[4] it too addressed a motoring public, though *Where Shall We Eat?* catered as much to the fashion for exploring the countryside as to gastronomic adventures.[5] Like Postgate's *Guide*, it was generated through a dialogue with members of the public in the letters page of *The Times*;[6] its aim was to literally to map good food – indeed to 'put English cookery on the map' (White 1937: 255) – and it was driven by the same crusading impulse to improve access to what was 'good' to eat. Like Postgate, White enjoyed referring grandly to the sweep of English high culture: Elvers cakes in Keynsham are described simply as 'famous here since the time of Defoe' (White, 1936: 94). And she too cultivated an exasperatedly doctrinaire air: 'There is a right and a wrong way of [preparing] every English dish' (p. 174). Broadly, whatever was different about the economic and political circumstances of the nation in which Postgate and White found themselves, much was comparable. Like the scene of rationed Britain in the late 1940s and early 1950s, life in the 'Hungry Thirties' was characterized by middle- and upper-class tensions with respect to questions of national tradition.

Interestingly, though, Postgate showed no interest in White's work – and not, I would guess, because it might have seemed to have stolen his thunder fifteen years before his own *Guide* appeared. Most obviously, White had not written the standard narrative of English inferiority to French food and poor 'service' to which the restaurant-going classes had long been dedicated. On the contrary, it was the survival of a vibrant if scattered tradition of national cooking that she wished to celebrate and not the traces of the 'Hotel Magnifique experience'.

The differences between Postgate's and White's texts are more fundamental than this, however. *Where Shall We Eat?* produces a very different understanding of the consumption of food and its relationship to class, gender and national identity. Part of the reason for this has to do with Postgate's and White's differing modes of discourse. Postgate's background was a privileged one, but, as ever within the tradition of gastronomy and indeed the tradition of satire, he presented himself as a figure marginal to the irrational, turbulent mainstream of the modern world. The authority lent by distance was limited, though. Over ten years before writing the *Guide*, Postgate explained his unwillingness to write an imaginative 'tour' of 1930s Britain, writing that 'the understanding of modern Britain depends at least on knowing the rest of the world as in visualising the internal condition of the country' (Cole and Postgate, 1938: 595). In the *Guide* itself, Postgate (1951: 5) argues that he cannot provide a 'gastronomic tour' of Britain, because the country is unexplored. Postgate, in short, feeling himself unequal to the portraiture of the modern nation, could not create the figure of a successful roving consumer within it.

White's position was very different. She was the déclassé daughter of a London dealer in lace, brought up in some comfort in the London suburbs, but faced subsequently with the challenge of achieving financial security as a single woman through a range of jobs: journalist, broadcaster, writer and teacher, but also housekeeper and cook. White's uncertain social status caused her personal and professional frustration, but it also placed her a range of social situations and gave her little reason to identify taste with class position. *Where Shall We Put Up?* draws together a wide range of encounters with food, both those open to the wealthy and those open to far less identifiable passers-by. So, for example, we have the following entry for Frome in Somerset:

> When trekking through England I was stranded one afternoon near the railway station for the want of a cup of tea; there seemed no hope so I knocked at the door of a wayside inn and discovered a treasure: a landlady who was a top-hole cook and served a most delicious tea consisting of wonderful seed cake, jam, bread and butter, all home-made. ... I think the name of the inn was the Great Western Railway Inn, but am not sure. (White, 1936: 94)

This is a world of eating out in which both the restorative function of food and the pleasure of fellow feeling are foremost, and in which the country appears as a space to be traversed and experienced in a quest for the most profound experience of its qualities. The quality of folk tale – the context of the search, the knocking on the stranger's door, the perfect repast, the transient experience that can only be half remembered – lends the research into good food in England a depth of meaning, collapsing any sense of identity achieved through choice. It evokes an ideal of interaction between people, devoid of surprise, and certainly of class distinction, an 'unravelling [of] the complicated strands of human intercourse, so that human beings could communicate freely and directly' (MacCarthy, 1981: 11).

Plainly, White's guide had its ideological roots in a very different scene to that of the gastronome. Her view of food was imbued with the ideals of the Arts and Crafts Movement: ideals not only of the dignity of manual work, of work as craft, but also of engagement with materials as a sensuous experience. As hostile as Postgate to the world of mass production, White ignores the 'artist' chef, and the cookery of the 'English gentlewoman' beloved of the nostalgic nationalist discourses of the period,[7] focusing instead on the creativity of the less privileged rural woman.

But if White's work was a late flowering of a movement that had, by the late 1920s and 1930s, largely been transformed into a handicrafts revival with a largely recreational function, it was nonetheless a radical intervention within the Arts and Crafts scene. Cooking was not a craft form favoured by the Arts and Crafts *cognoscenti*, associated as it was with drudgery and the kitchen, rather than with craft and the workshop. While forms of stitch brought women into the world of 'art' and creativity, cooking tended to keep them in the respectable world of social work or below stairs. White was bent on recuperating cooking and eating as activities eluding distinction and mending class difference.

White's work claimed an elevated purpose as part of a mission to find common ground through recovering and – literally – consuming England's shared heritage. The eccentricity of her idealism is demonstrated all too clearly by the failure of her attempt to get her English Folk Cookery Association affiliated either with Charles Herman Senn's Fabian 'Universal Cookery and Food Association', which had a mission to educate the cooking, as opposed to the dining, classes; or with Cecil Sharp's English Folk Song and Folk Dancing Associations, which also promoted a version of Englishness through 'expert' recovery of a live tradition of folk art.[8] Yet, like Sharp and many other of her contemporaries, White gloried in a vision of a common, consensual culture that could be accessed by 'townies' through immersion in the (culinary) world of Old England:

> SALISBURY
> West Harnham Old Mill Club owned by Mrs. Lionel Fox-Pitt is a survival of some fourteenth-century monastic building which its owner has converted into an ideal country club open to the public. ... It is noted for its good Wiltshire cookery. Augustus John says, "It is the best cookery in England." One of the specialities is samphire cooked like asparagus. Another is DEVIZES PIE. It has a mill stream where one can fish, a sun garden and a dovecote. It is a favourite resort of artists, musicians and men of letters.
>
> The Haunch of Venison, Poultry Cross, Salisbury, noted for its grills and good English Cookery generally. "The best grilled steak in Salisbury."
>
> When I was travelling all over England in search of Food and Cookery Lore, when in Salisbury, I made the Old George my headquarters. Once I occupied the very room occupied by Pepys when he stayed there 200 years ago ... The meat is English, and another boon is that free garage is given during the luncheon hour to all motorists who takes [sic] luncheon at the George.
>
> Pepys wrote in his diary: Came to the George Inn where lay in a silk bed, and very good diet. ... The George is also referred to by Dickens in *Martin Chuzzlewit.* The County Hotel is highly recommended by F. J. (White, 1936: 129)

Here, the experience of dining out is not separated from other activity – motoring, working, travelling, holidaying, reading – so the weight of expectation is diminished, the emphasis on correct ritual dispelled. The views of people, named and anonymous, are printed alongside White's own experiences in a way that evokes a democratic vision of random pleasures.

The confidence of White's tone is all the more striking, given that the cookery of the nation's womenfolk was subject to an intensely critical response during this period. When White published her article 'Country Climate and Cookery' in *The Listener* in 1931, she was writing a riposte to a well-trodden discussion of food and gender in England. *The Listener*, bastion of upper middle-class values, was engaged in a protracted commentary on the failure of domestic cookery to draw on, much less emulate, the 'artistry' of the (male) chef. White engages with this discussion in explicit terms. She insists on a national tradition of cookery situated beyond the gaze of the metropolitan authorities: '[G]o down to the West Country; there are no hams to beat those of Gloucestershire, but they never came to London' (White, 1931: 768). *Where Shall We Put Up?* privileges the cooking and the reviews of women, and surrounds comments on restaurants with information about a range of foodways, regional specialities and notes that are no more or less relevant to home cooking as to dining out:

> WARMINSTER
> The best meat in the Kingdom, according to Cobbett. Noted for lambs'
> tails pie and lambs' tails stew, 'solid syllabubs' called here 'whips.'
> Beer and ale.
> The Bath Arms, Warminster, is a small hotel where good
> simple well-cooked food is cooked in a cheerful manner. (White, 1936:
> 129)

The space White describes remains loosely but distinctly constituted into a nation, defined most distinctly by its boundaries with foreign nations. Thus, rice pudding in her *Listener* article is not a single thing, but a series of possibilities linked with different and disparate spaces in the nation:

> Baked Rice Puddings, another national dish (made with raisins and eggs
> in Cumberland, and known as Chipping Time Pudding), made also with
> raisins in Warwickshire, and with a number of other local variations in
> other districts. (White, 1931: 768)

Visions of 'the folk' were put to many uses in the 1930s. White's Anglo-Saxon nation of 'fine upstanding people' is part of a racialized conception of Englishness, into which others cannot be integrated (p. 767). But whatever she wishes for in terms of proofs of English superiority, she represents the task of finding Englishness as a piecing together of fragments, 'a scrap here, a thread there' (p. 767), by one who – with some justification – portrayed herself as a 'roaming' woman acting against the grain of the English social system:

> It seemed to me that life was a policeman who kept moving me on
> directly I had found a comfortable doorstep on which to sit, down and
> rest awhile. There was always some sting that bade me 'not sit nor stand
> but go!' (White, 1937: 258)

The Restaurant Guide as Romance

White wrote of the compilation of her guide as a 'romance' (1936: 5). This description of the restaurant guide is apt, for romance is, classically, a form which deals in stories of the pursuit and defence of goodness. The contemporary popular fictions we call romances are narratives that press their readers to be hopeful and idealistic in a world of disappointment, and this is also part of these guides' project.[9] Postgate's and White's guides are both concerned with evoking the possibility of a sense of fulfilment and pleasure achieved through the choice and consumption of food and they do so with a seriousness that recognizes the significance of the activity. Part of that significance lies in the way in which England may be understood, even possessed, through choosing food. In Postgate's *Guide* the quest is scattered and satisfaction dispiritingly elusive, in White's guide goodness is more easily found but she is always constrained to move on. Much of what we understand about lifestyle and lifestyle texts is shaped by our sense of the possibilities of self-invention in circumstances of mobility that allow the self to enter 'multiple milieux of action' (Giddens, 1991: 81-3). Postgate's and White's romances of fulfilment have a darker and more perplexing context.

Notes

1   See, for a recent discussion that foregrounds the trials of travelling, Holland and Huggan (1998), especially pp. vii-xiii.
2   See Mennell (1996) for a study of English attitudes to French cuisine.
3   See, for a discussion of this scene, Floyd (2003).
4   This summary of the inception of the 'Good Food Registers' is taken from White's introduction to *Where Shall We Eat Or Put Up?* (5-8); and from her autobiography, *A Fire in the Kitchen* (315-23). I cannot find the date of the demise of the Register, although White died in 1940.
5   O'Connell (1998), in *The Car in British Society* (especially pp. 81ff and 178), paints an evocative portrait of motoring holidays and the important place that inns, hotels and teashops played in the experience.
6   White began the process of eliciting accounts of local and regional specialities from the general public through writing to the *Times* on September 10 1931, promising to give anyone who corresponded with her details about particular local delicacies (White, 1936: 6; White, 1937: 320).
7   See Giles and Middleton (1995: 8ff), for a discussion of this context.
8   Senn's work is discussed in Mennell (1996: 185-86, 221), while the most comprehensive recent analysis of Sharp's work may be found in Boyes (1993).
9   See, for this latter argument, Radway (1984).

References

Ainsworth, J. (ed.) (2003) *Good Food Guide to Restaurants in England, Scotland and Wales*, London: Consumer's Association.
Bourdieu, P. (1984) *Distinction*, trans. R. Nice, London and New York: Routledge.
Boyes, G. (1993) *The Imagined Village: Culture, Ideology and the English Folk Tradition*, Manchester: Manchester University Press.
Campion, C. (2004) *The Rough Guide to London Restaurants 2004*, London: Rough Guides.
Capper, W. B. (1950) *Dining Out?* second edition, London: Rockliff.
Chaney, D, (1996) *Lifestyles*, London and New York: Routledge.
Cole, G. D. H. and Postgate, R. (1938) *The Common People, 1746-1938*, London: Methuen.
Driver, C. (1983) *The British at Table 1940-1980*, London: Chatto and Windus.

Finkelstein, J. (1989) *Dining Out: A Sociology of Modern Manners*, Cambridge: Polity Press.

Floyd, J. (2003) 'Simple, Honest Food: Elizabeth David and the Construction of Nation in Cookery Writing', in J. Floyd and L. Forster (eds) *The Recipe Reader: Narratives – Contexts – Traditions*, Aldershot: Ashgate Press.

Giddens, A. (1991) *Modernity and Self-Identity: Self and Society in the Late Modern Age*, Cambridge: Polity Press.

Giles, J. and Middleton, T. (eds) (1995*) Writing Englishness, 1900-1950: An Introductory Sourcebook on National Identity*, London and New York: Routledge.

Holland, P. and Huggan, G. (1998) *Tourists with Typewriters: Critical Reflections on Contemporary Travel Writing*, Ann Arbor: University of Michigan Press.

Inglis, F. (2002) 'The Good Food Guide 50 Years on', *The Good Food Guide 2002*, London: Consumer's Association.

Klugmann, J. (1979) 'The Crisis of the Thirties: a View from the Left', in J. Clark *et al.* (eds) *Culture and Crisis in Britain in the Thirties*, London: Lawrence and Wishart.

MacCarthy, F. (1981) *The Simple Life: C. R. Ashbee in the Cotswolds*, London: Lund Humphries.

Mennell, S. (1996) *All Manners of Food: Eating and Taste in England and France from the Middle Ages to the Present*, second edition, Urbana and Chicago: University of Illinois Press.

O'Connell, S. (1998) *The Car in British Society: Class, Gender and Motoring 1896-1939*, Manchester: Manchester University Press.

Postgate, R. (1951) *The Good Food Guide, 1951-2*, London: Cassell and Co.

Ronay, E. (1963), *Egon Ronay's Guide: 1000 Eating Places in Great Britain and Ireland including 200 London Pubs*, London: Gastronomes Ltd..

Spang, R. L. (2000) *The Invention of the Restaurant: Paris and Modern Gastronomic Culture*, Cambridge, Mass.: Harvard University Press.

Warde, A. and Martens, L. (2000) *Eating Out: Social Differentiation, Consumption and Pleasure*, Cambridge: Cambridge University Press.

White, F. (1931) 'Country, Climate and Cookery', *The Listener*, May 6, pp. 767-8.

White, F. (1937) *A Fire in the Kitchen: The Autobiography of a Cook*, London: Dent.

White, F. (1938) *Good English Food, Local and Regional*, London: Dent.

White, F. (1936) *Where Shall We Eat Or Put Up? A New Edition of the English Folk Cookery Association Good Food Register*, London: Practical Press.

Yaeger, P. (1996) 'Introduction', *The Geography of Identity*, Ann Arbor: University of Michigan Press.

Chapter 4

Presenting the Black Middle Class: John H. Johnson and *Ebony* Magazine, 1945-1974

Jason Chambers

When a young John Johnson arrived in Chicago in 1933 he had little idea what to expect. Born in the South, he had heard stories of Chicago from letters sent to Arkansas by earlier migrants, but they likely did little to prepare him for the bustling metropolis. As a young man in Arkansas, his father had been a mill worker and his mother, Gertrude, a labourer in various occupations. The daughter of two ex-slaves, she had encouraged him throughout his young life to do whatever he could to better his situation in life and standing in the world. More importantly she was a living example of that kind of determination and a significant force in his life. But, although his desire for improvement was strong, the racism and dire economic situation throughout Arkansas in the 1920s and early 1930s restricted the opportunities both mother and son sought. Finally, seeing no other choice, Johnson's mother decided to move the family North. While the family arrived in Chicago at the height of the Great Depression, the economic and labour opportunities present were better than those in Arkansas. Soon after arrival his mother found work and Johnson and the family settled into the city's predominantly African-American south side. Although it would have seemed unlikely at the time, in less than fifteen years this rural migrant went on to found the most successful African-American magazine in history. In the course of that effort Johnson not only became wealthy and a recognized business leader, but his flagship publication, *Ebony* magazine, helped define the parameters of middle-class lifestyle for generations of African Americans (Ingham and Feldman, 1994).

Historians and theorists alike have characterized the lifestyle of the 1950s as a period of conformity (Cohen, 2003; Featherstone, 1991; Weems, 1998), an era in which the mass in mass consumption and market led to a stultifying sameness in which there was little differentiation of which to speak. In contrast, the decades following were ones in which greater senses of individuality and self-determination allowed for consumers to break from the limited styles of the past to craft new individualistic selves. Problematic in these analyses, however, is that few offer any critical examination as to how those consumers specifically left outside of the consumerist visions of American media and advertising acted within their prescribed place in the consumer society. Specifically, how did black consumers orient themselves to the consumerist lifestyle when they could see themselves reflected in it in so few places? How, if at all, did the developing post-World War Two black middle class interpret the consumer society for themselves?

The lone theorist and scholar to examine the black middle class of the post-WWII period, E. Franklin Frazier (1962), had little good to say about the group. This group, a small portion of which he labeled the bourgeoisie, engaged in wild levels of conspicuous consumption and had little desire to have any connection with the larger black populace. Instead, this bourgeoisie was incensed and ashamed that their colour often left them victim to the same racism and discrimination as their poorer racial brethren. Consequently members of this class lived in a 'world of make believe' in which they used consumption to attempt to show their equality with whites. In short, Frazier implied that middle-class blacks wanted to be white. But a careful analysis reveals, as Dave Berkman (1963: 62) noted, that middle-class African Americans found 'appealing those items whose consumption most clearly says "white" – *but only because they also say middle class*' (original emphasis).

After Frazier's scathing account of the black middle class the group remained largely overlooked in scholarly examinations. As Mary Pattillo-McCoy (1999: 1) noted, 'Post-civil rights optimism erased upwardly mobile African Americans from the slate of interesting groups to study'. Yet in the last several years the development of the black middle class has once again come under examination. Recent scholars such as Pattillo-McCoy (1999) and Weems (1998) have tempered Frazier's assessment of the black middle class, but have concurred that blacks have used consumption and a consumer lifestyle to 'buy respectability'.

However, to simply argue that African Americans sought to buy respectability without recognizing the historical context is vacuous. The consumer activity of African Americans has long had political and economic ramifications. Throughout the twentieth century, blacks used consumption to press for greater access to employment and fair treatment within the marketplace. It is no coincidence, for example, that some of the earliest points of contestation in the civil rights movement were within consumer spaces (Cohen, 2003; Hale 1999; Weems, 1998). Consequently the consumer lifestyle of African Americans, specifically the black middle class, cannot be read in the traditional manner. Instead, through critical examination of the leading periodical of the post-war black middle class, *Ebony*, reveals a more complex purpose at work.

As the leading African-American-focused magazine for over four decades, *Ebony* has been fertile field for scholarly examination. Yet the magazine has primarily been examined in a comparative manner, most often to its guiding mainstream counterpart *Life* magazine (Berkman, 1963). Rarely have scholars examined the magazine in terms of its message content (Brooks, 1998; Hirsch, 1968; Pendergast, 2000). Even within those studies that have focused on message content, there has been no emphasis on the magazine's appeals to the black middle class. Scholars have not critically interrogated *Ebony*'s contents in terms of their instruction to (and, by relation, construction of) the black middle-class lifestyle. *Ebony* contained a myriad of instructions and examples to guide blacks on post-war modern living and hence it contradicts the traditional argument that lifestyle magazines are a format only recently created.

This chapter examines the development of *Ebony* magazine, the most successful magazine in the history of African-American publishing. The chapter is comprised of three distinct parts. First, there will be a description of Johnson's life and activities leading up to his decision to become a publisher. Second, there is an examination of Johnson's efforts to solidify the creation of *Ebony* magazine. Third, and by far the largest portion of this chapter, is an analysis of *Ebony* as a publication that described the accoutrements of a black middle-class lifestyle. Through *Ebony* John Johnson projected a middle-class mainstream. Though often criticized for stressing consumption over and above any other strategy, a careful analysis suggests something much more complex. Specifically, through *Ebony* magazine Johnson promoted and supported blacks' active participation within the existing consumer society. Further, though, *Ebony* politicized consumption as a lifestyle activity among blacks in that Johnson urged blacks to not only display their consumer potential, but also to press for equality as consumers. Therefore buying a consumer product could become more than a purchase alone, but also could become a statement in the larger fight for equality. So *Ebony* in many ways became a handbook for blacks' role as consumer citizens.

Early Professional Background

If one were to meet the young Johnson in Chicago in the 1930s it is unlikely that he would have been pegged as a future business leader. In fact, while settling into life in the new city Johnson initially stood out for the wrong reasons – a thick southern accent and homemade clothes. While both of the aforementioned drew little attention in Arkansas, they made him the object of some ridicule on the streets of Chicago. As she would at other points in his life, Johnson's mother provided the solution. When she learned of his difficulties she quickly made sure that he had clothing suitable to allow him to fit in among his peers. After he had adopted more urban fashions and as he diligently worked to temper his accent, Johnson became a leader among his classmates. Eventually he became the head of the student council and president of his senior class. It was in this latter position that Johnson experienced a turning point in his life. As one of the leading black students in the city, Johnson was invited to an Urban League dinner. The speaker that evening was Harry Pace, president of the Supreme Liberty Life Insurance Company. After the speech the young wide-eyed Johnson approached the business leader to tell him how much he valued his remarks. Sensing his admiration, Pace pressed Johnson on his plans following graduation. Johnson replied that though he had received partial scholarships to attend college he lacked the money to do so full-time. In response Pace offered Johnson the opportunity to work at Supreme Life part-time to earn money and attend school the balance of the time. This proved an important experience because working at Supreme Life not only gave Johnson the money to attend college, but also provided the seeds for his future publishing company.

As a young employee, Pace took Johnson under his wing as an assistant. Johnson thrived under the tutelage of the aging executive. At the time Supreme Life was the largest black-owned company in Chicago and it was at the centre of black life in the city. Almost all of the major events and persons of importance in black Chicago came into contact with the company in some way. This meant that the closer Johnson stayed to Pace, the closer he was to the epicentre of the important events affecting blacks in the city. Through his affiliation with the company, Johnson met the important black leaders in Chicago and came to be recognized as a young man with potential. This was not an unimportant distinction because it gave Johnson access to interactions and ideas seemingly incongruent with his youth. Nonetheless, the young man was well on his way to becoming an important figure in the black community.

In addition to involving him with black leaders throughout Chicago, Johnson's employment at Supreme Life provided him with lessons in business operation that he later replicated in his own company. Specifically, employment at the company gave Johnson the chance to see other African Americans operate as capitalists without the restrictions of racism. As one of the few large companies that issued policies to blacks, Supreme Life not only survived the depression but also it maintained its growth rate throughout its duration. As Johnson recalled, the company 'wheeled and dealed' its way through the Depression and he was there to witness it all. More importantly, it was during this time that he was tasked with the seemingly innocuous responsibility of gathering material for the company newspaper.

Although the majority of the material Johnson gathered for the company focused on Supreme Life, he also collected information about issues involving blacks throughout the country. When he told friends about the stories he was gathering he was surprised at the interest they showed. In fact, more often than not, his friends pressed him to bring them a copy of the paper so that they might read the story for themselves. Consequently, Johnson seized upon an idea. He began to envision a magazine that would include stories of the type he had gathered for the Supreme Life newspaper. The magazine he imagined would be different from a conventional newspaper in that it would have no staff to research stories, but instead would offer reprints from sources around the country. With the idea firmly in hand Johnson set out to establish his enterprise.

A Small Success in Publishing

Despite his enthusiasm, though, Johnson found that actually starting the magazine was much more difficult than crafting the vision for it. With the difficulties of starting any African-American publication in mind, several black business leaders were un-enthusiastic him about the venture. In addition to those who discouraged the idea, he found than banks were unwilling to lend him any capital for the effort. On the verge of abandoning the idea Johnson found a bank willing to lend him the money – provided he secure some collateral. As he had done in the past Johnson turned to his mother. Cautious, but encouraging, Johnson's mother allowed him to use her furniture to secure a $500 loan. With the money in hand Johnson convinced Pace to allow him to use the Supreme Life mailing list to seek subscriptions. He received an almost overwhelming response. Within a few weeks of the first mailing Johnson secured 3000 subscriptions at two dollars each. Now with nearly $7000 he set about printing and distributing the new magazine, the *Negro Digest*, modeled on *Readers' Digest*, the highly successful publication that offered various stories and slice-of-life vignettes. Johnson offered almost the same type of material as the original *Digest*; he simply focused his attention on stories involving blacks (Johnson, 1992).

Though he found the initial months of the business difficult, Johnson continued to print the magazine. Sales were not as brisk as he wished, but they were nonetheless steady. Further, when he convinced Eleanor Roosevelt to contribute an essay to the magazine, circulation exploded. By 1943 sales of *Negro Digest* were sufficient enough to allow him to quit his job at Supreme Life and focus on his publishing company. But, while sales remained steady, the magazine could not seem to become the runaway success that Johnson wanted. Moreover, the magazine lacked any significant advertising revenue with revenue instead coming from subscriptions. Consequently, a few years later he decided to start another magazine, this time modeled on *Life*, the successful general interest picture magazine. In November 1945 Johnson began publishing the magazine he would become most known for, the black-oriented picture magazine *Ebony*.

From the first issue Johnson focused *Ebony* on the 'happier side' of black life in America. Reserving *Negro Digest* for articles critically examining racism and discrimination, *Ebony* instead contained stories about other areas of life where blacks were actively involved. The inaugural issue set the tone the magazine followed for the next several decades: 'We're rather jolly folks we *Ebony* editors. We like to look at the zesty side of life. Sure, you can get all hot and bothered about the race question (and don't think we don't) but not enough is said about all the swell things we Negroes can do and will accomplish. *Ebony* will try to mirror … the positive everyday achievements from Harlem to Hollywood' ('Ebony Marks 5th Anniversary', 1950: 490). The initial print run of 25,000 issues sold out within a few hours, as did a second run of an additional 25,000. Within a few weeks circulation for the magazine topped 100,000 per issue. The time had come to secure advertising schedules.

The Search for Advertising Schedules

While Johnson had never worked in the newspaper business he knew of the difficulties black papers had in securing advertising. Often overlooked by national corporations, all but the largest black papers, such as the *Pittsburgh Courier* or *Chicago Defender*, lacked any significant or consistent level of national advertising. Consequently, when he began *Ebony* he crafted a multi-phase marketing program designed to secure national advertising. The first phase of the program called for *Ebony* to increase circulation without relying on any advertising whatsoever. From the beginning he wanted *Ebony* to be a 'first-class' magazine and to have the types of advertisements that went with such an organ. This meant that he initially refused to accept the small, classified-type advertisements that dominated much of the advertising in other sectors of the black press. Instead he wanted to secure the type of large four-colour advertisements that were present in *Life* magazine. So, Johnson waited until *Ebony*'s circulation crested 100,000 readers and then he began to approach advertising agencies and asked them to recommend advertising schedules in *Ebony*. The silence to his requests was deafening. Despite the large circulation numbers, Johnson found that agency executives did not view his magazine as a viable source for advertising placement. Further, even though African-American income had risen significantly since the end of the Second World War, many did not believe blacks to be a viable consumer market. Certainly some executives were wary of recommending any new magazine that lacked a significant publishing history. Many more, however, simply refused to chance offending their clients by recommending an advertising schedule in a black publication. Therefore, despite his best sales and marketing efforts among agencies, advertising in *Ebony* was severely limited (Dingle, 1999).

Although some large advertisers like Chesterfield cigarettes and Kotex feminine products were in the magazine by early 1946, they were the only such national advertisers in *Ebony*. Thus, Johnson was losing money with each issue sold and he was desperate to attract other national advertisers to the periodical or to produce revenue through other means. One source of revenue he found was through promoting various sundry goods sold by mail order and with advertisements in *Ebony*. Johnson recalled, 'I sold vitamins, wigs, dresses, and hair-care products. I sold anything that I could sell in order to get enough capital to keep *Ebony* going' (quoted in Dingle, 1999: 15). In fact, Johnson was just barely able to keep *Ebony* published while the mail order companies kept the company afloat; without greater advertising revenue the magazine would not survive. Finally, in 1947, after stretching his credit with lenders to near breaking point, Johnson hit on the idea of going 'over the heads' of advertising agency executives and approaching their clients direct for advertising schedules. He began to contact corporate executives and described the profits that were available in the black consumer market. This was a pioneering approach because at that time there was not much information available about the buying habits of black consumers. Therefore, he found several executives who were at least willing to listen to a discussion about unknown outlets where they could increase corporate profits. The most significant meeting Johnson secured through this approach was with Commander Eugene McDonald, head of Zenith Radio. McDonald not only personally approved an advertising schedule from his company, he also recommended to the heads of other companies that they take out advertising in *Ebony*. From that point forward advertising schedules in *Ebony* consistently increased, sometimes to the point that advertisements had to be rejected for lack of space (Johnson, 1992).

Capturing regular advertising schedules for a black-oriented magazine made *Ebony* unique in publishing history, in that it was the first such magazine to receive substantial revenue from advertising. Before its creation the only other long-running black magazines were the *Crisis* and *Opportunity*, organs of the

National Association for the Advancement of Colored People (NAACP) and the Urban League respectively. Both lacked any significant advertising and relied instead on their institutional affiliations to spur circulation and provide revenue. With *Ebony*'s rising advertising revenue, Johnson now had the freedom to follow the editorial course he wished and to move on with his development plans (Pendergast, 2000).

With individual advertising schedules secured, Johnson moved into the second phase of his plan. He now sought to make *Ebony* and the black consumer market a distinct target for corporations. Throughout the 1950s and 1960s Johnson and his staff launched what can be considered as an early integrated marketing campaign. He not only continued to directly seek advertising from corporate executives, but he also wrote articles in the trade press about marketing 'dos and don'ts' to black consumers; spoke before trade organizations; began a merchandising program that placed point-of-purchase endorsements (stickers announced 'You saw this advertised in *Ebony*') with products advertised in the magazine; organized a research centre to compile and disseminate information about black consumers; produced sales films on reaching black consumers; and maintained an advertising schedule for *Ebony* and other Johnson publications in the trade press ('Nation Within a Nation', 1957: 29). Those who viewed *Ebony*'s trade press advertisements were reassured that *Ebony* was not a 'protest organ' but a magazine that provided 'positive, informative, and entertaining' coverage of black life. The comprehensive program Johnson developed overwhelmed and overshadowed anything done by any other black publisher and he dominated his competitors ('Johnson Publishing', 1951). Through this process Johnson also became the recognized authority on the black consumer market and *Ebony* was regarded as the leading popular information source about blacks. Articles from *Ebony* were often picked up by the Associated Press or reprinted in general interest magazines such as *Time*, *Newsweek*, or *Readers' Digest*. Further, much to Johnson's delight, *Ebony* soon was recognized as the key vehicle for those interested in reaching black consumers (Johnson, 1952).

The Black Consumer Market

In its initial years Johnson filled *Ebony* with sensationalistic stories and features on black sports and entertainment stars. As a newsstand periodical Johnson knew he had to attract the attention of passersby, so pictures of attractive young women and flashy headlines were often on covers of the magazine. Inside *Ebony* were articles with suggestive titles such as 'Is It True What They Say About Models?' or 'Weep for the Virgins' (Reichley, 1968). While the contents of these articles were much more conservative than the titles suggest (models were in fact not excessively promiscuous, the article concluded), they served to attract the attention of newsstand readers. However, while attracting the attention of newsstand readers helped the magazine to grow, they did little to attract home subscribers. The recession of 1954 led Johnson to change the format of the magazine to try to reach home subscribers.

When the recession hit it led to a precipitous drop in *Ebony*'s newsstand sales. In the span of a single issue circulation fell from 500,000 to 400,000. Because the magazine failed to reach its advertising guarantee Johnson was forced to return a large portion of money to his advertisers, much of which he had already spent. Consequently, from that point onward he was determined to solidify the circulation base of *Ebony* with home subscribers. Increasing the number of home subscribers (then only 20 per cent of the circulation base) meant he would not be dependent on the whims of newsstand buyers and the immediate changes of the economy (Reichley, 1968).

To appeal to home subscribers Johnson toned down the sensationalism of the magazine. While the aforementioned types of article and cover did not disappear, they played a less prominent role in the magazine. The changes quickly attracted attention. Home subscriptions increased rapidly and church groups – who had once publicly avoided the magazine – began to sponsor subscription campaigns. Within a few years Johnson succeeded in making subscriptions 80 per cent of his circulation base with newsstand sales responsible for the remaining percentage (Reichley, 1968).

Regardless of the circulation base, however, the basic focus of *Ebony* remained largely unchanged for the first several years of its existence. As a general interest periodical Johnson focused the majority of attention on stories detailing the lives of black celebrities. From actress Lena Horne to former boxing champion Joe Louis, readers learned of celebrity choices in clothing, cars, favourite nightspots and brands of liquor enjoyed. Other celebrity portrayals often showed the stars at home and articles consistently mentioned the cost of the home and its furnishings ('At Home', 1954). The focus on the successful aspects of the celebrities' lives was part of a carefully crafted editorial policy, one that would be followed over the next several decades.

Of *Ebony*'s editorial policy Johnson remarked, 'Essentially our policy is an inspirational one. We try to motivate those who are coming up in the world, to show that there are no barriers, no restrictions, that they have as much right to become a professional golfer as to become president of the US' ('Color Success Black', 1968: 32). While such a policy drew him an ever-increasing number of critics, the magazine was an undeniable success. By the early 1950s circulation had crested over 400,000 copies per issue. *Ebony* was clearly the leading black magazine in the country and it became the handbook to define exactly what a middle-class lifestyle meant in black America.

Combined with its position as the leading black magazine, Johnson's focus on the 'happier side of life' quickly brought him an array of critics. However, what critics failed to take into account was that Johnson's overriding interest was to craft a commercially successful magazine. This meant that, unlike some black newspaper publishers, he did not criticize a company's employment policies in an article and then expect company executives to approve a full-page advertisement later in the magazine. Instead, in the first several years of *Ebony*'s existence the magazine largely avoided controversy as he chose to focus on the accoutrements of success more than the struggle that it took to achieve that success in the first place. For example, stories about Eddie Anderson, the black actor who played Jack

Benny's faithful employee, focused more upon his home, maid and cars than it did on his struggles with racism as one of the few blacks in Hollywood. Johnson felt that this editorial course was appropriate for two reasons. First, *Ebony* was the leading black periodical, but it was far from the only one. This meant that while *Ebony* articles might not be the highly critical pieces that some desired, there were other outlets (including *Negro Digest*) for that type of material. *Ebony* was far from alone in the black publishing arena, as other periodicals existed to address the serious racial problems in America.

Second, Johnson believed that blacks were better off in America than in any other country in the world. While true there were serious problems facing African Americans, he believed his own experience proved that at least some opportunities were present. In editorials he sometimes attacked blacks that had a 'colour complex' that led them to believe that whites opposed them at every turn. Johnson moderately counselled, 'our blessings far outweigh any hardships and the future is bright with hope for a truly democratic America' ('Time to Count', 1944: 44). Also, Johnson believed that if blacks only viewed the limits they faced in America they would fail to experience any achievements whatsoever. Consequently, rather than following a course of slashing attacks on the American system (and likely alienating advertisers in the process), through *Ebony*, Johnson urged blacks to aspire to achieve and implicitly urged a moderate course.

Third, Johnson felt the cautious editorial course he pursued in *Ebony* simply mirrored the prevailing desires among his readers. His readers were moderate, so his editorial tone was moderate. This is not to say the magazine was devoid of any serious analysis of the issues facing African Americans; such articles were sometimes included in its pages. But as members of the African-American middle class became more militant and engaged with civil rights protests, the tone of *Ebony* followed suit. When questioned about the content change Johnson caustically responded, 'Maybe we were tired. I'm not speaking for looters and burners, though I can understand them. They are less disciplined than we are, less educated, have much less to lose. But they're tired too' ('Uncle Tom Magazine', 1968: 70). Johnson was always responsive to the wishes of his readers and he was loath to be left behind and risk irrelevance. So, while he did not abandon a focus on glamour, fashion and entertainment, *Ebony* eventually included larger numbers of serious articles examining the situation facing blacks in America. Additionally, alongside articles detailing African-American successes in sports and entertainment, the magazine now included similar stories for blacks in business, politics, and education. Thus by the late 1950s *Ebony* aimed for an array of ingredients of African-American middle-class lifestyle (Hirsch, 1968; Rosen, 1964).

Defining a Lifestyle

There were three factors central to *Ebony*'s definition of lifestyle: pride, individual and group aspiration, and consumption. Editorials and articles in *Ebony* urged blacks to take pride in their individual accomplishments as well as those of other blacks. Articles often highlighted blacks that were the first or only ones employed by a particular company or in a specific role. Each individual success furthered the cause of blacks as a group. One writer argued, 'Every black person born in America is born with a responsibility – the responsibility to do everything within his or her power to improve the lot of all black people born into a nation in which the majority of whites still consider all blacks inferior' ('Responsibilities', 1973: 180). This was not a departure from material pursuits to be sure, because that action was accepted and expected from those who had achieved the means to obtain them. It was, however, an urging for blacks to have a sense of pride and responsibility in black achievement, organizations, and institutions. Also, this pride was to extend internationally and include the achievements of people of African descent worldwide. While not a full expression of Pan-Africanism, it was an effort to have blacks see themselves as part of a larger group.

Advertising in the magazine reflected blacks' middle-class aspirations. Advertisements for automobiles, watches, clothing and alcoholic beverages urged blacks to adopt more and more of the accouterments of middle-class living. A significant portion of each issue was also dedicated to cooking and entertaining. So, while true the African-American hostess might hold a full-time job, she was expected to be knowledgeable of the latest recipes and to maintain a modern kitchen and home. This was a clear emphasis on an urban and suburban lifestyle for blacks. Visits to museums, membership at country clubs, and attendance at parties were part of the lifestyle of the smarter set. Given the income and education of the average *Ebony* reader, many belonged to the group most likely to benefit immediately from the gains of the civil rights movement. They were the ones most likely to take advantage of newly available jobs, educational opportunities, and desegregating suburbs. Consequently, advertisements and articles urged readers to adopt the conspicuous trappings of success. To get the newly available job, for example, one had to dress in the right type and make of suit or drive the right kind of car. But, by the early 1960s, *Ebony* consistently featured articles urging readers to aspire for the freedom and achievement of the entire group, not just individual members. For individual success, while important, was not a signal that racism and discrimination had died in America. An editorial critically noted, 'The undramatic Negro is so happy over his personal acceptance into a limited fellowship of white people that he often chooses not to identify with the less fortunate dark people to whom even a small measure of privilege comes hard' ('The Discontent', 1961: 70). So, while it might be the African-American youth or poor leading and taking part in the protest efforts, the freedom of the black middle class depended on their success. Articles in the magazine consistently reminded individual blacks that their opportunities for a new job or a suburban home was directly tied to the actions of other African Americans. This meant that blacks had to aspire for both individual and group achievement ('Case Studies', 1951).

While pride and aspiration were important factors in the lifestyle *Ebony* defined for middle-class blacks, each was dwarfed by its emphasis on consumption. Over and above anything else *Ebony* was a consumer lifestyle handbook for African Americans. Through the articles and advertisements blacks learned of the latest cars, clothes, alcoholic beverages, appliances, and other aspects of consumer living. However, while scholarly critics of Johnson and *Ebony* often end their analysis with a description of the emphasis on consumption (Weems, 1998), a careful analysis reveals something more complex at work. Specifically, Johnson was clearly operating within the tradition of African-American politicization of consumption for goals beyond those inherent in the immediate act of consuming.

In the 1920s and 1930s, African-American protesters had used their spending power to achieve various socio-economic goals. During this period blacks used their spending to press for employment, fair prices, or better treatment from store employees. As Lizabeth Cohen (2003) has explained, by the 1940s the consumer was a recognized agent of change in America. From the catalyzing point of consumer rights, groups could and did branch their efforts into other areas of change. So, for blacks, the initial issue may have been the opportunity to buy goods at a local store, but the eventual goal was to create employment in that store or within the management of the corporation. Thus, through their consumer activity, blacks had a tradition of developing 'a strategy to achieve economic power [and] political equality' (Cohen, 2003). So, while Johnson may not have verbalized his efforts via *Ebony* in this manner, he was in fact acting within an important tradition. Certainly he was self-interested and needed to earn a profit, but the net impact of *Ebony* and of black consumer purchases, he urged, was greater access to the social, political and economic rights for which they strove. Johnson was implicitly urging blacks to assert their rights within the public spaces in America and to adopt a politicized form of consumption as part of their lifestyle. Quite simply, if blacks could not succeed in winning equal rights in the marketplace, where the objective rules of capitalism supposedly applied, what hope did they have for doing so in subjective arenas such as employment or education where acceptance could be given based on subjective criteria? For while discrimination led to blacks receiving fewer dollars for doing the same work as whites, once those dollars were received they were supposed to be equal in their spending power. If they were not then what hope did blacks have for their other social and political struggles to be achieved? Simply put, none. In fact, blacks had to achieve victory in the consumer arena at least simultaneously, if not before, victory in the socio-political one. As civil rights leader Ella Baker argued, it was 'crystal clear that the current sit-in and other demonstrations are concerned with something bigger than a hamburger ... The Negro and white students ... are seeking to rid America of the scourge of racial segregation and discrimination – not only at the lunch counters but in every aspect of life' (Cohen, 2003: 190). So, there were larger issues than spending and access to accommodation, but Johnson chose to focus his efforts on the area in which he could both earn a profit and have the greatest possible impact. That such a focus also endeared him to potential advertisers was simply a significant and profitable bonus.

Fighting for Equality and Status

At first glance the advertisements and articles within *Ebony* seem to point to an uncritical emphasis on consumption for consumption's sake. However, when one examines the magazine over several years, pays careful attention to the editorial content, and juxtaposes that material alongside the socio-cultural events ongoing in America, a very different picture emerges. Careful examination reveals Johnson placing a measured emphasis on the potential impact of consumption on blacks' status in the United States. Simply put, material gains were not defined as a cure all for the issues blacks faced in America. Fundamentally, one editorial observed, 'material gains do not alter the Negro's status. They are but a compensation for his lack of standing and he is still groping and grasping to find the illusive happiness which is the aspiration of people everywhere' ('The Fable', 1949: 60). Material gains were simply part of the information that signaled where one stood socially and financially, and blacks had to adhere to the same (if not higher) standards as whites.

Johnson's view of blacks' consumption was further expressed in late 1949 in what became one of his most widely reprinted editorials. Entitled 'Why Negroes Buy Cadillacs' (1949: 34), Johnson argued that a Cadillac was a tool to further blacks (at least in terms of image) along the road to equality. He wrote, 'The fact is that basically a Cadillac is an instrument of aggression, a solid and substantial symbol for many a Negro that he is as good as any white man. To be able to buy the most expensive car made in America is as graphic a demonstration of that equality as can be found'. The Cadillac had no prejudice. If one had the money he or she could buy one and drive as long and as far as their money would allow. It was the supreme symbol of automotive quality and for blacks to acquire one meant that they had scaled the highest peak of consumer goods. They might be limited in engaging in other areas of life and leisure, but there were few prescriptions on their purchases. Hence the Cadillac in Johnson's mind was an integral part of blacks' 'uphill fight for status'; it was a 'weapon in the war for racial equality'. But Johnson was not blithely placing car ownership above social, political and economic goals. Instead it was a practical recognition that just as blacks strove to achieve those lofty goals, Americans judged one another based on their clothes, homes, choice of liquor, and the cars they drove. Therefore, an African American that drove a Cadillac gave an immediate impression of lofty status. Further because blacks were judged as a group rather than as individuals, the success of one translated in some small way to improving perceptions of the group.

Johnson also reasoned that only those who could afford the cars should ponder buying them, though all should aspire for such a purchase. He did not encourage blacks to forgo mortgage payments to make car payments. He wrote that those who bought unwisely were 'paying a mighty high price for racial pride' and that such action was a mark of 'misplaced values' ('Why Negroes Buy', 1949: 34). Those who could afford the car, though, should buy one. But, in a nod to the expected racial solidarity, he counselled that besides buying the car, blacks were expected to give liberally to racial organizations. Beyond that point, however, was one more way that individual blacks could 'reach for equality on every level of

U.S. life' ('Why Negroes Buy', 1949: 34). The Cadillac was simply one more step on blacks' quest to become first-class citizens.

Consumption and economic power went hand in hand in *Ebony*'s vision of a middle-class lifestyle. Money meant the potential access to power. Combined with consumption it gave blacks another tool to use in their press for equality. An *Ebony* writer noted, 'To the American money talks. And if it can talk loud enough, is powerful enough, it will demand respect. It will make even the white man lay his racial prejudices down' ('Why Negroes Overtip', 1953: 96). Still, Johnson did not celebrate the centrality of money unswervingly, noting that it was 'unfortunate' that money was so central a determinant in one's life choices. But he pragmatically concluded 'that is the way it is'. Further, he knew from personal experience that while it did not dissolve one's problems, it was far better to have money than not and that, without economic clout, blacks had little chance of achieving their other goals.

Readers and other contemporary critics of Johnson's approach suggested that he was reproducing a white middle-class inspirational vision for African Americans. Implicit in such critiques is that Johnson simply considered blacks as dark-skinned whites. Such criticisms obscure the nuances of the socio-cultural reality existing when Johnson published *Ebony*. Johnson saw material goods for what they were, clear markers of status within a consumer society. Therefore, if the world thought more highly of the man who drove the Cadillac, then blacks should aspire to drive Cadillacs. Certainly his approach was only a press for an increased consumer status. But, with the interweaving between the consumer and citizen that began in the US during the Great Depression, Johnson adroitly recognized that in the minds of many Americans the two were synonymous. As he told a group of advertising representatives, 'you must understand his [the black consumer's] desire for recognition, his yearning for courtesy and attention, and his unrelenting efforts to be accepted and treated as a citizen and as a man' (Johnson, 1963). This meant that, though admittedly less important than many of the other measures blacks were fighting for, consumer equality was important as well because it was a clear indicator of blacks' status within society.

Besides projecting a more nuanced vision of consumption as a lifestyle choice for blacks, critics have failed to note the evolution of Johnson's consumer vision during his tenure as publisher and chief editor. A measured analysis of the magazine reveals that, while true that consumption was a significant portion of the lifestyle touted by *Ebony*, it involved several other factors including education, employment opportunities, an end to discrimination, and continued pressure to secure political equality. Hence, success equaled more than just consumption, it also included the capacity to live one's life in the free manner that one chose. Also, Johnson never equated consumption with political and social equality, instead presenting it as a separate type of equality. Johnson recognized that the ability and opportunity to consume were part of the definition of full citizenship. So, while others pressed for equality in those areas, Johnson used *Ebony* to encourage readers to live a lifestyle of conspicuous, but politicized, consumption and to place their consumer equality on full display. Moreover, by the late 1960s, Johnson had began urging blacks to buy homes, complete college educations, and invest in stocks and bonds so as to have a more complete level of economic equality: 'Petty signs of class and caste are but temporary distractions from the humiliation of racial segregation and discrimination' ('The Negro Status Seeker', 1960: 96).

Criticisms of *Ebony* Magazine

Given Johnson's success it should not be surprising that both he and *Ebony* have been both highly lauded and heavily criticized. The nature of *Ebony*'s general interest format meant that it had to contain subject matter designed to attract the widest possible readership. Some made the criticism personal: '*Ebony* is very much a reflection of Johnson's own estimation of the black intellect – and it's a perception not much different from whites. He thinks black people must be entertained. He thinks you must make them sing and dance. He doesn't view them as serious people who want to be informed about the world around them' (Ingham and Feldman, 1994: 377). Other critics pointed specifically to advertisements in the magazine for products designed to bleach the skin, in the process supposedly making it lighter in colour. Combined with other advertisements for products that straightened African-American hair, Johnson and *Ebony* were accused of promoting black self-hatred or white standards of beauty. In *Black Bourgeoisie*, Frazier (1962) singled out *Ebony* for particularly vehement criticism. He argued that the magazine perpetuated blacks' sense of unreality by focusing only upon the consumer habits of those it portrayed rather than the effort that lay behind their accomplishments. So, rather than focusing upon the educational achievements of a surgeon, for example, essays drew attention to the car he drove and the expensive home he had purchased.

Further, as the leading black periodical, *Ebony* was targeted by contemporary critics for not doing more, the definition of which depended on the position of the critic in question. During the period under study in this chapter that often meant more on the issue of civil rights. But it is important to remember that, while it was the flagship publication, *Ebony* was only one of the periodicals Johnson published. Although *Ebony* was the most successful of the Johnson publications he continued to publish *Negro Digest*. While he had a history of abandoning unsuccessful ventures, he continued to offer this money-losing periodical into the 1970s (by the late 1960s *Negro Digest* lost between $80-100,000 per year in publishing costs). Johnson did so because he believed the booklet offered an important outlet for black writers. Though often criticized for the celebratory overtones of *Ebony*, Johnson countered that the types of articles critics sought were published in *Negro Digest*. For example, while articles in *Ebony* critically, but judiciously, examined the 'white problem', articles in *Negro Digest* were not as charitable; rather than examining the issues, a writer in *Negro Digest* offered 'Every white throat cut is a success in itself' ('Color Success', 1968: 32). Such an incendiary argument would never have been found in the advertiser-reliant *Ebony* magazine.

Conclusion

By the early 1970s Johnson controlled the largest black publishing company in America. He also owned a radio station, a successful cosmetics firm (whose products were advertised in *Ebony*) and had become chairman of his first corporate employer, Supreme Life. Still, by this time *Ebony* was no longer unchallenged in the black magazine field. Early in the decade two new publications, *Essence* and *Black Enterprise*, found their way to store shelves. Catering to black women and black businesspeople respectively, by the mid-1970s it was clear the two newcomers were here to stay. Thus, *Ebony* was no longer alone in detailing for blacks the accoutrements of their lifestyle. Although *Ebony* remained the magazine with the largest circulation, descriptions and depictions of black lifestyle were no longer its alone to define. As the publishers of his original inspiration, *Life* magazine, soon found, the era of the general interest magazine was over and the time of specialized publication had arrived. But, for nearly three decades, Johnson and *Ebony* had dominated the black publishing field and had guided generations of African Americans on the definitions of middle-class lifestyle. Johnson was also a key figure in expanding corporate interest in African Americans as a distinct consumer market. Also, whether one agreed with *Ebony's* editorial approach, it was an undeniable boost to the morale of African Americans to have a source to turn to that showed that they too could be successful in America. For that fact alone, Johnson deserves a large measure of appreciation and credit.

Acknowledgements

Many thanks to my research assistants Linda Manning, Marisa Randle and Erica Smith for their hard work in compiling the material for this essay.

References

'At Home with Marian Anderson' (1954), *Ebony*, February, pp. 52-57.

Berkman, D. (1963) 'Advertising in *Ebony* and *Life*: Negro Aspirations vs. Reality', *Journalism Quarterly*, Vol. 40, pp. 53-64.

Brooks, D. (1991) 'Consumer Markets and Consumer Magazines: Black America and the Culture of Consumption, 1920-1960', Dissertation, University of Iowa.

'Case Studies: How Several Firms Have Succeeded in Selling the Negro Market' (1951), *Tide*, July 20, p. 44.

Cohen, L. (2003) *A Consumers' Republic: The Politics of Mass Consumption in Postwar America*, New York: Alfred A. Knopf.

'Color Success Black' (1968) *Time*, August 2, p. 32.

Dingle, D. (1999) *Black Enterprise Titans of the B.E. 100s*, New York: John Wiley and Sons.

'Ebony Marks 5th Anniversary of Publication' (1950), *Advertising Age*, October 23, p. 49.

Featherstone, M. (1991) *Consumer Culture and Postmodernism*, London: Sage.

Frazier, E. (1962) *Black Bourgeoisie: The Rise of a New Middle Class in the United States*, New York: Collier Books.

Hale, G. (1999) *Making Whiteness: The Culture of Segregation in the South, 1890-1940*, New York: Vintage Books.

Hirsch, P. (1968) 'An Analysis of *Ebony*: The Magazine and Its Readers', *Journalism Quarterly*, vol. 45, pp. 261-270, 292.

Ingham, J. and L. Feldman (eds) (1994) *African-American Business Leaders: A Biographical Dictionary*, Westport: Greenwood Press.

Johnson, J. (1952) 'Does Your Sales Force Know How to Sell the Negro Trade? Some Do's and Don'ts', *Advertising Age*, March 17, pp. 73-75.

Johnson, J. (1963) 'The New Negro Consumer: A Challenge, Responsibility and Opportunity', in J. Walter Thompson Marketing Vertical File, 1940-1999, Box 22, Hartmann Center, Duke University.

Johnson, J. and Bennett, Jr., L. (1992) *Succeeding Against the Odds*, New York: Amistad Press.

'Johnson Publishing Launches Merchandising Program for "*Ebony*", "Tan" Advertisers', (1951) *Advertising Age*, October 22, p. 23.

'Nation Within a Nation' (1957) *Premium Practice*, May, p. 29.

Pattillo-McCoy, M. (1999) *Black Picket Fences: Privilege and Peril Among the Black Middle Class*, Chicago: University of Chicago Press.

Pendergast, T. (2000) *Creating the Modern Man: American Magazines and Consumer Culture, 1900-1950*, Columbia: University of Missouri Press.

Reichley, A. (1968) 'How John Johnson Made It', *Fortune*, June, pp. 53-54.

'Responsibilities of the Black Middle Class' (1973), *Ebony*, August, p. 180.

Rosen, B. (1964) 'Attitude Change Within the Negro Press Toward Segregation and Discrimination', *The Journal of Social Psychology*, Vol. 62 (February), pp. 77-83.

'The Discontent' (1961) *Ebony*, August, p. 70.

'The Fable of the Happy Negro' (1949) *Ebony*, January, p. 60.

'The Negro Status Seeker' (1960) *Ebony*, January, p.96.

'Time to Count Our Blessings' (1944) *Ebony*, November, p. 44.

'Uncle Tom Magazine Removes the Kid Gloves' (1968) *Business Week*, March 23, pp. 70-73.

Weems, R. (1998) *Desegregating the Dollar: African-American Consumerism in the Twentieth Century*, New York: New York University Press.

'Why Negroes Buy Cadillacs' (1949) *Ebony*, September, p. 34.

'Why Negroes Overtip' (1953) *Ebony*, July, p. 96.

Chapter 5

The Politics of *Playboy*: Lifestyle, Sexuality and Non-conformity in American Cold War Culture

Mark Jancovich

It has now become commonplace for social theorists to present contemporary lifestyles as the product of a radical break with the past, even of an epochal shift from modernity to postmodernity. In the process, critics contrast 'the 1950s as an era of grey conformism, a time of *mass* consumption' with the post-1960s, and claim that the consumer culture of the latter is distinguished not by mass consumption and mass conformity but by diverse and heterogeneous lifestyles (Featherstone, 1991: 83).[1] The implications of these claims are massive and it is frequently suggested that these changes represent a shift from one form of social differentiation to another: class, it is alleged, is neither central nor significant within contemporary society. As Bocock puts it:

> [If] modern implied an industrial, urban, capitalist society, in which socio-economic class was still the determining feature of people's lives, of their sense of who they were, their identity, 'post-modern' implied a post-industrial, suburban, even post-capitalist social formation in which old, stable points for establishing people's sense of identity had been displaced. Identities in post-modern conditions become more flexible and float around in a state of potential, if not actual, change. (1993: 3-4)

As a result, it is argued, identity is no longer defined through one's productive work but through one's consumption:

> Consumption has been seen as epitomizing this move into postmodernity, for it implies a move away from productive work roles being central to people's lives, to their sense of identity, of who they are. In place of work roles, it is roles in various kinds of family formations, in sexual partnerships of various kinds, in leisure-time pursuits, in consumption in general, which has come to be seen as more significant to people. (*ibid.*)

Ignoring the problematic gender-blindness of such a statement, identity here is not something that is imposed on one by one's social position, but something that can be chosen or constructed through one's consumption practices.

For some, postmodern consumer society is therefore a world with 'no rules only choices'. Even Featherstone, who refutes this point, claims that:

> The new heroes of consumer culture make lifestyle a life project and display their individuality and sense of style in the particularity of the assemblage of goods, clothes, practices, experiences, appearance and bodily dispositions they design together into a lifestyle. The modern individual within consumer culture is made conscious that he speaks not only with his clothes, but with his home, furnishings, decoration, car and other activities .... The preoccupation with customizing a lifestyle and a stylistic self-consciousness are not just to be found among the young and affluent; consumer culture publicity suggests that we all have room for self-improvement and self-expression whatever our age or class origins. (1991: 86)

In other words, while Featherstone is critical of the claim that lifestyles are purely defined within consumption and that social hierarchies have dissolved, he still identifies postmodernity, consumer culture and lifestyle with one another, and associates them with an era that comes sometime after the 1960s.

However, Don Slater (1997) has not only shown that similar claims about consumption date back at least until the late eighteenth century, but also that claims about lifestyle were central to cold war rhetoric within the United States during the 1950s. If, as we have seen, the 1950s is often identified by contemporary critics as 'an era of grey conformism' and '*mass* consumption', the features of modernity which they contrast with contemporary postmodernity, within the 1950s itself, many saw consumer choice as a distinguishing feature of the period. In other words, consumer choice was one of the key ways in which the United States sought to distinguish itself from the Soviet Union, and associate itself with pluralism (and the Soviets with totalitarianism).

This can be clearly seen in the 'Kitchen Sink debate', where, as Karal Ann Marling points out, Nixon and Khrushchev 'locked horns over spin cycles, in-house intercom systems, and American household gadgetry in general' rather than over the arms race:

> To Nixon, the latest in kitchen consumerism stood for the basic tenets of the American way of life. Freedom. Freedom from drudgery for the housewife. And democracy, the opportunity to choose the very best model from the limitless assortment of colours, features, and prices the free market had to offer. (Marling, 1994: 243)

For many cold warriors, mass society was associated with Europe, where identity was ascribed rather than achieved, and people therefore lacked the freedom to choose their identities and distinguish themselves from others (Bell, 1988). In contrast, consumer capitalism in the United States, it was often claimed, provided individuals with the freedom not only to choose between consumer items but, in so doing, to reject conformity and choose their identities.

This position was clearly articulated in *Playboy* magazine, which was first published in 1953. This year is significant as it marks the moment of transition from the period of the McCarthy witch trials, in which the United States engaged in an anxious and paranoid confrontation with the Soviet Union, to the period of economic affluence that followed, in which the United States was more confident and assured of its own moral and political superiority to Soviet Communism. Furthermore, this celebration of consumption as a means of rejecting conformity and defining one's own identity was powerfully argued through the magazine's sexual politics. Rather than an apolitical titillation, the magazine's sexual materials were not only integrated into its politics of lifestyle, but became the central signifier of this politics.

Andrew Ross claims that the problem that faced many cold war intellectuals was the simultaneous, but potentially contradictory, requirements to demonstrate political responsibility while also defending intellectual freedom. The solution, he suggests, was that '*responsibility* became redefined as the protection of an intellectual's "freedom" at all costs' (Ross, 1989: 219). It was by defending intellectual freedom that cold war intellectuals presented themselves as demonstrating political responsibility. In other words, it was by refusing to allow art and ideas to become dominated by political interests that these intellectuals claimed that they were challenging totalitarianism. By defending intellectual freedom, they presented themselves as taking a stand against those ideologues of the left or the right who, it was claimed, sought to repress all aspects of life and make them subservient to authoritarian doctrines. Similarly, art itself was often praised as politically responsible precisely through its refusal of politics: it was by refusing to become mere propaganda that it demonstrated the limits of totalitarian discourses and, in so doing, offered a critique of them (see, for example, Jancovich, 1993).

In much the same way, *Playboy* sought to defend the autonomy of sex and sexuality. By freeing them from the demands of other social discourses – by claiming an autonomy for sexual tastes – they not only figured in classed struggles, as I have argued elsewhere (see Jancovich, 2001a, 2001b), but also articulated a cold war rejection of totalitarianism. The pursuit of sexual pleasure was claimed to be justifiable as an end in itself without recourse to other systems of value. The pursuit of pleasure without purpose became a stand against totalitarian attempts to make all aspects of life service politics.

However, it would be wrong to dismiss *Playboy* as simply an anti-Communist cold war publication. On the contrary, it rarely positioned itself against the Soviet Union but rather used cold war rhetoric to challenge aspects of American society and culture. However, for *Playboy*, this position was based on an attempt to establish a pure and uncontaminated sexual pleasure that was not only outside forms of social power, but also a direct challenge to them. In other words, it sought to recapture a natural unrepressed sexuality and use it to reject the supposed perversion of this natural state by social and political repression. It was for this reason that the magazine had such great problems in its dealing with feminism in the later 1960s: its commitment to the belief that sexual pleasure was opposed to social power meant that it tended to regard feminist critiques of sexuality as anti-sex, as repressive and totalitarian.

Lifestyle, Consumption and Sexuality in *Playboy*

Playboy's belief in the liberating powers of lifestyle consumption is probably best summed up by Hefner himself:

> I think it was the right idea in the right place at the right time. A great many of the traditional social and moral values of our society were changing, and PLAYBOY was the first publication to reflect those changes. We offered an alternative lifestyle with more permissive, more play-and-pleasure orient-ation. People get less sense of identity out of their jobs now than ever before, and with increasing affluence, how one spends one's time and finds value in it is more important than ever. (quoted in Anon., 1974: 66)

Despite Hefner's inevitable over-estimation of the magazine's originality, he clearly associates individual freedom and identity with the capacity to choose between different objects of consumption. Indeed, this passage is remarkably similar to Bocock's description of the postmodernity that supposedly follows the modernity of the 1950s. Furthermore, it associates consumption with the 'aestheticization of life', that is seen as central to postmodern culture, and in which the choice between objects of consumption is made on the basis of the pleasures that they offer, pleasures that are usually associated with the appreciation of style (see, for example, Featherstone, 1991).

The magazine even made this association between style and freedom explicit. For example, an article on college fashions praised 'the current national acceptance of the trim, tapered, natural look in men's clothing', but it also stressed that 'this year, any playboy-about-campus … will take full advantage of the New Freedom that is abroad in the land' (Kessie, 1955a: 18). If the traditional look had its virtues, *Playboy* warned that many women felt that 'men are boring to look at'. Fortunately, it also claimed that

> assuming our man is not totally color blind, possesses most of the necessary appendages upon which to hang assorted articles of apparel, earns more than $60 a week, and takes a shower at least as often as he receives his pay check, there is no reason why he can't look as tastefully attired as that fellow who sells Schweppes. (Kessie, 1955b: 39)

Instead of looking boring, *Playboy* called for men to distinguish themselves, but it warned against getting 'caught up in a perplexing phantasmagoria of color combinations, patterns, styles, designs, fabrics and cuts'. Instead it favoured 'those distinctive details of styling that point up that a man is being *quietly* well dressed' (*ibid.*).

Despite its appreciation of the quietly distinctive conservative look, the magazine also satirized the epitome of this look, Brooks Brothers. Dedman (1954: 17) claimed that the 'Brooks Brothers look is not merely a *look* – it's a religion' and, given the magazine's distrust of religions, this claim implied that the look was fanatical and conformist. Once someone had acquired the look, 'it remains unchanging throughout prep school, college, marriage, divorce, remarriage, and death'. It was not only that the individual never changed but also that they became just like everyone else in their milieu: 'At college (eastern, again) you don't make a fraternity unless you've conformed to the venerable BB formula. It has its advantages, for during rush period it's easy to detect "your type" the kind with whom you can "really get along". Naturally, he's wearing a Brooks Brothers suit' (*ibid.*). The Brooks Brothers suit becomes a badge or uniform that is worn by all members of a closed and conformist social group.

In contrast, *Playboy* suggested that clothing should be seen as a way for a man to distinguish himself from others and assert his identity. It was for this reason that the magazine objected to a whole host of different types of apparel: 'Like twin sets of anything, the belt-tie duo indicates a stamped out approach that belies your high IQ (individuality-quotient)' (Anon., 1957b: 65). Clothes were seen as a way of expressing the self but, consequently, a man had to be careful about what his clothes said about him:

> After all, the average urbanite gets few chances to exhibit his penetrating philosophy of life or reveal his blinding pyrotechnics of wit. But if he is well turned out ('rich but not gaudy') and the cut of his jib is trim ('but not express'd in fancy'), he is immediately proclaimed a lad who knows his way around. The duds he wears do much to conceal or reveal the kind of gink he is. (Rutherford, 1957: 47)

If urban life offered people few opportunities to distinguish themselves, consumption was one way in which individuals could reject conformity and assert their individuality.

As a result, while the first edition of the magazine declared that 'Affairs of state will be out of our province' and that it would 'emphasize entertainment', it was nonetheless clear that it was 'filling a publishing need only slightly less important than the one just taken care of by the Kinsey Report' (Anon., 1953a: 3). In this way, consumption and entertainment were seen as important, despite their separation from 'affairs of state', and they were also crucially linked with issues of sexuality. Hefner is fond of telling the press that 'Paul Gebhard, director of the Institute for Sex Research, once said that the genius of *Playboy* was that it linked sex with upward mobility' (quoted in Anon., 1974: 66), but this claim only tells half the story. It is not simply that the magazine suggested that upward mobility would give one greater access to sex, or even that sex was simply reduced to another consumer item, but rather that sexual tastes were recognised as one element in the ensemble of different dispositions that make up a lifestyle (Jancovich, 2001a). As a result, Hefner pointedly rejected the separation of sexuality from other lifestyle choices, and opposed those who presented the magazine as 'schizophrenic' in its juxtaposition of articles with a 'sophisticated patina' and nudes that cater 'to peepshow tastes' (Hefner, 1962: 169).

On the contrary, the magazine turned the pursuit of pleasure into a moral stance in itself, and strongly distanced itself from mere hedonism:

What is a playboy? Is he a wastrel, a ne'er-do-well, a fashionable bum? Far from it: he can be a sharp-minded young business executive, a worker in the arts, a university professor, an architect or engineer. He can be many things, provided he possesses a certain point of view. He must see life not as a vale of tears, but as a happy time, he must take joy in his work, without regarding it as the end of all living; he must be an alert man, an aware man, a man of taste, a man sensitive to pleasure, a man who – without acquiring the stigma of the voluptuary or dilettante – can live life to the hilt. This is the sort of man we mean when we use the word playboy. (Anon., 1956e: back cover)

As I have argued elsewhere, sexuality became one of the key ways in which the new middle classes of the post-war period sought to distinguish themselves from the old middle classes (Jancovich, 2001a), but sexuality was also important to this class for another reason. As Featherstone observes, the new middle classes are characterized by the 'quest for the new and the latest in relationships and experiences' (Featherstone, 1991: 86) and, in the pages of *Playboy*, sex signified an intensity of experience and intense experiences signified sex. For example, in an article that introduced readers to the culinary delights of curry, the experience of eating is heavily sexualized: 'curry is deceptive and full of sensuous surprises. It warms at first, then provokes, bites, singes, sears, explodes and satisfies' (Mario, 1956a: 49).

It is for these reasons that the magazine's first edition had so directly associated itself with the Kinsey Report. For Hefner, the Kinsey Report demonstrated the disjuncture between the accepted norms of sexual behaviour and the actual patterns of sexual activity and, in so doing, it 'makes obvious the lack of understanding and realistic thinking gone into formation of sex standards and laws. Our moral pretences, our hypocrisy on matters of sex have led to incalculable frustration, delinquency and unhappiness' (quoted in Brady, 1974:39). The magazine therefore promised to liberate its readers from repressive codes of sexual behaviour and promote the pursuit of sexual experience as both healthy and natural when uncontaminated by social and political power.

It is this authentic sexuality that the magazine's first centrefold, Marilyn Monroe, was supposed to represent: as the magazine asked, 'what makes her *the real article*?'. Although they stress that there is 'no denying that the young lady is very well stacked', they stress that her body's curves 'aren't *that* spectacular'. Nor is her face claimed to account for her importance: it is 'sweet, wide-eyed and innocent' but not much different to a host of other actresses. Instead, her power was supposed to derive from being 'natural sex personified', which made 'her the most natural choice in the world for our very first *Playboy Sweetheart*' (Anon., 1953b: 18).

From the start, then, *Playboy* was opposed to censorship. In 1955, Hefner was forced to take on the post office but this was as much for economic and promotional reasons. However, in April 1954, the magazine also published Ray Bradbury's *Fahrenheit 451* and, in October 1954, it ran an article on 'Nudity and the Foreign Film'. As Barbara Wilinsky (2000: 37) has noted, during this period European films often identified with 'obscenity and perversity' by some while, for others, their sexual content was often seen as proof of their adult seriousness. The *Playboy* article takes the latter approach and observes that while the 'movie censors of America have considered the human body and concluded it is immoral … the greatest artists of all time have always contended that the human body is a thing of beauty' (Anon., 1954a: 41). While the censors are accused of hiding from reality and creating an 'ideal species', 'a spayed, denavelled, breast-free, unbuttocked creature who cannot possibly offend anyone', the foreign film is deemed to be 'interested in realism'. In the process, Europe is made the positive other of a repressive United States in which 'poor, unenlightened European audiences, never having been told that nudeness and lewdness are one and the same, sit through it all without apparent ill effects' (Anon., 1954a: 43). Indeed, images of the continent as a positive alternative to the United States turn up repeatedly in the magazine throughout the 1950s, whose travel section often celebrated European culture.

These concerns with censorship also featured in September 1954, when an article on Gina Lollobrigida condemned attempts to censor René Clair's *Beauties of the Night*, and it is therefore hardly surprising that the subscription page for that month identified Thomas Bowdler as 'the anti-playboy'. As it argued, Bowdler

> would never have approved of PLAYBOY. The man who made 'bowdlerize' synonymous with 'censorship;' whose edition of Shakespeare omitted 'those words and expressions which cannot with propriety be read aloud in a family;' who expurgated Gibbon's *Decline of the Roman Empire* to conform with the narrowness of his own mind – this man would have been horrified by PLAYBOY. (Anon., 1954e: 51)

It therefore suggested that 'If, like Bowdler, you feel all literature should be made proper for six-year olds and elderly ladies, please *don't* subscribe to this magazine' (Anon., 1954e: 51).

In contrast to Bowdler, Molière is identified as the sort of man who would have appreciated *Playboy*, and he is identified as 'a man of sparkling wit who poked fun at prudery, satirized hypocrisy and laughed at censors'. These qualities, it is argued, make him 'a man very much like the PLAYBOY subscriber of today; a man of good humour with a broad mind and a great capacity for pleasure; a sophisticated man; an aware man; a man of taste' (Anon., 1954b: 51). J.S. Bach is also seen as a forerunner of *Playboy*, although in this case he is identified with the magazine rather than the reader: he is identified as 'a man of more than usual sexual energy', who 'was not above shocking little minds by inserting a hilarious aria into a staid cantata'. Similarly, it is claimed, '*Playboy* has no compunctions about shocking little minds, and it feels that sexual energy is a very good thing' (Anon., 1954d: 51).

In this way, the magazine sought to identify itself with a series of iconic figures that were claimed to represent an appreciation of the same values as the magazine. Issak Walton is identified as a *bon vivant* who 'liked to live well' (Anon., 1954c: 51), while Rabelais is claimed to be 'one of Playboy's favorites … a brilliant sensualist, [who] was a devote respecter of the human appetite' (Mario, 1955a: 27). They also praise Benjamin Franklin, who, it is claimed, was a man who 'enjoyed life's many pleasures, and when he was sent to France as a special commissioner, his charm and ready wit won the hearts of many Parisian ladies' (Anon., 1954f: 51). However, the reference to Franklin also allows them to humorously misinterpret his advice that those that love life should not 'squander time'. This advice is interpreted as an encouragement to live life to the full and to not defer gratification, but Hefner knew that Franklin's position was quite different. Indeed, in his account of lifestyles, Hefner makes an overt comparison between *Playboy* and Franklin's *Poor Richard's Almanac*:

> Franklin was writing a guidebook to coping with life when a more frugal work-oriented Puritan ethic was essential to survival in a frontier society; *Playboy* came along and offered a new set of ethical values for an urban society. The editorial message in *Playboy* came through load and clear: enjoy yourself. (quoted in Anon., 1974: 66)

In this way, the reference to Franklin works to distinguish between the restraint of the old middle class and the 'fun-morality' of the new middle classes (Bourdieu, 1984; Hollows, 2002; Jancovich, 2001a).

In addition to those with a capacity for pleasure, the magazine also associated itself with a series of more contemporary figures. In June 1954, it ran a profile on Orson Welles, who was celebrated as a professional non-conformist, but it had rather more problem with the beats towards the end of the decade. On one hand, *Playboy* and the beats had much in common. Both were anti-conformist and were devoted aficionados of jazz. But they also had very different value systems. *Playboy*'s commitment to the good life presupposed an investment in corporate America. Material success was necessary for the consumption of fine wines, fine foods, and stylish clothes on which the lifestyle depended. The beats, by contrast, displayed a rejection of corporate American and a calculated anti-fashion in their consumption practices: 'about half were tricked out as bohemians, the pure stuff, complete with sandals, paint-stained suntans, work shirt, beard and clutched roll of manuscript paper' (Clad, 1958: 22). If the playboy was a model of grooming, the beat was determinedly anti-grooming.

However, while *Playboy* was critical of the movement in February 1958, by July 1959 it had published pieces by Kerouac, Corso and Ginsberg, and in the same month featured a 'beat playmate'. The criticism of the movement largely revolved around the supposed emptiness of the scene. Described as the 'new nihilism', the beats are frequently seen as people who have simply failed to grow up. It is claimed that most have 'lived on the G.I. Bill, 52-20, state unemployment, on-the-job training and a 200-dollar advance from Random House' since the end of World War II, and still engage in 'the college talk of 10 year ago', a endless tired round of pretentious pointless prattle (Clad, 1958: 22). Their cool is presented as little more than boredom, which leads them to play spiteful tricks on others:

> In Denver a gaggle of young lads, not knowing what to do on a warm spring evening, steal a car each, drive them to the other side of town, park, steal a few more, drive back to the starting point, park, and then

settle down to giggle about the confusion of the owners and the police.
Silence. Return of boredom. Yawn. (Gold, 1958: 20)

Furthermore, as this circular prank suggests, for *Playboy*, the beats are 'nothing
going nowhere, coolly' (Anon., 1958: 20). Worst of all, for *Playboy*, they are even
too cool for sex. It is only after they have driven cars back and forth across town
that one of the lads in Denver 'says softly, "Pops, why didn't we think of picking
up some chicks?"' (Gold, 1958: 20).

However, the presentation of beat playmate Yvette Vickers is quite
different. Instead of the listless boredom discussed in the earlier articles, the
presentation of Vickers is one of independence and energy. The article even gently
mocks the magazine itself. It starts with the magazine's researchers and
photographers as they prepare for an earlier article on *The Coffee Houses of
America*, during which they 'saw many beauteous bohemiennes sipping expresso'.
However, as 'thoroughly indoctrinated company men', they remained undecided
about these girls until they met Yvette. However, while Yvette wins them over, she
is not an aberration but fully 'representative of the girls who inhabit the beat coffee
houses of Hollywood'. She is serious and smart with a interest in 'serious acting,
ballet, the poetry of Dylan Thomas, classical music ("Prokofiev drives me out of
my *skull!*")'. She is also 'a bit of a rebel' who is 'reckless and uninhibited enough
to race a Jag in the desert for kicks'. However, she is in no sense a passive and
unthreatening scene follower: 'she has strong opinions' and is given to 'frowning
prettily on conformity' (Anon. 1959: 47).

Consumption, Conformity and the Problem of Gender

If the *Playboy* male was supposed to define his identity through his consumption,
he also needed to avoid the dangers of consumption. Over the course of the 1950s,
Playboy published numerous articles, including contributions from Philip Wylie
and Vance Packard, which warned that advertising and mass consumption was
producing an increasingly conformist society. As Hefner himself argued:

> We know that *Playboy* has always stressed – in our own way – our
> conviction of the importance of the individual in an increasingly
> standardized society, the privilege of all to think differently from one
> another and to promote new ideas, and the right to hoot irreverently at
> herders of sacred cows and keepers of stultifying tradition and taboo.
> (1962: 168-9)

However, the danger of the magazine was that while it sought to present itself as a
'pleasure-primer styled for masculine taste' (Anon., 1953a: 3), it often found itself
accused of being a 'dictatorial tastemaker' (Hefner, 1962: 73). For example,
Harvey Cox claimed that *Playboy* produced Riesman's 'other-directed person':

> Within the confusing plethora of mass media signals and peer group
> values, *Playboy* fills a special need. For the insecure young man with

newly acquired time and money on his hands who still feels uncertain about his consumer skills, *Playboy* supplies a comprehensive and authoritative guidebook to this foreboding new world to which he now has access. It tells him not only who to be; it tells him *how* to be it, and even provides consolation outlets for those who secretly feel that they have not quite made it. (1961: 57)

Playboy stood accused of creating conformity rather than individuality, and of being a response to gender confusion rather than authenticity: '*Playboy* speaks to those who desperately want to know what it means to be a *man*, and more specifically a *male*, in today's world' (*ibid.*).

Although the postmodern consumer culture of the 1980s is often associated with a masculinity crisis, which is often opposed to the 1950s as a period of in which masculinity was both dominant and assured, the 1950s itself produced a torrent of writing on a supposed 'crisis of masculinity'. As Barbara Ehrenreich has argued, the debate about conformity in the period was itself a debate about a crisis in masculinity, given that the

> traits that Riesman found in the other directed personality – the perpetual alertness to signals from others, the concern with feelings and affect rather than objective tasks – were precisely those that the patriarch of mid-century sociology, Talcott Parsons, had just assigned to the female sex ... The other directed *man* was a Parsonian *woman*. (Ehrenreich, 1983: 34)

In other words, although critics of conformity may not have stated it explicitly, conformity in women was assumed to be right and proper – 'other-directedness was built into the female social role as wives and mothers' – and it was only in relation to men that it was seen as a problem. As Ehrenreich puts it: conformity 'meant a kind of emasculation' (p. 32).

Thus, while *Playboy* repeatedly stressed that people should make their own choices – 'No one should dictate your choice of chair any more than he picks out your clothes' (Palmer, 1954: 12) – the magazine's success was heavily dependent on college students, a group that were often represented as the epitome of the conformist and other-directed personality within the period (Reisman, 1961). Although a youth market, this group was the polar opposite of the rebellious youth subcultures associated with juvenile delinquency in the period, or the student radicals of the 1960s. On the contrary, they were the next generation of grey flannel corporation men that caused intellectuals so much anxiety at the time.

Furthermore, the magazine's attempt to distance itself from certain types of masculinity has also led some to regard the *Playboy* male as a 'domesticated male' (Kimmel, 1997). For example, in its first edition, the magazine distinguished itself from the rugged masculinity of the outdoorsman:

> Most of today's 'magazines for men' spend all their time out-of-doors – thrashing through thorny thickets or splashing about in fast flowing streams. We'll be out there too, occasionally, but we don't mind telling

you in advance – we plan on spending most of our time inside. (Anon., 1955a: 3)

In contrast to the rugged outdoorsman, the *Playboy* male enjoyed the creature comforts that consumer society made available: 'We like our apartment. We enjoy mixing up cocktails and an *hors d'oeuvre* or two, putting a little mood music on the phonograph, and inviting a female acquaintance for a quiet discussion of Picasso, Nietzsche, jazz, sex' (*ibid.*). The magazine also distinguished itself from other rugged masculinities and proudly reprinted a letter from a reader under the heading 'NO BLOOD AND GUTS':

> On a recent trip to Fort Worth, I discovered your handsome new magazine for men. I think it's great (and so does my wife.) I've become so disgusted with all the other 'men's magazines' I never buy them anymore. They're crammed with sensationalism, blood and guts stories, and hot rods, not to mention the gyp advertising on each page. (Rutherford, 1954: 3)

The *Playboy* male did not prove his masculinity through physical labour or conflict and was associated with the intellectual and symbolic labour of the white-collar worker. Nonetheless, he was in no way a domesticated male.

On the contrary, as Ehrenreich has pointed out, *Playboy* was a key player in the revolt against the family, in an attempt to reject its domesticating and feminizing associations. While some have seen the 1950s as the crest of the traditional family, as Elaine Tyler May (1988) has shown, the family of the 1950s stands out as a singular and unique case that was the creation of the broader political culture. Furthermore, attitudes to the family were highly ambivalent in the period. On the one hand, it was seen as a guarantor of security, individuality and freedom in a world of disruption, alienation and conformity. However, on the other hand, it was also frequently seen as precisely the opposite: an institution in which women were responsible for dominating and castrating their men and turning them into conformist automatons (see Hollows, 2000).

In such a situation, *Playboy* offered the obvious solution: a rejection of the family. To enjoy the *Playboy* lifestyle, the male had to disconnect himself from familial responsibilities and, even at Thanksgiving, he did not return to familial home but ate 'the Rock Cornish Game Hen' with a female companion (Mario, 1956b: 38). Moreover, in its rejection of conformity, the magazine constructed the housewife as its conformist other, so guaranteeing its identity. It is for this reason that Ehrenreich has claimed that '*Playboy* loved women – large-breasted, long-legged young women, anyway – and it hated wives' (Ehrenreich, 1983: 42).

If conformity 'meant a kind of emasculation', it was also suggested that the problem was the dominance of women: 'the matriarchy' (Mario, 1955b: 22). For example, the first edition contained an article, 'Miss Gold-Digger of 1953', which suggested that women were simply after men's money: 'All American womanhood has descended on alimony as their natural heritage' (Norman, 1953: 6). The author warns the reader not to 'mistake *alimony* for *child support*', and claims that it is

> a throwback to the days when grandma was a girl. A couple of
> generations ago, this was a man's world, and a nice young woman
> without a husband had a difficult time making her own way. Nothing
> could be further from the truth in 1953. (Norman, 1953: 7)

In this way, wives were seen as a problem because they were irrational consumers
who wanted to spend men's money, while *Playboy* insisted that women not only
had the opportunity but also the responsibility to be financially self-sufficient.

However, in his articles for the magazine, Philip Wylie made an
alternative suggestion. If he warned of 'a womanization of America' he also
suggested that men were controlled *through* women rather than *by* them, or rather,
as his subtitle puts it, 'the gray flannel mind exploits him through his women'
(Wylie, 1956: 23). According to Wylie, adverts targeted at men often use women's
sexuality, but he also claims that many adverts are also aimed at women, who he
presents as the ideal consumers. For them, status is everything and they will buy
whatever products will have the right connotations. However, he also claims that
advertisers address women because 'the ladies have the lucre': 'Economists and
statisticians have figured out that American Womanhood controls about 80% of the
capital wealth of the nation and does more than 80% of America's buying' (p. 24).
Thus, while he suggests that men are exploited through women by advertisers,
Wylie ultimately ends up seeing the problem as being the virtual enslavement of
men by their women: 'Why have American men built a civilization for women,
then sweated themselves into early graves to set it to women, and finally willed
their earnings to women? What is the method of this calamity?' (p. 50) His answer
is that women trade on their sexuality, withholding or promising sex in the hope of
financial reward, and he presents the modern male as a castrated drone working to
satisfy the appetites of the dominant female.

However, despite the obvious problems of this kind of position, it should
be noted that it was the basis of Friedan's feminist bestseller, *The Feminine
Mystique*, which was published in 1963, and had been published in article form
from the late 1950s onwards. For Friedan, the role of housewife forces women to
live through others and to lose their sense of self. In the process, they become
dependent, possessive and materialistic. As Friedan puts it:

> there is increasing evidence that woman's failure to grow to complete
> identity has hampered rather than enriched her sexual fulfilment,
> virtually doomed her to be castrative to her husband and sons, and
> caused neuroses, or problems as yet unnamed as neuroses, equal to those
> of sexual repression. (Friedan, 1963: 70)

Furthermore, Freidan argues that the solution to this problem is the rejection of
conformity and the search for identity, both of which can only be achieved through
a rejection of femininity and domesticity. If *Playboy*'s othering of femininity and
domesticity is problematic, it is similar to that of many feminist critics.[2] Like
Freidan, it did not object to women but rather to the social roles dictated by the
family.

If the magazine saw the social role of wife as problematic, this role was not just distinguished from the figure of the playboy but also from the positive representation of femininity, the playmate. As a result, the magazine spent much of its time teaching its readers how to discriminate not only between different consumer items, but also between different types of women. Furthermore, as Joanne Hollows (2002) has pointed out, if the playboy spoke his identity through his consumption, he could also learn to read women through their consumption. As one article observed:

> Any man can be his own private eye. All he needs is a menu. The next time you are sufficiently interested in a young lady to wants to explore some of the more hidden facets of her personality, follow this simple procedure. Invite her to a restaurant. (Mario, 1954: 39)

If she is 'the diamond digger who is determined to make you spend a month's salary in an evening', you don't want her. However, she may equally be 'a two-way tootsie who is out to impress you with her extreme frugality and thoughtfulness when she actually doesn't possess these qualities at all'. Others are indecisive, self-obsessed, while the ideal playmate 'is the girl whose eyes glisten when you hand her a menu because she sees a good time ahead'. The ideal playmate is a woman as sensitive to pleasure as the playboy himself: 'This girl simply loves to eat. It's the kind of uncomplicated love with which every healthy male feels a direct bond' (p. 40). Similarly,

> Powderhouse fluffs who expect you to brush the seat before they sit down to eat mincingly will snub a hamburger. But girls who like to snuggle up in a roadster, who do not mind walking onto a sawdust floor, who like to sit at high barstools and drink Munchner beer and who love rare meat cooked over charcoal will do the grand beefsteak justice. (Mario, 1955c: 21)

The ideal companion for the playboy should be a woman who shares the same attitude to life as him, who is as sensitive to pleasure and as independent.

Although the magazine relied on established glamour photographers at first, as soon as it was able it produced the playmate of the month section itself, and, in the process, the magazine distinguished this section from traditional glamour pictorials. As the magazine claimed in an article on its first two-dozen playmates:

> In the early issues, she wasn't very different from any other pin-up picture, but as the months passed she began to develop a personality distinctly her own; she became more sophisticated; she left a little more to the reader's imagination; and though some kidded her about her new found bashfulness, they loved her more than ever. (Anon., 1956f: 53, 55)

Instead of the 'unreal, highly stylized projections of male fantasies' that had constituted the 'rich tradition of pin-up art in American', Hefner has claimed that the playmate pictorials were 'an attempt to *humanize* the pin-up concept'. Instead of 'using movie stars and glamour girls', the magazine 'changed all that': it 'choose girls from everyday life – secretaries, college students, airline stewardesses – instead ... and we pose them naturally, in real life settings' (Hefner quoted in Anon., 1974: 68).

One of the major innovations of the playmate pictorial was precisely that, however 'improbable' (Miller, 1981: 67), the pictorial was accompanied by a profile of the playmate. She was given a narrative, a context and a personality:

> Accompanying the pictures is a story about the girl that adds to her reality as a person. The entire girl-next-door concept that we created for our centerfold was intended to make the Playmates more a part of real life for our readers. (Hefner quoted in Anon., 1974: 68)

The playmate had a life of her own beyond the pages of the magazine, and just as sex was part of a more general lifestyle for the playboy, so it was for the playmate. For example, the December 1955 pictorial on Janet Pilgrim is complemented with an article that accompanies her on a holiday evening out. Similarly, the November 1955 pictorial on Barbara Cameron presents her as an ordinary girl that the staff had run into in a record shop and with whom they had discovered a mutual interest in music. It is also stressed that she had never posed professionally before, although she had caused a rumpus on campus and become the focus of an article in *Life* when she posed for a college magazine. Finally, it is stressed that while she had initially been coy about posing for *Playboy*, she had been persuaded that the magazine preferred non-professionals.

However, if the magazine did not want professional models, the ideal playmate was often portrayed as an independent and professional woman. Certainly, many of the playmates were supposed to work in supportive or creative professions, but the fact that they were seen as working women at all is highly significant. Some fitted the predictable role of the aspiring actress such 'Playboy's TV Playmate', who is described as 'a little girl with big ambitions' (Anon., 1956c: 35), while others were professional office workers like Miss November 1956, who worked as a office manager in Los Angeles, although it is significant that she is clearly distinguished from the role of secretary through her designation as a 'buxom boss' (Anon., 1956a: 42). Similarly, Janet Pilgrim, one of the magazine's most popular playmates of the 1950s, 'supervises subscription fulfilment for Playboy' and 'runs her department efficiently, which may surprise some who expect beauties to try getting by on beauty alone'. She not only has 'five girls [working] under her' but has even refused 'a number of modelling and similar job offers' because she 'loves her work and being subscriptions manager of Playboy is more important than being a celebrity'. Instead of the aspiring actress or model, she is a 'very level headed girl' who 'lives in a smartly decorated, modern apartment', which she 'shares ... with an airhostess'. She dates on weekends, but likes to spend other evenings 'at home, listening to music, reading'. She is professional, independent and cultured (Anon., 1955: 29).

However, not all the playmates had professions like these. One was a designer (Anon., 1960), and another a writer, whose fiction is even published in the magazine. Given the magazine's concern to develop its reputation for quality fiction, the implication is clearly that she is a serious writer, and the article on her presents her as a woman with an agenda: '*The Deal* expresses some potent opinions on sex and we asked her if she considered it an anti-sex story. "Not at all," she insisted. "It's anti-commercialized sex, but its pro-sex"' (Anon., 1956b: 35). In this way, both the form and the content of the pictorials sought to present them as natural and healthy, and to distinguish them from the commercialization of sex that many commentators were criticizing in the period.

Certainly, these profiles were largely ways of eroticizing the playmate by constructing elaborate fantasies around her. Miss April 1956, for example, is the familiar buxom country girl: 'Our tastes rarely run to the rural, being city-bred and all, but when a corn-fed critter as cut as Rusty Fisher comes down the pike, we feel obliged to make an exception' (Anon., 1956d: 35). Similarly, Miss August 1957 is a wealthy sophisticate:

> Much has been said and written about the 'girl next door' quality of Playboy's playmates, even in literate journals like The Nation and Saturday Review, and we've done a goodly bit of the saying ourselves.[...] Lately though, we've been wondering if the lot of us haven't been guilty of sloppy thinking in this area. For *every* girl (unless she's a hermit, and we don't know many of those) lives next door to someone; and, in this sense, every girl is a girl-next-door. Take Dolores Donlon, our August playmate, for instance. This lithe, long limbed, languorous, luscious blonde drives a snow white T Bird and a baby blue Cad and lives in a two storey Spanish-style house with a swimming pool and 20 rooms (eight of them bedrooms). [...] But does this make her any less of a girl-next-door. Not if you happen to live next door to her in Beverley Hills, California, it doesn't – and we know a couple of lucky lads who do. (Anon., 1957a: 34)

However, professional women were not simply celebrated as part of the titillation, and it was not just the girls who appeared in the pictorials who were the subject of articles about their professional lives. The magazine also ran an article on one of its photographers, Bunny Yeager, in which it celebrated her status as a professional photographer and even claimed that it gave her an edge over her male colleagues. (Yeager has gone on to become a cult figure in the world of glamour photography.)

Conclusion

Playboy was therefore very self-consciously a lifestyle magazine that did not address an audience of mass consumers, but consumers who yearned for distinction. The *Playboy* consumer sought to make 'lifestyle a life projection and display their individuality and sense of style in the particularity of the assemblage of goods, clothes, practices, experiences, appearance and bodily dispositions' that they mobilized, and he was fully 'conscious that he speaks not only with his clothes, but with his home, furnishings, decoration, car and other activities' (Featherstone, 1991: 83).

As a result, *Playboy* disturbs the narrative of many histories of consumer culture. Nor is the magazine's own attempt to present itself as the heroic forerunning of future developments any solution. On the contrary, *Playboy* drew upon a central plank of US cold war rhetoric that sought to distinguish consumer capitalism from Soviet communism, and to privilege the former over the latter. Certainly, *Playboy* transformed this rhetoric and turned it against aspects of American society and culture, which it presented as conformist and totalitarian, but it is nonetheless the case that rather than promoting mass consumption and mass conformity, American political discourse of the 1950s overtly championed consumer choice and individualized lifestyles as the inverse of totalitarian conformity.

However, while *Playboy* is not justified in its claim to have been the vanguard that led America from the mass conformity of the 1950s into the brave new world of the 1960s, its specific use of the discourse of lifestyle was significant. Indeed, *Playboy* made two key interventions. First, it directly distinguished the *Playboy* consumer from the figure of the mass consumer, through its explicit masculinization of his consumption practices. In most criticisms of consumerism, even most feminist criticisms, the problem with the mass consumer is directly associated with femininity, through its supposed irrationality, conformity and passivity. The *Playboy* consumer, in contrast, was clearly distanced from this figure and was presented as a heroic figure who displays his masculine expertise and proficiency through consumption. Certainly this privileged the masculine over the feminine in highly problematic ways but, as we have seen, similar positions can also be found within the feminist work of the period and, as Ehrenreich demonstrates, *Playboy* was not anti-women but anti-wives, a position that prefigured many of the central tenets of Friedan's feminist classic, *The Feminine Mystique*.

Ironically, it is the second intervention which has not only been the focus of most attacks but has also proved most productive. By claiming autonomy for sexual tastes, the magazine profoundly politicized sex and sexuality, and sexual pleasure came to represent a realm of freedom that opposed totalitarian politics. However, equally ironically, while this position established the groundwork for more radical forms of sexual politics over the following decades, it is the magazine's sexual politics that has been the most common focus of attack and has left it most vulnerable to these attacks. The magazine not only came to represent sexual conservatism to the sexual radicals that followed it, but its very formulation of sexuality as that which resisted power precisely through its refusal of politics meant that it frequently interpreted later radical critiques of sexuality as 'anti-sex', and hence as indistinguishable from the repressive and the totalitarian.

Notes

1   The periodization of this break remains profoundly unclear. For many it is clearly associated with the 1980s while many simultaneously associate it with the 1960s radicalism of their own pasts: see, for example, Jameson (1984) and Sayres *et al.* (1984).

2   For work on the othering of femininity and/or domesticity, see Brunsdon (1997) and Hollows (2000).

References

Anon. (1953a) 'Announcement', *Playboy*, December, p. 3

Anon. (1953b) 'Sweetheart of the Month', *Playboy*, December, p. 18.

Anon. (1954a) 'Nudity and the Foreign Film', *Playboy*, October, pp. 41-44.

Anon. (1954b) Subscription page, *Playboy*, August, p. 51.

Anon. (1954c) Subscription page, *Playboy*, June, p. 51.

Anon. (1954d) Subscription page, *Playboy*, July, p. 51.

Anon. (1954e) Subscription page, *Playboy*, October, p. 51.

Anon. (1954f) Subscription page, *Playboy*, September, p. 51.

Anon. (1955) 'A Holiday Evening With Janet Pilgrim', *Playboy*, December, pp. 29-36.

Anon. (1956a) 'Buxom Boss', *Playboy*, November, pp. 42-8.

Anon. (1956b) 'Miss July is a Writer', *Playboy*, July, pp. 35-39.

Anon. (1956c) 'Playboy's TV Playmate', *Playboy*, March, pp. 35-39.

Anon. (1956d) 'Rusty is a Rustic Girl', *Playboy*, April, pp. 35-39.

Anon. (1956e) Subscription Page, *Playboy* April, back cover.

Anon. (1956f) 'The First 2 Dozen Playmates', *Playboy*, January, pp. 51-59.

Anon. (1957a) 'The Girl Next Door', *Playboy*, August, pp. 33-39.

Anon. (1957b) 'The Waistland', *Playboy*, January, p. 65.

Anon. (1958) 'The Beat Mystique', *Playboy*, February, p. 20.

Anon. (1959) 'Beat Playmate', *Playboy*, July, pp. 47-51

Anon. (1960) 'Designing Playmate', *Playboy*, August, pp. 55-59.

Anon. (1974) 'Playboy Interview: Hugh M. Hefner', *Playboy*, January, pp. 63-84, 288-290.

Bell, D. (1988) *The End of Ideology: On the Exhaustion of Political Ideas in the Fifties*, Cambridge, MA: Harvard University Press.

Bocock, R. (1993) *Consumption*, London: Routledge.

Bourdieu, P. (1984) *Distinction: A Social Critique of the Judgement of Taste*, trans. R. Nice, London: Routledge.

Brady, F. (1974) *Hefner: The Unauthorized Biography*, New York: Macmillan.

Brunsdon, C. (1997) *Screen Tastes: Soap Operas to Satellite Dishes*, London: Routledge.

Clad, N. (1958) 'A Frigid Frolic in Frisco', *Playboy*, February, pp. 21-22, 74-5.

Cox, H. (1961) '*Playboy*'s Doctrine of Male', *Christianity in Crisis: A Christian Journal of Opinion*, May, pp. 56-60.

Dedman, J. (1954) 'That Brooks Brothers Look', *Playboy*, February, pp. 16-17.

Ehrenreich, B. (1983) *The Hearts of Men: American Dreams and the Flight from Commitment*, London: Pluto.

Featherstone, M. (1991) *Consumer Culture and Postmodernism*, London: Sage.

Friedan, B. (1963), *The Feminine Mystique*, New York: Dell.

Gold, H. (1958) 'What it is – Whence it Came', *Playboy*, February, pp. 20, 84-87.

Hefner, H.M. (1962) 'The *Playboy* Philosophy', *Playboy*, December, pp. 73-74, 166-170, 196.

Hollows, J. (2000) *Feminism, Femininity and Popular Culture*, Manchester: Manchester University Press.

Hollows, J. (2002) 'The Bachelor Dinner: Masculinity, Cooking and Class in *Playboy*, 1953-61', *Continuum*, vol. 16(2), pp. 143-55

Jameson, F. (1984) 'Postmodernism: or the Cultural Logic of Late Capitalism', *New Left Review*, vol. 146, pp. 59-92.

Jancovich, M. (1993) *The Cultural Politics of the New Criticism*, Cambridge: Cambridge University Press.

Jancovich, M. (2001a) 'Naked Ambition: Pornography, Taste and the Problem of the Middlebrow', *Scope: An Online Journal of Film Studies*, June: http://www.nottingham.ac.uk/film/journal

Jancovich, M. (2001b) 'Placing Sex: Sexuality, Taste and Middlebrow Culture in the Reception of *Playboy* Magazine', *Intensities: A Journal of Cult Media*, Autumn/Winter: http://www.cult-media.com

Kessie, J. (1955a) 'Summa Cum Style', *Playboy*, October, pp. 18-19, 52.

Kessie, J. (1955b) 'The Well Dressed Playboy', *Playboy*, January, pp. 38-9.

Kimmel, M. (1997) *Manhood in America: A Cultural History*, New York: Free Press.

Mario, T. (1954) 'Is She Your Kind of Dish?', *Playboy*, October, pp. 39-40, 50.

Mario, T. (1955a) 'Consider the Crab', *Playboy*, April, pp. 27-9.

Mario, T. (1955b) 'The Cocktail Hour', *Playboy*, October: 22-24, 58.

Mario, T. (1955c) 'The Naked Hamburger', *Playboy*, February, pp. 27-9.

Mario, T. (1956a) 'The Curry with the Singe on Top', *Playboy*, March, pp. 49, 54.

Mario, T. (1956b) 'The Holiday Dinner', *Playboy*, November, pp. 38-40, 87.

Marling, K.A. (1994) *As Seen on TV: The Visual Culture of Everyday Life in the 1950s*, Cambridge, MA: Harvard University Press.

May, E. Tyler (1988) *Homeward Bound: American Families in the Cold War Era*, New York: Basic.

Miller, R. (1981) *Bunny: The Real Story of Playboy*, London: Corgi.

Norman, B. (1953) 'Miss Gold-Digger of 1953', *Playboy*, December, pp. 6-8.

Palmer, P. (1954) 'One Wonderful Chair', *Playboy*, December, pp. 12-14.

Riesman, D. (1961) *The Lonely Crowd: A Study of the Changing American Character*, New Haven, CT: Yale University Press.

Ross, A. (1989) *No Respect: Intellectuals and Popular Culture*, London: Routledge.

Rutherford, B. (1957) 'The Marks of the Well-Dressed Man', *Playboy*, February, p. 47.

Rutherford, J.E. (1954) Letter, *Playboy*, May, p. 3.

Sayres, S., Stephanson, A., Aronowitz, S., and Jameson, F. (eds) (1984) *The 60s, Without Apology*, Minneapolis, MN: University of Minnesota Press.

Slater, D. (1997) *Consumer Culture and Modernity*, Oxford: Polity.

Wilinsky, B. (2000) *Sure Seaters*, Minneapolis, MN: University of Minnesota Press.

Williams, L. (1990) *Hard Core: Power, Pleasure and the 'Frenzy of the Visible'*, London: Pandora

Wylie, P. (1956) 'The Abdicating Male and How the Gray Flannel Mind Exploits Him through his Women', *Playboy*, November, pp. 23-24, 50, 79.

Chapter 6

Rapture of the Deep: Leisure, Lifestyle and the Lure of Sixties Scuba

Bill Osgerby

The water may be the turquoise Mediterranean, an ice-skimmed quarry in
Vermont, the translucent waters off Bermuda, the Pacific rolling in
majestic rhythm toward the shores of San Diego. Around the world and
across the nation, swimmers are sinking beneath the surface to fly like
angels through an alien realm. This fascinating new playground, alive with
beauty and tinged with danger, belongs to the skindiver. (*Time*, 1960: 66)

'An Invasion of Eerie Sea Dwellers'

'Like an invasion of eerie sea dwellers', *Life* magazine wistfully related in 1959,
'divers in rubber suits and breathing devices emerge from the ocean' (Anon., 1959:
104). *Life*'s full-colour, double-page photo-feature on the North Shore Frogmen's
Association was part of the magazine's 'Special Double Issue on the Good Life' –
a bumper, extra-length edition released to celebrate 'our new-found good life,
growing out of our new-found leisure'. In an effusive survey of the 'Big and Busy
US Playground', *Life* described 'a vast *new* economic force, the Leisure Business,
which could not exist if everyone worked at "useful things" and which, by the
buying power it releases and by the dreams it satisfies, has filled the whole
economy with energy and ambition' (Coughlan, 1959: 69). The postwar leisure
boom, *Life* estimated, represented a spending power of around $40 billion a year –
or more than 8 per cent of America's GNP (p. 70) – and the magazine profiled an
explosion of fun pastimes sweeping through the country, from golf and skiing to
mountaineering and dinghy sailing. Diving also caught the magazine's eye. 'This
year', *Life* enthused, 'a million skin and scuba divers will plunge into US waters,
there – weightless in an alien element – to drift, glide and pry into the mysteries of
the sea' (Anon., 1959: 105).

    Indeed, once the preserve of military specialists and seafaring roughnecks,
diving underwent phenomenal growth as an American recreation during the late
1950s and the 1960s. A multi-million dollar leisure industry developed as diving
equipment manufacturers, training organizations and holiday firms all cashed in on
a wave of enthusiasm for undersea excitement. Across a range of popular texts,
moreover, diving was celebrated as a totem of hedonism, exhilaration and

exoticism. Numerous Hollywood movies and TV shows featured scuba diving as a spectacle of alluring adventure, while glossy magazines and advertising campaigns regularly deployed scuba images and allusions as they courted consumers eager to see themselves as members of a hip and vibrant jet set.

This chapter argues that the cultural purchase of scuba diving during the late 1950s and the 1960s was a facet of shifts within the composition and values of the American middle class. The growth of recreational diving and its representation in the popular media was constituent in the emergence of a new petit bourgeois faction that defined its social status and sense of cultural identity through distinctive, consumption-driven lifestyles; their values and codes of behaviour laying an accent on stylistic self-expression, freewheeling hedonism and self-conscious display. Dripping with exhilarating and glamorously sexy connotations, the 1960s scuba phenomenon was an ideal expression of the habitus and ideals of this new middle class, who embraced scuba diving as one of their pre-eminent lifestyle sports.

The Taste of Pleasure: 'Lifestyle Sports' and the 'Ethic of Fun'

The terms 'lifestyle sport', 'extreme sport' and 'alternative sport' entered both popular and academic discourse during the late 1990s. In North America the 'extreme' moniker was adopted by the popular media as an all-embracing label for new, avant-garde, individualistic and youthful sports – for example, snowboarding, windsurfing, skateboarding, kite-surfing, sky-diving and B.A.S.E jumping (using a parachute to jump from fixed objects) – recreations whose qualities of dynamic exhilaration were perceived to transcend the more mundane experiences of 'conventional' sport. The notion of 'alternative' sport was preferred by scholars such as Robert Rinehart and Synthia Sydnor (Rinehart, 1998, 2000; Rinehart and Sydnor, 2003), who used the term to denote a range of recreations stretching from indigenous folk games to ultra-marathons, beach volleyball, jet-skiing and scuba diving. What this diverse range of activities shared in common, Rinehart and Sydnor argued, was their departure from the ways sport had been traditionally understood and practiced. Alongside Rinehart and Sydnor, authors such as Bale (1994), Maguire (1999) and Midol and Broyer (1995) all cast 'alternative' sports as diverging from traditional, rule-bound and competitive sports cultures through their effacement of regulations and institutional controls in favour of an emphasis on participation, experience and the intrinsic enjoyment of taking part.

As Belinda Wheaton (2004: 3) has pointed out, however, to understand the cultural significance of 'alternative' sport necessitates moving beyond 'simplistic and constraining dichotomies such as traditional versus new, mainstream versus emergent, or other related binaries such as sport versus art'. For Wheaton, the term 'lifestyle sport' better encapsulates the way recreations such as windsurfing and snowboarding are sites 'of identity politics, a politics that is expressed around competing and passionate claims about the right to belong, and to be recognized' (p. 9). Emphasizing the 'locally situated identity politics' of lifestyle sports, she argues they are a source of a particular kind of social identity for their participants, offering a sense of autonomy, distinctiveness and 'alternative' nonconformity (p. 5).

According to Wheaton (pp. 11-12), 'lifestyle sports' tend to embrace (even fetishize) notions of risk and danger, yet are usually non-aggressive activities that involve little bodily contact. They are invariably based around the consumption of new commodities or technologies, and often involve the appropriation of outdoor 'liminal' zones without fixed or created boundaries. 'Lifestyle sports' are also, Wheaton argues, predominantly (though not exclusively) individualistic and, rather than being oriented around spectatorship, emphasize 'grassroots' participation and are characterized by 'a participatory ideology that promotes fun, hedonism, involvement, self actualization, "flow", ... living for the moment, "adrenalin rushes" and other intrinsic rewards' (*ibid.*).

Moreover, with their surfeit of symbols and distinctive signifiers (brand names, logos, eye-catching designs), 'lifestyle sports', Wheaton argues, exemplify the character of postmodern consumer culture (p. 6). According to theorists such as Mike Featherstone, late-modern or postmodern societies have seen the development of a close affinity between consumption and identity, so that people increasingly 'display their individuality and sense of style in the particularity of the assemblage of goods, clothes, practices, experiences, appearance and bodily dispositions they design together into a lifestyle' (Featherstone, 1991: 86). Wheaton's notion of 'lifestyle sports' epitomizes exactly this kind of relationship between identity and commodity consumption:

> In the emergence and evolution of lifestyle sport activities what is being sold to the consumer is not merely a sport or leisure activity but a complete style of life, one which is saturated with signs and images that emphasize many of ... [the] aspirations of postmodern consumer culture. (2004: 6)

The increased significance of consumption in the construction of (post)modern self-identity has been seen by some theorists as displacing social class as a key point of identification. Zygmunt Bauman (1992), for example, has suggested that in the social relations of production, class relationships have been increasingly overshadowed by lifestyle affiliations, while Michael Maffesoli (1996: 76) has developed the concept of the 'neo-tribe' to denote the way individuals express collective identity through distinctive rituals and consumption practices, people wandering through multiple group attachments, so that collective identity is 'less a question of belonging to a gang, a family or a community, than of switching from one group to another'.

Wheaton, too, sees the proliferation of consumer culture as begetting a kaleidoscope of different options for self-expression and identity formation, characteristics 'reflected in lifestyle sport's cultures, identities and styles of life' (2004: 6). Yet Wheaton also insists that lifestyle choices have not become an autonomous set of 'free-floating' options, but remain socially and culturally constructed acts that are 'structured by and contingent on factors such as age, class, gender and ethnicity' (*ibid.*). Here, Wheaton concurs with Scott Lash's view of postmodern culture as not simply being the product of market dynamics and autonomous consumer preferences, but also as representing a distinctive set of social and cultural expressions associated with the 'post-industrial middle-classes'

(Lash, 1990: 252). Indeed, 'lifestyle sports', Wheaton argues, have a close affinity with this new socio-cultural formation and, as such, are characteristically 'dominated by the privileged white male middle classes' (2004: 6).

Wheaton's research on 'lifestyle sports' largely focuses on their contemporary manifestation, social relationships and associated practices of identity formation (Wheaton, 2000, 2003a, 2003b, 2004). Nevertheless, in discussing their historical antecedents, Wheaton insightfully suggests that modern 'lifestyle sports' developed as a facet to social and cultural transformations of the kind Pierre Bourdieu has identified as taking place in the fabric of French bourgeois culture after the Second World War. In *Distinction* (1984), his classic survey of the shifting texture of bourgeois life in France, Bourdieu argued that the post-war period had seen the rise of a new form of capitalist economy in which power and profits were increasingly dependent not simply on the production of goods, but also on the continual regeneration of consumer desires (Bourdieu, 1984: 310). According to Bourdieu, by the late 1960s these processes of economic and cultural transformation had laid the basis for the rise of a specific section of the French middle class – a group he termed the 'new petite bourgeoisie' (p. 311). Lacking the economic, cultural or social capital that distinguished the traditional petite bourgeoisie, this new class fraction established its distinctive status by colonizing new occupations based on the production and dissemination of symbolic goods and services, Bourdieu coining the term 'cultural intermediaries' to denote the new petit bourgeois cohort that rose to dominate fields such as the media, advertising, journalism and fashion.

In its quest to secure its class position and status, Bourdieu argued, the new petite bourgeoisie broke away from the 'morality of duty' associated with the traditional middle class. Puritanical and production-oriented, this ethos had induced 'a fear of pleasure and a relation to the body made up of "reserve", "modesty" and "restraint", and associate[d] every satisfaction of the forbidden impulses with guilt' (p. 367). In its place the new petite bourgeoisie elaborated their own 'ethic of fun' – a new 'morality of pleasure as a duty', in which it became 'a failure, a threat to self-esteem, not to "have fun"' (*ibid.*).

Conceiving of themselves as connoisseurs in 'the art of living', Bourdieu argued, the new petite bourgeoisie laboured to promote the legitimacy and prestige of their 'new model lifestyles' centred on freedom, pleasure and the fulfilment of consumer desires. This new middle class habitus expressed itself through a gamut of behaviour, attitudes and tastes, embracing everything from food and fashion to music and interior design. Sport, too, was an arena in which the new petite bourgeoisie expressed their characteristic 'art of living'. Indeed, for Bourdieu, the divide between the old and new middle class could be 'retranslated into the opposition between traditional sports and ... all the new sports', the latter encompassing adventuresome pursuits such as 'foot-trekking, pony trekking, cycle-trekking, motorbike trekking, boat-trekking, canoeing, archery, windsurfing, cross-country skiing, sailing, hang-gliding, microlights etc.' (1984: 220). Blending conspicuous consumption and thrilling nonconformity, these sports demanded 'a high investment of cultural capital in the activity itself, in preparing, maintaining and using the equipment, and especially, perhaps in verbalizing the experiences', but they also 'typically cultivated cults of the natural, the pure and the authentic' (*ibid.*). This, then, was a combination of wild individuality and hedonistic consumerism that became a trademark of modern 'lifestyle sports'.

Bourdieu's analysis was focused fairly exclusively on cultural shifts in post-war France. But comparable developments also took place elsewhere. Indeed, it is significant that Bourdieu termed the new recreations of the French middle class 'Californian sports', suggesting they had often been 'imported from America by members of the new bourgeoisie and petite bourgeoisie' (*ibid.*). For, like France, the United States underwent a set of dramatic economic, social and political changes during the 1950s and 1960s, developments that laid the way for the emergence of a new middle class fraction similar, in many respects, to Bourdieu's new petite bourgeoisie.[1]

After the Second World War, the US developed into the world's largest consumer-oriented economy. National output of goods and services doubled between 1946 and 1956, and doubled again by 1970, with expenditure on private consumption accounting for two-thirds of the gross national product throughout the period (Cohen, 2003). The middle class were particular beneficiaries. Between 1947 and 1957 the number of salaried workers increased by 61 per cent as white-collar career opportunities multiplied among the expanding business corporations. The number of solidly middle-class families (with an annual income of between $4,000 and $7,500) grew from 12.5 million to 18 million between 1947 and 1953, while the percentage of those earning between $7,000 and $10,000 per year rose from 5 per cent to 20 per cent between 1947 and 1959 (US Bureau of Census, 1975).

Crucially, however, the American middle class not only expanded, but also changed in composition and cultural outlook. The American economy's growing dependence on the servicing of consumer demand brought a major expansion in the number of salaried managerial and technical workers and 'culture producers' of all kinds: administrators, academics, journalists, advertisers and other professions whose economic role centred around the production and dissemination of symbolic goods and services. This professional-managerial group embraced a diverse range of occupations but, Barbara and John Ehrenreich argue, were bound together by common experiences, interests and worldviews, coming to represent a distinct and recognizable middle-class formation that constituted around 20 per cent of the American population (Ehrenreich, 1990: 12; Ehrenreich and Ehrenreich, 1979: 14).

Like Bourdieu's 'new petite bourgeoisie' of 1960s France, the ascending middle class of postwar America established its status as a social formation through the consumption of distinctive cultural goods and signifiers. Its cultural priorities were exemplified by the new popularity of the concept of 'lifestyle'. By the 1950s the term was already being deployed by market researchers to denote the spending patterns of particular consumer groups. But it was the developing tastes of the new middle class with which the notion of 'lifestyle' became most closely associated. Among advertisers and marketeers, especially, the concept of 'lifestyle' was used to denote the mores of 'a new middle class of college-bred administrators, professionals and managers' who were oriented to a culture of 'play, fun and excitement' and who took 'endless delight in pursuing a lighthearted existence of interpersonal repartee and pleasure' (Bensman and Vidich, 1971/1995: 249-52).[2]

Just like Bourdieu's new petit bourgeois fraction, then, the emergent American middle class defined their social status and cultural identity through distinctive, consumption-driven lifestyles, their values and codes of behaviour laying an accent on stylistic self-expression, self-conscious display and (to use Bourdieu's terminology) an 'ethic of fun'. Expressive and liberated, this hedonistic 'art of living' embraced a new world of racy consumption, narcissism and leisure. The exciting 'Californian sports' mentioned by Bourdieu were a notable ingredient. Motorcycling, surfing and (later) windsurfing and hang-gliding were all on the menu. So, too, was scuba diving – and, as diving pioneer Hans Hass reflected in 1975, the sport positively boomed during America's new leisure age:

> What was at first merely the eccentric behaviour of a few daredevils became a trend which gathered momentum until it exceeded all bounds. … New industries were called into being to manufacture masks, snorkels, flippers, diving apparatus, harpoons, and underwater cameras. Today it is a business worth millions. The annual world turnover for amateur diving equipment already amounts to 500 million dollars and there is hardly a coastline where amateur divers do not go under water. (Hass, 1975: 10)

Fathoming the Scuba Phenomenon

As Wheaton (2004) argues, then, the rise of 'lifestyle sports' such as diving can only be fully understood when they are considered within their broader socio-historical context. Nevertheless, while patterns of economic, cultural and political change are decisive influences, the role of technological development must also be acknowledged. Of course, technology does not condition changes in culture and social behaviour. As Raymond Williams (1974) argued in his general critique of technological determinism, new technologies do not emerge from self-generating research and development, but are the practical outcome of pre-existing relations of production, distribution, ownership and control. Yet, while historical and social context were crucial to the growth of recreational diving, technological development also played a key role in facilitating the scuba phenomenon.

Since the Victorian age, diving had been a gruelling, cumbersome and dangerous business. Relying on air pumped through a hose from the surface, divers were encumbered by air lines, hefty lead boots and a brass helmet, and they were sealed from the elements in a heavy, watertight suit of sheet rubber and twill. In the late nineteenth century greater diving freedom was offered with the development of self-contained 're-breathing' apparatus that used caustic soda to 'recycle' pure oxygen. This equipment was much favoured for military sabotage (because its 'closed-circuit' system produced no telltale bubbles of exhaled air), but its uses were limited due to the toxicity of pure oxygen when breathed at depths below 10 metres. It was, then, not until the 1940s that divers were given true freedom and flexibility through the development of a safe, reliable system of Self-Contained Underwater Breathing Apparatus – or 'scuba' (an acronym first coined in 1954).

New equipment had already improved the capabilities of breath-hold divers (usually known as 'skin divers' or 'free divers') during the early 1930s. Guy Gilpatrick, an American journalist living on the French Riviera, had developed an early form of the diving mask by waterproofing a pair of pilot's goggles (lining the edges of the lenses with glazer's putty), which he used for swimming underwater and spearing fish. Writing up his exploits in a series of articles for *Saturday Evening Post*, Gilpatrick won a firm following in the US and went on to publish *The Compleat Goggler* (1938), probably the first book to extol the pleasures of amateur diving.[3] Commercial versions of Gilpatrick's goggles were soon available, together with Louis de Corlieu's new broad-bladed swimming fins (patented in 1935 and sometimes known as 'flippers'), worn on the feet to improve the speed and manoeuvrability of intrepid 'goggle' divers. But the key technological breakthrough that laid the way for the growth of recreational diving came during the early 1940s, with the development of effective scuba equipment by a French duo – Jacques-Yves Cousteau and Emile Gagnan.[4]

During the Second World War, Cousteau was a French naval officer and an experienced diver. Gagnan, meanwhile, was an industrial gas control systems engineer with L'Air Liquide (a company whose Board of Directors included Cousteau's father-in-law) and had expertise in the mechanics of gas valves. Working together, the duo perfected a revolutionary diving device, a demand regulator valve that could control the flow of compressed air from a cylinder worn on the diver's back. During the summer of 1943 Cousteau and two close friends (Philippe Tailliez and Frédérik Dumas) tested prototypes of the new scuba system in the Mediterranean. Christened the Aqua Lung, the equipment proved to be safe, reliable and remarkably simple to use. Patented in 1946, the new Aqua Lung was put to the ultimate test in October 1947 when Frédérik Dumas made a record 94-metre dive off the coast of Marseilles.[5]

The physiology of diving was also better understood. During the early twentieth century research by John Scott Haldane, a Scottish physician, had revealed that decompression sickness (the notoriously painful, often fatal, 'bends') was caused by nitrogen bubbles forming in the blood of divers as they ascended from long dives. Haldane's discoveries had allowed the development of the first dive tables, introduced by the US Navy in 1912, making longer and deeper dives possible through the introduction of gradually staged ascents to the surface. Haldane's original calculations were steadily refined, and in 1956 diving became much less treacherous with the US Navy's publication of improved dive tables. The secrets of nitrogen narcosis – the mysterious 'rapture of the deep'– were also unlocked. While at depth divers often felt sensations akin to intoxication, Cousteau describing 'the glow of depth rapture' as resembling 'the giggle-party jags of the nineteen-twenties when flappers and sheiks convened to sniff nitrogen protoxide' (Cousteau, 1953: 23). While some relished the buzz, 'rapture of the deep' often proved deadly by impairing a diver's judgment and skills, and ultimately causing unconsciousness. But during the 1940s experiments by Jack Haldane (John's son) revealed that the narcosis resulted from breathing nitrogen (the major component of air) under pressure, the discovery allowing for the development of diving practices that reduced the risk of lethal 'rapture'.

Technological and scientific advances, then, certainly made recreational diving a possibility. But it was the wider nexus of social and economic change during the 1950s and 1960s that turned scuba diving into a cultural phenomenon. Indeed, while the Aqua Lung developed by Cousteau and Gagnan was undoubtedly a superb innovation, the pair had initially struggled to market their new equipment. During the late 1940s the Aqua Lung was manufactured by La Spirotechnique (a subsidiary of L'Air Liquide) but, while the military were keen, civilian interest was limited. The Aqua Lung was marketed commercially in France and Britain, but in Europe the austerity of the postwar years choked the growth of a consumer market and sales were slow. Instead, La Spirotechnique (like many European manufacturers of consumer goods) increasingly turned their attention to export markets – especially the US, where the postwar consumer boom promised fruitful returns.

In America, small but hardy clubs of free divers (such as San Diego's Bottom Scratchers) had existed since the early 1930s and, after World War Two, enthusiastic amateurs tinkered with underwater breathing apparatus built from assorted garden hoses, metal buckets, tyre pumps, fire extinguishers and surplus high altitude oxygen gear.[6] Interest in the French Aqua Lung, however, began slowly. In 1947 six models were imported by René Bussoz, the owner of an up-market sports store in Westwood, a stylish quarter of Los Angeles. At first Bussoz regarded the Aqua Lung as a novelty gadget and (legend has it) after selling his first six examples declined further shipments from the French manufacturer on the grounds that 'the US market was saturated' (Parry and Tillman, 2001: 70). But Bussoz's mind was soon changed by a torrent of interest from customers (including two swimming champions turned Hollywood stars – Buster Crabbe and Johnny Weissmuller). As a consequence, Bussoz went on to import over 1,000 Aqua Lungs during the late 1940s and early 1950s, setting up a new company – U.S. Divers – with exclusive rights to manufacture and sell the equipment in America. Big orders from the US Navy were a boon to the fledgling company, but even more significant was the surge of popular enthusiasm for scuba diving.

Amid America's postwar 'leisure boom', recreational diving became a thriving consumer industry. By 1953 some $250,000 worth of Aqua Lungs had been sold in the US and the country boasted as many as a million amateur divers (Parry and Tillman, 2001). During the 1950s retail diving stores opened across the nation. California was at the forefront, with Hermosa Beach's 'Dive 'n' Surf' emporium opened in 1953, followed by the 'Water Gill' store in Venice; 'Mel's Aqua Shop' in Torrance; and the 'San Diego Divers Supply' further down the coast. In the East, Florida also became a diving Mecca, and Paul Arnold's 'Aqua-Lung, Inc.' opened for business, followed by Jordan Klein's 'Underwater Sports' and Lou Maxwell's 'Florida Frogman' store. The late 1950s saw further growth as the diving bug spread to the mid-West. Jack Blocker opened 'Jack the Frogman' in Minneapolis, while Ralph West opened 'Sport Diver' in Milwaukee. Even the arid Southwest discovered diving when Boris Innocenti opened his 'Aqua Sports' store in Phoenix (Dorfman, 2004).

U.S. Divers also began facing stiff competition from a new wave of dive equipment manufacturers. During the early 1950s Gustav dalla Valle (the émigré son of an aristocratic Italian family) began importing diving gear made in Italy by

Eduardo Cressi, while 1955 saw Sam Davison launch his own equipment manufacturing company, Dacor. In 1958 Sherwood Manufacturing also began producing scuba gear, and in 1963 dalla Valle joined forces with Dick Bonin (a former Navy diver and scuba retailer) to form what became one of the world's biggest diving equipment companies, Scubapro.

A proliferation of new products helped ensure the scuba phenomenon remained big business. In 1956 scientists at the University of California developed neoprene, and the rubber-like fabric was quickly used in new 'wetsuits' (as they became known), diving wear more user-friendly than the traditional, watertight diving suit.[7] First marketed by the Beaver company of La Jolla, California, wetsuit manufacture soon became a million-dollar money-spinner. In 1961, meanwhile, Maurice Fenzy patented an inflatable buoyancy compensator (similar in look to a life jacket and originally developed by the French Navy) that quickly became a standard piece of diving kit, and the shelves of diving stores steadily bulged with new lines of underwater scooters, torches, depth gauges, cameras and spearguns. The rapid growth of scuba diving in America prompted equipment manufacturers to form the Organization of Underwater Manufacturers in 1958, with a view to managing industry practice and procedure. The idea, however, developed little momentum until it was revived in 1963 when the Diving Equipment Manufacturers Association (DEMA) was formed 'to promote, foster and advance the common business interests of the members as manufacturers of diving equipment', DEMA subsequently emerging as a potent force in the burgeoning business of recreational diving.

Training systems for amateur divers also became a major industry. Profit had not been a key motive in the earliest diver training programmes. The first forms of recreational scuba tuition were non-profit courses launched by the Los Angeles County Department of Parks in 1955 and the YMCA in 1959. And in 1960 the National Association of Underwater Instructors (NAUI), another non-profit body, was founded to develop nationally recognized training programmes for diving instructors. For several years NAUI dominated American diving, but by the mid-1960s its training courses seemed slow and demanding, while NAUI's non-profit philosophy frustrated its more business-minded members. John Cronin (CEO of U.S. Divers) and Ralph Ericson (a seasoned diving instructor) were especially keen to develop sport diving's commercial possibilities, and in 1966 they splintered from NAUI to form a new training agency – the Professional Association of Diving Instructors (PADI). PADI maintained a dedication to safety and education, but it was also thoroughly commercial in orientation, developing quick and simple training courses that could be sold easily to customers through affiliated dive stores. It proved a winning formula and, by the beginning of the 1970s, PADI's coffers were swelling as it developed into America's leading diver training agency.

PADI's phenomenal growth was testimony to the increasing significance of leisure-oriented consumption within the American economy. The success of PADI's rigorously commercial ethos was also indicative of the way US sport and recreation was becoming increasingly business-oriented as American consumerism shifted into high gear. Elsewhere, however, the business of recreation grew more falteringly. As Frank Mort (1997) argues, for example, the development of British consumerism was slower, partial and more uneven than the American experience.

And, as a consequence, the commercialization of British recreation was much slower and less intense than in America. This was certainly evident in the case of scuba diving. While the inexorable rise of PADI during the 1960s and 1970s put the US scuba scene on an avowedly commercial footing, the British diving fraternity remained wedded to a spirit of robust amateurism for decades. Founded in 1953, the British Sub Aqua Club (BSAC) was Britain's leading diving organization throughout the 1950s and 1960s, and maintained a proudly Corinthian outlook until the late 1970s when PADI's hardnosed expansion impelled moves towards a more market-oriented attitude in BSAC's organizational structure and training programmes.[8]

The growth of scuba diving in America during the 1950s and 1960s, then, was indebted to a number of factors. Technological and scientific innovations played their part, as did the development of new equipment manufacturers and retailers, together with the rise of commercially oriented training agencies that prospered amid the growth of consumer spending and the increasing commodification of recreation. But also important was the rich mythology of adventure, glamour and sexy hedonism that surrounded the scuba phenomenon.

During the 1950s and 1960s, scuba diving was something new and exciting. Exclusive and exotic, it was tailor-made to the 'ethic of fun' championed by America's emergent middle class. Scuba diving flourished because it captured the imagination of this new petite bourgeoisie through its promise of action and adventure in spectacular locations, and its reliance on the consumption of expensive and à la mode consumer goods (in 1960 a full set of diving gear would set you back several hundred dollars). As the first 'lifestyle sport', therefore, scuba diving was embraced by the upwardly-mobile and style-conscious middle class as an avenue through which they could express their individuality, autonomy and pleasure-oriented 'art of living'.

Diving to Adventure: Representing the Aquatic Allure

From the outset, the media played a key role in promoting scuba diving as a recreation for the adventurous and affluent jet set. During the early 1950s best-selling books such as Hans Hass's *Diving to Adventure* (1951) and *Manta* (1952), together with Jacques Cousteau's *Silent World* (1953) tempted readers with lush travelogues that cast diving as the passport to a wonderland of daredevil excitement. In 1951 the launch of *Skin Diver* magazine also helped popularize the new sport. Published by Californian diving enthusiasts Chuck Blakeslee and Jim Auxier, *Skin Diver* had humble beginnings. Issue one was a slim sixteen pages, and its 2,000 copies were put together in Auxier's garage, but by 1953 circulation had already shot up to 57,000 and continued to climb steadily.

In 1963 publishing mogul Robert Petersen bought out Blakeslee and Auxier, and *Skin Diver* was added to Petersen Publications' empire of hot rod, hunting and surfing titles. Under Petersen's ownership the magazine's production values soared, and *Skin Diver* was transformed into a glossy, colourful celebration of sybaritic leisure amid sun-kissed beaches and crystal oceans. Indeed, travel to far-flung, tropical shores became a stock feature of *Skin Diver* as international holidays became a major facet of the scuba diving industry. The first dedicated dive resort (Small Hope Bay in the Bahamas) opened for business in 1960, while in 1964 the first dedicated live-aboard dive boat (the Marisla) was launched by dive guide Richard Adcock in La Paz, Mexico. And by 1969 the first dedicated diving travel agency – Dewey Bergman's Sea and Sea Travel in San Francisco – was doing a roaring trade, offering package diving tours to (at the time) such off-the-beaten-track destinations as Bonaire, Grand Cayman and Cozumel.

At the cinema, too, scuba diving made a splash. Jacques Cousteau led the way. In 1950, financed by Loel Guinness (of the wealthy brewing dynasty), Cousteau purchased the Calypso – a decommissioned navy minesweeper – and had it refitted as a combined oceanographic laboratory and floating film studio. Cruising the world's marine beauty spots, Cousteau captured his undersea adventures on film, winning the Golden Palm at the Cannes Film Festival in 1956 for his documentary, *Le Monde Du Silente* (*The Silent World*). In 1957 the first international underwater film festival was held in Los Angeles, followed by events in Mexico, Miami and the Virgin Islands, the artistic aura of undersea documentaries helping cement scuba diving's urbane and esoteric connotations, displacing the sport's early association with burly seadogs. On the big screen scuba diving was also used as a vehicle for glamour and exotic adventure. In 1953, for example, Robert Wagner, Gilbert Roland and Peter Graves (and a belligerent rubber octopus) starred in *Beneath the 12-Mile Reef*, a tale of young swashbucklers diving for sponges off the Florida coast. The movie was panned by critics, but was a hit with audiences and received an Academy Award nomination for its underwater cinematography. In 1954, meanwhile, Kirk Douglas, James Mason, Paul Lukas and Peter Lorre starred in Walt Disney's popular version of *20,000 Leagues Under the Sea*, the film winning Academy Awards for its lavish art direction and breathtaking undersea special effects. Scuba diving's most glamorous appearance on the big screen, however, came in 1955 with the release of Howard Hughes' aquatic epic, *Underwater!* Premiering in a swimming pool to a group of journalists wearing diving gear, *Underwater!* starred Richard Egan and Gilbert Roland as a pair of island-hopping treasure hunters, with Jane Russell and newcomer Jayne Mansfield adding a large measure of sex appeal (see Figure 6.1).

Television also took the plunge. Again, underwater documentaries cast scuba diving as opening a door to a world of thrilling and mysterious beauty. TV's first undersea documentary series, *Kingdom of the Sea*, debuted in 1954, but it was a genre that Jacques Cousteau made his own. Running from 1966 to 1973, Cousteau's prime-time documentary series for ABC TV, *The Undersea World of Jacques Cousteau*, followed the adventures of the Calypso's crew as they voyaged across the world's oceans. The series' educational veneer established Cousteau's credentials as a crusading environmentalist, but the programmes were also a sumptuous odyssey that took audiences into an azure nirvana of spectacle and sensuality, the journey given added cosmopolitan flair by the Gallic lilt of Cousteau's narration.

Figure 6.1 'Skin Diver Action!': theatre poster for *Underwater!*, 1955

Scuba diving's associations with racy high-living also bubbled up in TV action series. Beginning with *77 Sunset Strip* (1958-64), the late 1950s and early 1960s brought to American TV a wave of new adventure series focused on the exploits of charismatic playboy-adventurers. *Sea Hunt* (1958-61) gave the formula an aquatic spin. Through *Sea Hunt's* 155 episodes, Lloyd Bridges starred as chisel-jawed Mike Nelson, a freelance underwater trouble-shooter who travelled the world in his private yacht ('The Argonaut') solving mysteries and fighting crime for salvage companies, insurance firms and even the US government. Other playboy-adventurers also followed in Mike Nelson's wake. In *Assignment Underwater* (1960-61) Bill Williams starred as Bill Greer, a scuba diving private eye, while *The Aquanauts* (later re-titled *Malibu Run*, 1960-61) chronicled the adventures of two footloose scuba divers in Hawaii.

Above all, however, it was James Bond who stood out as the playboy-adventurer who most fully embodied the values of the new, leisure-oriented jet set. As Tony Bennett and Janet Woollacott (1987: 111) have observed, Ian Fleming's secret agent cast off the dead hand of tradition in favour of a more dynamic and hedonistic approach to life:

> His attitudes towards sex, gambling and pleasure in general are distinctly liberal and his tastes and lifestyle have a decidedly international and cosmopolitan flavour. In a word, Bond is not old fashioned ... Bond belongs not to the Breed but to a new elite ... committed to new values (professionalism) and lifestyles (martini).

Agent 007, then, could be seen as a standard-bearer for Bourdieu's new petite bourgeoisie and their 'morality of pleasure as a duty'. The James Bond of Fleming's original novels, however, was still relatively conservative in his outlook and lifestyle. The Bond movies, in contrast, were more geared to an American market (the first 007 movie, *Dr No*, opened in the US in 1963) and, as a consequence, the cinematic Bond was configured more fully as an agent of swinging consumerism – denoted by the character's voracious appetite for nightclubs, sports cars and martinis. And, unsurprisingly, scuba diving also regularly figured in 007's hectic hedonism. Most obviously, *Thunderball* (the fourth Bond movie, released in 1965) won an Academy Award for its spectacular undersea visuals, as a scuba-equipped 007 decamped to the Bahamas to battle a legion of evil frogmen. Bond's most profitable triumph at the American box office, *Thunderball's* aquatic escapade testified to the affinity that had developed between scuba diving and the 'ethic of fun' espoused by the new, consumption-driven middle class – the film also giving a renewed push to the scuba phenomenon, as a horde of aspiring 007s began honing their diving skills.

Throughout the late 1950s and 1960s, a stream of advertising campaigns also featured scuba references in their appeals to consumers eager to identify themselves with the hip and happening good life. In 1960, for example, Pepsi-Cola's 'Sociables' ad campaign announced 'They do lively things with lively people, these debonair moderns', a watercolour tableau depicting young couples at the beach cheerfully preparing their scuba gear (see Figure 6.2). Other advertisers

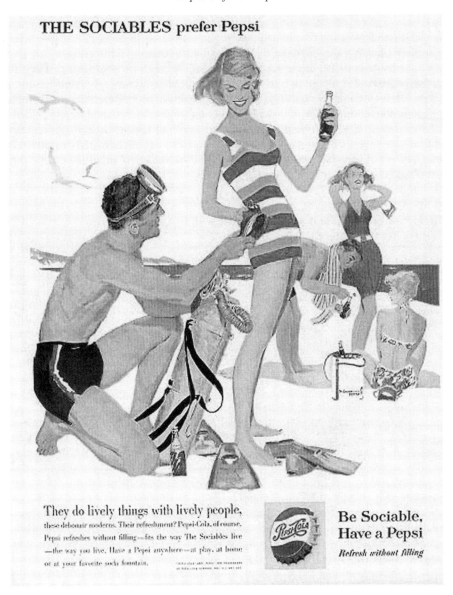

THE SOCIABLES prefer Pepsi

They do lively things with lively people, these debonair moderns. Their refreshment? Pepsi-Cola, of course. Pepsi refreshes without filling—fits the way The Sociables live —the way you live. Have a Pepsi anywhere—at play, at home, or at your favorite soda fountain.

Be Sociable,
Have a Pepsi
Refresh without filling

Figure 6.2 'The Sociables Prefer Pepsi – They Do Lively Things With Lively People': advertisement for Pepsi-Cola, 1960 (Reprinted with permission)

followed suit. In 1962, for example, a campaign for Wrangler's jeans proclaimed 'Skin Divers Wear Wranglers' alongside a picture of a kid wearing denim shorts and diving gear, while in 1963 an ad for Honda placed a scooter on the beach, alongside a diver in full scuba regalia, complete with spear gun. The trend continued throughout the sixties: 1966 advertising campaigns for Fiat and Pontiac, for example, both featured car drivers in wetsuits and scuba gear, while in 1968 an ad campaign for Canadian Club Whiskey featured an athletic young couple out skin-diving.

By the 1960s, then, scuba diving had become an abiding signifier for consumer lifestyles rooted in lively and stylish pleasure seeking. A 'lifestyle sport' surrounded by connotations of exclusivity, exoticism and exhilaration, the scuba phenomenon developed as an ideal expression of the values of the new middle class and their taste for conspicuous consumption and hedonistic non-conformity. And it was an association that scuba manufacturers themselves eagerly capitalized upon, their ads invariably promoting diving as the essence of an affluent, sexy and excitingly distinctive lifestyle (see Figure 6.3).

Immersed in Action and Acquisition: Masculinity, Consumerism and the Sixties Scuba Phenomenon

In Bourdieu's original analysis of the new petite bourgeoisie, Marxist perspectives were writ large, the French theorist identifying socio-economic class as the pre-eminent force in the organization of relations of social distinction and cultural power. His position has drawn justifiable criticism from a number of theorists who have argued that it marginalizes relationships that might have an equally important bearing on configurations of taste and the mapping of cultural boundaries. John Frow (1995: 74), for example, has questioned the way such approaches privilege the determining role of class over those of gender and race, while Beverley Skeggs (1997: 16) criticizes Bourdieu's tendency to view gender as little more than a distributive mechanism operating within class groups.

Yet this critique need not force abandonment of Bourdieu's analytical framework. As Leslie McCall (1992) maintains, the strength of Bourdieu's work in respect of gender may actually have been overlooked.[9] In Bourdieu's model, she argues, gender is seen as having a less immediately visible impact on social and mental structures yet is still acknowledged as a crucial influence on the social structure. According to McCall, therefore, Bourdieu's notions of taste as a marker of cultural boundaries offers a potentially profitable way of making sense of gendered social dispositions and symbolic practices. From this perspective, the consumption-oriented lifestyles that arose in America during the 1950s and 1960s can be seen as being mediated not only by factors of social class, but also by dimensions of gender.

Indeed, one of the most significant dimensions to the reconfiguration of the American middle class after 1945 was the emergence of masculine cultures that fervently endorsed a 'morality of pleasure as a duty', embracing hedonistic consumption as an acceptable – even highly desirable – focal point to their values, aspirations and social practices. According to Barbara Ehrenreich, from the mid-1950s the traditional, masculine ethos oriented around the family, hard work and sobriety was increasingly challenged by a model of American manhood that refused to succumb to the fetters of domesticity. Instead, this 'playboy ethic' prioritized a quest for personal gratification in a swinging world of endless leisure, luxury and indulgence (Ehrenreich, 1983).

Figure 6.3 'Nemrod Treasure Hunt Adventure': advertisement for Nemrod diving equipment, 1969

The scuba diving phenomenon of the 1950s and 1960s was closely allied with the rise of this new brand of leisure-oriented masculinity. It articulated perfectly the 'playboy ethic' and its emphasis on conspicuous consumption and narcissistic pleasure. Of course, women were not excluded from the scuba diving boom. In 1953 Eugenie Clark's account of her undersea exploits, *Lady With a Spear*, became an international bestseller, and throughout the 1950s and 1960s women such as Lotte Hass and Zale Parry were leading diving pioneers. But scuba diving remained a resolutely masculine domain. The majority of recreational divers were male, while in scuba-related magazines, advertising campaigns, films and TV shows, female divers were constructed as sexual objects, invariably posed erotically in form-hugging wetsuits or draped seductively over the latest piece of shiny scuba gear. Typical were *Skin Diver* magazine's pin-ups of the early 1960s. Called 'Miss Driftwood', the magazine's 'bathing beauty' pages led to a popular feature, the Miss Beach Temptress Contest, that showcased young women in revealing bikinis posing flirtatiously alongside assorted diving equipment.

It was, however, scuba diving's prominence in *Playboy* magazine that most vividly reveals the sport's affinity with new masculine identities rooted in consumer practice and desire. Launched by Hugh Hefner in 1953, *Playboy* was an immediate publishing success, its circulation soaring to a million a month by 1956 and rocketing to over 4 million by 1967. *Playboy* became best known for its nude pictorials – but these were just one ingredient in the magazine's universe of cosmopolitan hedonism (see Jancovich, this volume). *Playboy* was a paean to a masculine lifestyle of material pleasure, page after page crammed with images of fashionable menswear and mouth-watering consumer goods. And, nestling amid this lavish cornucopia, were regular scuba diving features and advertisements. In 1962, for example, a 'Scuba Gear and Scuba Dear' photospread included a 'skindiving belle … amply equipped for the occasion' posing alongside piles of deluxe scuba kit (Anon., 1962: 97). And in 1971, a wetsuited model struck an erotic pose on the cover of *Playboy*'s special 'Scuba-Do!' issue, while inside a sumptuous feature paraded a host of diving holidays available in the world's most exclusive resorts (Anon., 1971: 98-106).

But it was in one of *Playboy*'s 1966 promotional features that the links between the scuba phenomenon and masculine consumerism were made most explicit. 'What Sort of Man Reads Playboy?', asked the magazine's advertisement, beneath a luxurious beach scene. Resplendent in jazzy Bermuda shorts, a muscular Adonis was shown enjoying the fruits of the good life with a beautiful young woman, the couple surrounded by a sports car – and an array of polished scuba gear. This, the advertising copy explained, was the kind of lifestyle that distinguished the *Playboy* reader as a 'young man of action and acquisition' for whom 'the name of the game is fun' (*Playboy*, November 1966: 97). The advertisement, then, captured the essence of the 'new masculinity' that had emerged in post-war America. With its accent on glamour, fun and stylish hip – all neatly condensed in the totem of scuba diving – this was a construction of maleness tailored to the demands of the consumer society that blossomed in America during the 1950s and 1960s.

Lifestyle, Consumption and the Urge to Submerge

According to Nancy Midol and Gérard Broyer (1995), what have become known as 'lifestyle sports' trace their roots to the countercultural movements of the late 1960s and 1970s. The history of scuba diving, however, suggests that the distinguishing features of 'lifestyle sport' actually emerged earlier – during the late 1950s and early 1960s. Moreover, rather than being spawned by any rebellious *counter*culture, the case of scuba diving suggests that 'lifestyle sports' were originally generated within the habitus of a new, expressive and consumer-oriented middle class.

Of course, consumerism was not a force unique to American life during the 1950s and 1960s. The 'traditional' middle-class world that had originally emerged during the eighteenth and nineteenth centuries – with its emphasis on family life, the work ethic, moderation and probity – was already losing some of its authority by the 1920s as American capitalism steadily prioritized consumption, leisure and immediate gratification. In the period after the Second World War, however, these shifts accelerated and intensified, middle-class culture becoming more thoroughly permeated by a leisure-oriented consumer ethos. With its emphasis on individuality and conspicuous consumption, this was a middle-class value system adapted to the demands of the consumer economy. A new, commodity-driven bourgeois culture, it was perfectly attuned to modern capitalism's demand for an endlessly regenerating consumer market.

The cultural purchase of the scuba phenomenon during the 1950s and 1960s, then, was indebted to these shifts. The growth of recreational diving and its representation in the popular media crystallized the tastes and values of the new middle class, their lifestyle placing a premium on freedom, individuality and the fulfillment of consumer desires. And as this 'ethic of fun' established its hegemony over the following decades, so the scuba boom continued, with PADI issuing its ten millionth diving qualification in the year 2000, its retail sales soaring to over $250 million, and the company boasting 4,600 retail and resort operations located worldwide. This surging success of recreational scuba divining, then, testifies to the continuing growth of new petit bourgeois lifestyles predicated on individualism, style and – perhaps above all – leisure-oriented consumption

Notes

1   While Bourdieu's account offers a useful framework for understanding general shifts in American middle-class culture, there remain some important differences between the French experience and that in the US. In France, for example, Bourdieu highlighted cultural and socio-economic resources as key markers of bourgeois cultural boundaries, but Michèle Lamont (1992) has suggested that in America a more significant role has been played by moral imperatives based around the qualities of honesty, hard work and personal integrity. More generally, Lamont contends that cultural perimeters are more strongly demarcated in France than in America, where the presence of powerful ideologies of egalitarianism has meant that such boundaries are weaker and more loosely defined.

2   For a more extensive discussion of these developments, see Osgerby (2001).

3   See Norton (1999: 9-24) for an account of Gilpatrick's life and adventures.

4   In 1926 Yves le Prieur, an officer in the French Navy, had already patented a diving system based on compressed air carried in tanks, and in 1937 le Prieur's equipment had been further improved by Georges Comheines who had demonstrated his device in a 'human aquarium' exhibit at the Paris International Exposition. But the

Cousteau/Gagnan scuba system developed during the early 1940s was a considerable advance, being far more reliable and efficient than its predecessors.

5   Munson (1989: 42-64) gives a full account of these developments.

6   In June 1947 and July 1953 *Popular Science Magazine* included features on how readers could build their own underwater breathing equipment from various odds and ends. Perhaps understandably, product liability insurance was not included.

7   See Rainey (2001) for a history of early wetsuit manufacture.

8   In 1976 the Sub-Aqua Association (SAA) was formed to give a voice to Britain's independent diving clubs. Like the British Sub-Aqua Club, the SAA began as an avowedly amateur organization, but (like BSAC) adopted more a commercial approach to its ventures during the 1980s and 1990s.

9   Shi (2001) makes similar arguments.

References

Anon. (1959) 'Explorers of a Weird World Below', *Life*, 28 December, pp. 104-5.

Anon. (1960) 'Skindiving: Poetry, Pleasure and Pelf', *Time*, 28 March, pp. 66-77.

Anon. (1962) 'Scuba Gear and Scuba Dear', *Playboy*, June, pp. 97-101.

Anon. (1971) 'Scuba-Do!', *Playboy*, May, pp. 96-103, 112, 222-223.

Bale, J. (1994) *Landscapes of Modern Sport*, Leicester: Leicester University Press.

Bauman, Z. (1992) *Intimations of Postmodernity*, London: Routledge.

Bennett, T. and J. Woollacott (1987) *Bond and Beyond: The Political Career of a Popular Hero*, Basingstoke: Macmillan.

Bensman, J. and A. Vidich (1971/1995) 'Changes in the Life-Styles of American Classes', in A. Vidich (ed.), *The New Middle Classes: Life-Styles, Status Claims and Political Orientations*, London: Macmillan.

Bourdieu, P. (1984) *Distinction: A Social Critique of the Judgement of Taste*, trans. R. Nice, London: Routledge.

Clark, E. (1953) *Lady With a Spear*, New York: Harper.

Cohen, L. (2003) *A Consumers' Republic: The Politics of Mass Consumption in Postwar America*, New York: Alfred Knopf.

Coughlan, R. (1959) 'A $40 Billion Bill Just For Fun', *Life*, 28 December, pp. 69-74.

Cousteau, J. (1953) *The Silent World*, New York: Harper.

Dorfman, M. (2004) 'Time Line of Scuba: A Chronology of the Recreational Diving Industry', Hanauma Bay Dive Tours, http://www.hanaumabay-hawaii.com/About_scuba_diving.htm

Ehrernreich, B. (1983) *The Hearts of Men: American Dreams and the Flight From Commitment*, London: Pluto.

Ehrenreich, B. (1990) *Fear of Falling: The Inner Life of the Middle Class*, New York: Harper Perennial.

Ehrenreich, B. and Ehrenreich, J. (1979) 'The Professional-Managerial Class', in P. Walker (ed.), *Between Capital and Labor*, Boston: South End Press.

Featherstone, M. (1991) *Consumer Culture and Postmodernism*, London: Sage.

Frow, J. (1995) *Cultural Studies and Cultural Value*, Oxford: Oxford University Press.

Gilpatrick, G. (1938) *The Compleat Goggler: Being the First and Only Exhaustive Treatise on the Art of Goggle Fishing*, Bodley Head: John Lane.

Hass, H. (1951) *Diving to Adventure: The Daredevil Story of Hunters Under the Sea*, Garden City, NY: Doubleday.

Hass, H. (1952) *Manta: Under the Red Sea with Spear and Camera*, New York: Rand, McNally.

Hass, H. (1975) *Conquest of the Underwater World*, London: David and Charles.

Lamont, M. (1992) *Money, Morals, and Manners: The Culture of the French and American Upper-Middle Class*, Chicago: University of Chicago Press.

Lash, S. (1990) *Sociology of Postmodernism*, London: Routledge.

Maffesoli, M. (1996) *The Time of the Tribes: The Decline of Individualism in Mass Society*, London: Sage.

Maguire, J. (1999) *Global Sport: Identities, Societies, Civilizations*, Cambridge: Polity Press.

McCall, L. (1992) 'Does Gender Fit? Bourdieu, Feminism and Conceptions of Social Order', *Theory and Society*, Vol. 21, pp. 837-67.

Midol, N. and G. Broyer (1995) 'Towards an Anthropological Analysis of New Sport Cultures: The Case of Whiz Sports in France', *Sociology of Sport Journal*, Vol. 12, pp. 204-212.

Mort, F. (1997) 'Paths to Mass Consumption: Britain and the USA Since 1945', in M. Nava, A. Blake, I. MacRury and B. Richards (eds), *Buy This Book: Studies in Advertising and Consumption*, London: Routledge.

Munson, D. (1989) *Cousteau: The Captain and His World – A Personal Portrait*, New York: William Morrow.

Norton, T. (1999) *Stars Beneath the Sea: The Pioneers of Diving*, New York: Carroll and Graf.

Osgerby, B. (2001) *Playboys in Paradise: Masculinity, Youth and Leisure-Style in Modern America*, Oxford: Berg.

Parry, Z. and A. Tillman (2001) *Scuba America: The Human History of Sport Diving, Vol. I*, Olga, WA: Whalestooth.

Rainey, C. (2001) 'Wetsuit Pursuit: Hugh Bradner's Development of the First Wetsuit', *Historical Diver*, Vol. 9(1), pp. 22-24.

Rinehart, R. (1998) *Players All: Performances in Contemporary Sport*, Bloomington: Indiana University Press.

Rinehart, R. (2000) 'Emerging Arriving Sport: Alternatives to Formal Sport', in J. Coakley and E. Dunning (eds), *Handbook of Sport Studies*, London: Sage, pp. 504-519.

Rinehart, R. and S. Sydnor (eds) (2003) *To the Extreme: Alternative Sports, Inside and Out*, Albany: State University of New York Press.

Shi, C. (2001) 'Mapping Out Gender Power: A Bourdieuian Approach', *Feminist Media Studies*, Vol. 1(1), pp. 55-9.

Skeggs, B. (1997) *Formations of Class and Gender*, London: Sage.

U.S. Bureau of Census (1975) *Historical Statistics of the United States: Colonial Times to 1970*, Washington: USGPO.

Wheaton, B. (2000) 'Just Do It: Consumption, Commitment and Identity in the Wind-Surfing Subculture', *Sociology of Sport Journal*, Vol. 17(3), pp. 254-274.

Wheaton, B. (2003a) 'Windsurfing: A Subculture of Commitment', in R. Rinehart and S. Snyder (eds), *To The Extreme: Alternative Sports, Inside and Out*, Albany: State University of New York Press.

Wheaton, B. (2003b) 'Lifestyle Sports Magazines and the Discourses of Sporting Masculinity', in B. Benwell (ed.), *Masculinity and Men's Lifestyle Magazines*, Oxford: Blackwell.

Wheaton, B. (2004) 'Introduction: Mapping the Lifestyle Sport-scape', in B. Wheaton (ed.), *Understanding Lifestyle Sports: Consumption, Identity and Difference*, London: Routledge.

Williams, R. (1974) *Television: Technology and Cultural Form*, London: Fontana.

Chapter 7

Lifestyle Print Culture and the Mediation of Everyday Life: From Dispersing Images to Caring Texts

Sam Binkley

The cultures of advanced capitalist or postmodern societies are often characterized by their saturation with visual media (Brennan and Jay, 1996; Featherstone, 1991; Kellner, 1995; Lash, 1990a; Lash and Urry, 1987; Mirzoeff, 1998; Stephens, 1998). For millions of people, the spectacle of television, film, fashion, architecture, retail displays, themed environments, video and an array of new digital image technologies provides far and away the most abundant vehicles for imagination and escape, constituting a hegemony of the visual which, some argue, has eroded the centrality once ascribed to print and practices of reading. For many critics, the visualization of daily life has affected an epochal shift in the realm of identity, politics and representation, subjecting the most intimate realms of identity and selfhood to subtle and pervasive commodification processes (Leiss, Jhally and Klein 1986; Mirzoeff 1999). Such theories of the mediation of everyday life through visualization develop from Marx's theory of commodity fetishism, interpreted by proponents of the Frankfurt School, Benjamin, Lukács, and more recently by postmodernists like Jameson and Baudrillard, who variously link the visualization of culture with the dissolution and dispersal of personal identities and the eclipse of reflexive subjectivity understood in the classic modernist sense (Baudrillard, 1975, 1981; Debord, 1977; Jameson, 1991). Eulogies for the centred transcendental subjectivity of the modern self typically cite these commodification-visualization processes as the source of a postmodern dispersal or fragmentation of subjectivity, collapsed, as Frederic Jameson (1991: 16) ominously portends, into pure depthlessness, a pastiche of fragmented 'intensities' – sensations which are 'free floating and impersonal and tend to be dominated by a peculiar kind of euphoria' (see also Goldman and Papson, 1996; Kellner, 1992, 1995).

Versions of such a thesis have exercised a powerful influence on the cultural theory of the past few decades: the more visual our everyday lives, the more given we are to the fragmentation and dispersal of our identities across a range of imagined possible selves, which flicker, transform and disappear in a hallucination of mediated spectacle. This truism of postmodern scholarship, however, is typically posed as a theory of macro-level socio-economic transformation coupled with a micro-level assertion of these effects on audience subjectivities. As thinly modified versions of a Marxian economic determinism which moves breezily from late capitalism to fragmented subjectivity, such models gloss over the in-between realms of actors, social groups, institutions and cultural trends whereby visual cultures are produced and disseminated. In spite of many promising starts in this direction, much remains to be learned about the rise of mediated culture in the latter part of the twentieth century, and specifically about these new mediators themselves, whose growth in number and influence over the course of a transition from modern to postmodern, or Fordist to post-Fordist, consumer cultures affected so many fundamental changes (Du Gay, 1996; McRobbie, 1998; Nixon, 2003). Where such questions are asked, I will argue, empirical evidence arises which questions the presumed hegemony of the visual within the postmodern turn, and casts doubt on many assumptions concerning the decentring and fragmentation of identity in an increasingly mediated life.

Thus, the approach taken here attempts to redress this oversight by considering, first, the specific groups of professional mediators engaged in the dissemination of postmodern sensibilities through the mediation of daily life, and, second, the various non-visual media through which these groups have operated. From this it is possible to draw new conclusions about the nature of mediated identity in the culture of late capitalism, and reassess certain assumptions pertaining to the fragmentation of the self in a media-saturated culture. By taking up an approach to the sociology of postmodernism which considers cultural products as the affects of specific social groups (Featherstone, 1991; Lash, 1990a; Lash and Urry, 1987, 1993) – and specifically an analysis of culture which looks at the broader professional and institutional circuitry behind the production of culture (Du Gay, 1996) – the study that follows will examine some of the ways in which a lifestyle print media provides readers with exhortations and advice meant to deflect the decentring effect of visual culture, and unify personal identity around a coherent notion of individual authenticity through style of life.

More precisely, in what follows I will consider the case of a select cohort of professional mediators that emerged in the late 1960s and early 1970s, the approximate period typically cited as the point of rupture between modern and postmodern cultures. These mediators were hippies, and the media they produced was a hippie lifestyle print culture, wherein one was instructed on more real, healthy and authentic ways of living aimed not at the fragmentation of identity, but at the rendering of a 'whole self'. They were self-appointed, self-styled lifestyle specialists who shaped new ways of mediating life, not through advertisements, rock videos or any other forms of media typically cited by theorists of the postmodern, but by a print discourse on lifestyle which assumed a strong pedagogical tone, addressed to the suppressed authenticity of the reader as the practitioner of a thematically unified style of life. If, as Jameson wrote, postmodern visual media condemned us to depthlessness, these mediators worked hard to rescue what they perceived as our true, centred selves, buried deep in the ways we lived our daily lives.

In the pages of dozens of books, magazines, journals, brochures and news-papers, what I call a 'countercultural lifestyle print discourse' emerged from a grassroots publishing network based largely on the US west coast, and expanded to exert a broad influence on the American book market and on popular culture in general, shaping a mediating print culture on lifestyle and selfhood based not on images but on written, instructional texts. This literature consisted of how-to manuals, catalogues, books and magazines that offered advice on such topics as the management of diet, marriage and relationships, exercise, home furnishing, spirituality, travel, sex, home economics, cycling, recycling, gardening, massage, home birth and Volkswagen repair. In a postmodern culture of dispersing images, these lifestyle publications fill the function of what I call (lifting a phrase from the later Foucault) 'caring texts', ethical exhortations that sought to restore a thoughtful re-centring of identity through a rendering of the self and its daily conduct as an object of ethical problematization, cultivation and care (Foucault, 1986).

In the third volume of the *History of Sexuality, The Care of the Self*, Foucault immersed himself in a detailed and descriptive exploration of the many ways in which subjectivity among the Ancient world's ethical elites was shaped and produced through myriad and subtle techniques and methods pertaining to such domains as family and kinship, political activity, sexuality, sleep and the interpretation of dreams, and the care of the body. His concerns were with caring as a daily practice of an ethical life: writing on Marcus Aurelius, Foucault described a 'tranquility of a pleasant existence – [in] the possession of oneself' which was managed through rigorous effort and the enforcement of severe ascetic codes. But this was not a solipsistic or abstracted activity, removed from real relations with others. As Foucault describes it:

> Around the care of the self, there developed an entire activity of speaking and writing in which the work of oneself on oneself and communication with others were linked together … it constituted, not an exercise in solitude, but a true social practice … the interplay of the care of the self and the help of the other blends into preexisting relations, giving them a new colouration and a greater warmth. The care of the self – or the attention one devotes to the care that others should take of themselves – appears as an intensification of social relations. (Foucault, 1986: 351)

It will be argued here that countercultural lifestyle print culture assumes the functions of such caring texts, giving a 'new colouration and greater warmth' to a media whose effect is counterpoised to that of dispersing images.

New Cultural Intermediaries and the De-distanciation of Lifestyle

Scholars of contemporary culture have produced a surfeit of theories describing postmodern culture as an expression of visual, spectacular and imagistic media, whose ultimate end result is the decentring of a once unified subjectivity. One such account is found in Scott Lash's characterization of the contradictory tendencies embedded in the image and the text, loosely organized around the ascent of the 'figural' (or visual) over 'discursive' (or textual) regimes of signification (Lash,

1990b). Borrowing from Lyotard's work of the early 1970s, and from Sontag's cultural criticism of the 1960s, Lash finds two contrasting ideal-types in a language/image opposition: while the discursive, modernist sensibility 'operates through a distancing of the spectator from the cultural object' (Lash, 1990b: 175; see also Lyotard, 1984; Sontag, 1966), a hedonistic consumer culture of images erodes this distance, producing a certain instability in the field of meaning. Against the contemplative distance maintained by discourse, images 'operate through the spectator's immersion, the relatively unmediated investment of his/her desire in the cultural object' (Lash, 1990b: 175). Lash terms this process one of semiotic 'dedifferentiation', a process that runs counter to quintessentially modern tendencies toward institutional and social differentiation (Habermas, 1991). In short, for Lash, new forms of mediation are summarized under the decentring function of the visual. The cultures of print are, for Lash, regressive and anachronistic, pertaining as they do to a contemplative distance assumed in the thoughtful reception of meaning, while visual media are hegemonic, affecting a collapse of reflective distance and an immersion of subjectivity in the flux and flow of stimuli.

Indeed, the difference between visual and discursive lifestyle media is apparent: while texts anchor meanings in concrete narratives, images tolerate ambiguity and invite the active interpretive and associational work of viewers and consumers, who weave their own dreams of imaginary self-transformation into what they see. These qualities have been richly documented by advertising and media scholars, most notably Liess, Kline and Jhally (1986), in their expansive account of the ascendance of visual over discursive representations in twentieth-century advertising: 'Verbal imagery is discursive, while visual imagery is nondiscursive':

> Explicit in the former is an argument or a case for the association of the image with what it refers to, so that one could, if asked, spell out the relationship in a more extensive written text. In visual imagery, there is often an abrupt 'imaginative leap' and a freer play of associations that is difficult to put into words. (p. 287)

But the collapse of distance that characterizes visual culture is not solely the effect of visual media itself: it is also the specific product of identifiable social groups, professional mediators of culture, whose numbers have been steadily on the rise since the 1960s.

For Pierre Bourdieu and others following him, the dichotomy of distance and immersion is attributed not to specific media, but to social groups competing for cultural legitimacy. Bourdieu is credited with coining the term 'new cultural intermediaries' to describe a breakaway fraction of the new post-war middle classes, a group encompassing a broad swath of what can be termed the 'lifestyle' professionals – service sector experts in media, communications and marketing, therapists and social workers, public relations experts, stylists, designers and other professionals whose numbers have been steadily on the rise since the 1960s (Bourdieu, 1984: 354-372). For Bourdieu, the cultural disposition of this class was largely hedonistic: their lifestyles betrayed an ethical reorientation from what he called 'duty to the fun ethic', or from an implicit opposition to the 'charming and attractive, a fear of pleasure and a relation to the body made up of "reserve", "modesty" and "restraint"', that defined the older, traditional middle-class outlook, to a hedonism which 'makes it a failure, a threat to self-esteem, not to "have fun"' (Bourdieu, 1984: 367). The phrase 'new cultural intermediaries' has been taken up in scholarly discourse to designate a range of professional groups associated with this hedonistic lifestyle turn. The entry of new cultural intermediaries has been equated with a dissemination of postmodern sensibilities and a new culture of consumption, resulting from a radical expansion of visual culture, images and symbols (advertisers, stylists, lifestyle specialists), but also from a growth in the human services sector: pedagogues, therapists and others, whose aim, like their counterparts in the visual media, is primarily hedonistic – the stimulation of desire, the enhancement of self-expression and the removal of hang-ups and inner blocks that limit the experience of fun (Featherstone, 1991; Lash and Urry, 1993; Lury, 1996; Nixon and Du Gay, 2002; Slater, 1997).

Yet such fun, on closer study, is not handled the same way by seductive and pedagogical mediators respectively, nor is its net effect so easily equated with hedonism, if by hedonism we mean the commodification and aestheticization of daily life and the fragmentation of identity. On closer study, this fun ethic reveals not only a comprehensive technique of self-cultivation and care, but a concerted effort to sustain and consolidate clear public and personal identities. If the mediated life is the fun life, fun entails more work or care for the self than is commonly acknowledged. To unfold the full complexity of this lifestyle ethic, new cultural intermediaries must be understood in terms of the broader predicament facing the middle classes in post-industrial societies, and in terms of their location within a fundamental restructuring of middle-class cultural codes.

The Hedonistic Habitus

Sociologists of industrial capitalism have defined the middle classes by a certain lack of fixity, which has disposed them to the most duplicitous and pretentious strategies of self-legitimation. Neither wage labourers nor owners of the means of production, the middle classes occupy a liminal social position between labour and capital: they are salaried professionals who supervise, rather than directly execute, the production of goods and services without actually profiting from the production process (Burris, 1986; Ehrenreich, 1989; Vidich, 1995; Warner, 1949; Whyte, 1956). This in-between location inclines the middle class to a range of pretentious, self-classifying practices. They are 'other-directed', 'conspicuous' consumers of 'positional goods' meant to parade their tastes while affirming their distance from their immediate inferiors in the labouring classes, a quality summarized in Bourdieu's famous phrase, 'taste classifies the classifier'.

Under the conditions of late capitalism, however, the self-legitimation of the middle classes through culture becomes difficult. What were once stable cultural codes are eroded under the inflationary overproduction of status bestowing goods and practices in an accelerated culture of consumption, leading to a gradual weakening of the cultural canons of middle-class taste. Middle-class classificatory practices wane in their power to classify classifiers, to shape identities and to affirm social boundaries. This problem is exacerbated further in the 1960s and 1970s with the emergence of a range of oppositional social groups (economically independent women, minorities and countercultural youth), and a new cast of cultural intermediaries as producers of newer and more novel means of affirming cultural classifications (musicians and artists, film-makers, fashion designers and stylists of many kinds, whose appropriations from elite cultural canons confuse traditional distinctions of high and low). Paul DiMaggio has described this condition as one of cultural inflation:

> The system of classification of artistic goods is becoming more finely, but also less clearly, differentiated, less universal and less symbolically potent. The social structure continues to generate high levels of demand for the cultural goods with which social identities can be fashioned. But structural changes that weaken the institutional bases of cultural authority transform this demand into an inflationary spiral, undermining the cultural capital on which the symbolic economy has rested while proliferating weaker currencies. (1991: 142)

These weaker currencies were the product of the swollen ranks of the new cultural intermediaries, avatars of a new hedonism (which doubled as techniques of self-care), in the exploding lifestyle and media industries. Such sensual invocations, premised on a dismissal of the old protocols of middle-class taste, provided both an alternative schema for marking social differences and a personal ethic championing an authentic experience of the self in a presumably unmediated, more real present.

Bourdieu has famously analyzed the canons of middle-class taste as ordered by an implicit hierarchical schema in which distance, reserve and a contemplative withdrawal from the immediacy and impact of cultural materials affirm the aesthetic distanciation of the middle classes, who hold themselves at one remove from immediacies in general, in the fields of both cultural and economic life. Taste classifies the classifier, Bourdieu argues, through the affirmation of this distance, but under the conditions of cultural inflation induced by new cultural professionals, the habitus of the new post-industrial middle class becomes decentred: it sheds the hierarchical structure that once confirmed its distinction, and opens itself up to wild and 'inflationary' classifications and reclassifications of culture and taste, particularly among its younger, more cosmopolitan element (Featherstone, 1991: 70). These differences can be described as follows: while the old bourgeois disposition valued contemplation over sensation and thoughtful reserve over emphatic investment in cultural experiences, the new middle classes embraced the immediacy of experiences, rewritten as learning processes, exploratory adventures in the exoticism of cultural 'otherness', the feeling of newly sensualized mundane activities, and the sensuality of the body. The classificatory codes that regulate middle-class cultural hegemony are subjected to a process of what Scott Lash called cultural de-differentiation, resulting in a cultural *de-distanciation* among the middle classes, a new classificatory scheme which recuperates immediacy and lived experience as legitimate taste (Featherstone, 1991: 70-72). The new cultural intermediaries are, in this regard, champions of a de-distanciated self in everyday experience. They teach us how to let ourselves go, to live in the now, eroding distinctions between social classes in their openness to novelty and exoticism, and in their attention to the undervalued realm of the everyday. They find artistry in the most mundane places (the body, food, nature) and they collapse the alleged 'distance' demanded of middle-class connoisseurship in their embrace of immediacy, sensation, adventure and experience, reclassified as 'self-development', 'self-realization' or 'fun'.

In short, the lifestyles of the new middle classes and the new cultural intermediaries express the desire to relinquish the mechanisms of self-control which secure aesthetic distances and maintain outmoded classificatory schemes. They long to break free from the uptight world of their parents, to live in a de-distanciated habitus more attuned to consumption and lifestyle than tastes cultivated through higher learning and connoisseurship. As middle-class canons dissolved, the field was opened up to rich and adventurous modes of distinction and cultural classification (premised on the rejection of traditional canons of cultural classification itself), practiced by innovative and entrepreneurial cultural intermediaries and producers uncovering inventive ways of classifying social practices. More precisely, this process came to the fore during the 1970s, the Me decade so often invoked for its (mis)adventures with lifestyle and its appeals to new realms of narcissism and personal experience, wherein the invention of ever newer ways to live with authenticity by collapsing the distance on real experience powered an expansive cultural and political transformation.

Such an art of living was hedonistic to be sure, but it was also a hedonism meant to function symbolically by affirming social classifications and reproducing such classifications in a stable class habitus, even one that operated by evading the overt, hierarchical schemas through which such classifications were traditionally imposed. And as such, this hedonism, mediated by a host of expert hedonists, was a caring hedonism, shaped by an ethical discourse on the proper techniques of self-immersion. Seeking to classify the (non-)classifier, the one presumably too immersed in experiences of reality to classify at all, it required the mediation not just of fragmented and disjointed visual spectacles, but the consolidating mediation derived from a pedagogical text, relating a technique of living that appealed to a deep seated personal authenticity, realized through a philosophically unified way of life. The hedonistic lifestyles were for this reason accompanied by a discourse of expertise and control, in which one worked to relax oneself, monitoring oneself to prevent unexpected eruptions of, ironically, self-monitoring. What Featherstone (1991: 45), following Cas Wouters (1986), has called the 'controlled decontrol of emotion' involved elements both of release and constraint, and the new middle classes, Featherstone contends, blended the expressive, sensual and experiential releases associated with the carnival, with the self-management and self-monitoring ensured by a discourse of expertise and therapeutic control. Featherstone describes:

> the increasing capacity of the new middle class to display a calculating hedonism, to engage in more varied (and often dangerous) aesthetic and emotional explorations which themselves do not amount to a rejection of

controls, but a more carefully circumscribed and interpersonally responsible 'controlled de-control' of the emotions which necessary entails some calculation and mutually expected respect for other persons. (1991: 59)

Turning from such macro-level analyses to the particular groupings of cultural intermediaries themselves, we discover that the expanding ranks of mediators emerging in and around the moment of the postmodern turn, and specifically key groupings within those ranks, served many diverse functions and operated from a broader range of media. Looking at the lifestyle literature that surged to prominence in the early 1970s, we discover that while de-distanciation did serve as a means of classification between competing groups, it is neither limited to visual media, nor is it so quickly linked with decentring and dispersal of subjectivity. De-distanciation, the emersion of the reflective mind in the sensuality and immediacy of lived experience, expressed, in the pages of the lifestyle print culture of the 1970s, a mode of ethical instruction as a caring discourse on style of life.

West Coast Publishing: Classifying the Advisable Life

A discourse of lifestyle tied to the counterculture emerged in the US in a print culture that had many specific points of origin, from struggling rural communes to small urban cooperative groups (Binkley, 2002, 2003b). The intellectual and creative source that most broadly influenced the American mainstream, and that played a significant part in launching an alternative way of thinking, talking and writing about daily life choices, was undoubtedly to be found in San Francisco's burgeoning publishing community. Throughout the 1970s, this context developed a group of highly prolific lifestyle intellectuals and mediators of everyday life, largely without traditional institutional credential or any assertion of a specifically scientific knowledge of their topic. Their expertise was largely experiential and their capacity to speak with intimacy and familiarity to other lifestyle practitioners allowed their advice to penetrate the remotest spaces of daily life (Binkley, 2003a). The emergence of this discourse can be described in terms of a struggle for legitimacy between two fractions: on the one hand, the mainstream American book industry dominated by the big New York-based publishing houses and the Eastern literary establishment sought to uphold traditional standards of literary excellence for a cultivated East coast readership, while on the other, a nascent, emerging culture of lifestyle advanced by a younger fraction of lifestyle mediators which celebrated pragmatic knowledge of the immediacy of everyday life practices as itself a basis for legitimate literature. The contest for legitimacy between these groups expressed the competing values of a distanced regard for literary seriousness, and an immersive engagement with real, everyday experiences. To understand this struggle for legitimacy, we must inquire into the origins of this upstart publishing and literary movement.

The West Coast

Throughout the 1970s, the state of California was identified with a new culture of leisure and lifestyle that was fast transforming the country, challenging long-held patterns of middle-class distinction with a new style emphasizing openness, sensuality and self-authenticity through new forms of leisure. The explosion of lifestyle culture on the West coast was in part attributed to a boom in grassroots publishing ventures during that time, which saw dozens of small presses turn out hundreds of practical, how-to manuals and instructional texts on a range of lifestyle practices from cooking and exercise to Rolfing, massage, cycling and adventure vacations. In the business literature of the book industry, primarily written for the East coast publishing establishment, the California small press movement was alternately heralded as a lucrative opportunity to snatch up cheap book projects for potentially profitable distribution, or as an affront to its cultural authority, a surge of novelistic and trivial material with no redeeming literary value.

The consolidation of the West coast as a major national market for books began in the early 1970s with the consolidation of the counterculture of the 1960s into a durable informal economy, whose networks of small bookstores and grassroots presses had given the first intonations of the region's viability as a market for books. Large retail booksellers based in the East began to respond: B. Dalton Booksellers, Doubleday and Brentano's all moved to expand their presence in malls and shopping districts across the state, challenging the independent booksellers who had been steadily expanding their clientele over the last few years (Welles, 1972). 'As the hippie-trippy phase of West Coast publishing ends', one industry journalist reported, 'most publishers are scurrying to build a solid trade list and are determined to make the West Coast industry a national one' (Stuttaford, 1972: 40). In the years that followed, major houses from the East opened offices in West coast cities to better reach those markets, most notably the move in 1976 of Harper and Row's religious department to offices in San Francisco. But as appealing as the West coast was to many Eastern firms, it was nonetheless often perceived as an immature market, fraught with risks and logistical problems concerning distribution and advertising which hampered its full development.

The West coast, it was argued, lacked the traditional intellectual class of critics and commentators on literary products capable of serving the 'gate keeping' functions demanded of a mature book reading and book buying public. Such mediators provided an indispensable channel to consumers, and without them sales and promotion of new titles would be difficult. How would people hear about books? True, the West possessed powerful local networks and informal centres where books were discussed and promoted. Specifically, in an influential underground publishing network (evident, for example, in literary supplements appearing in college newspapers as well as other suburban dailies and regional publications), publicity for locally produced titles directed to specific timely and regional issues on local news and other media could propel sales without the usual book promotion spots. From a marketing standpoint, this network had its advantages: it fostered a more active and cooperative role for independent bookstores in arranging author tours, speaking events and in cooperating in larger promotional plans. But the view of the West as lacking in the intellectual stature of the East, and thus closer to the mass market model for books, permeated the trade press of the 1970s, carrying with it more than a dash of Eastern condescension. One visiting publisher described the market as strong in 'best sellers, how-to, pop-psych, self-help, occult – and most of them in trade and paperbacks. But not much hardcover, not much fiction, very few literary works of "heavy" nonfiction. It's an unsophisticated audience, and yes, it buys a lot of books, but it's not as varied or diverse or consistently responsive as general statistics might indicate' (Holt, 1976: 31).

Indignation (or what Bourdieu called a 'counter-refusal') of the chauvinism of the East coast establishment was deeply rooted in the identity of the West coast publishing culture, a sentiment expressed by Digby Diehl, book editor for the *Los Angeles Times,* in an article that appeared in a special issue of *Publishers Weekly* on the emerging West coast scene. Diehl, photographed for the article on the beach, surfboard in one hand, arm full of books and typewriter in the other, clearly removes himself from the cultural hierarchies he identifies with Eastern publishing, asserting that 'in New York, I am often treated to the joke that I was chosen Book Editor of the *Los Angeles Times* because I was the only person in California who could read without moving his lips' (Diehl, 1973: 36). Defending the West from charges of vulgarity, Digby Dheil writes:

> Ah, yes, the secret word is out: vulgarity. It's what the West has that everyone else seems to want in startlingly increasing proportions. No doubt it will be the secret of how the East was won. And in its best form… it is something to be joyously embraced… There is an energetic ferment in the Western book world that is revitalizing the national mainstream. This ferment has, in many ways, brought publishing out of its quaint New England cloisters to… the edge of history. (*ibid.*)

Yet vulgarity is linked here with a primitivism that retains its own unique distinction:

> Despite my flippancy, I hope that my praise of Western vulgarity is understood with the seriousness intended, for this vulgarity is not only vitality, but a sense of commonality often missing in our elite, high educated and snobbish book circles (from 'Vulgus, L., common people'). (*ibid.*)

But the West coast was desirable to the East coast establishment not only as a market for books produced in the regular manner, but for the kinds of books it generated locally, which were drawing an increasingly loyal readership nationally. These books celebrated fun as a way of life, and offered careful, sustained instruction on the fun life as an ethical technique, a view of life shaped and advanced in a grassroots publishing and bookselling industry that seemed to conform to very different rules covering everything from the development of content to production and distribution. Nowhere is the uniqueness of this industry better illustrated than in the case of the Bay Area publishing and book selling business.

The Bay Area

Just before Christmas in 1972, San Francisco's Golden Gate Park was host to a gathering that in many respects resembled dozens of others over the preceding years. Organic food stands set up next to bookstalls, rock bands and poets performed from an open air stage and pot smoke wafted out into the open air while bottles of wine were surreptitiously passed between groups of vendors and their customers. But this was not a Be-in or Gathering of the Tribes in the tradition of the Haight-Ashbury scene: it was the First International San Francisco Book Fair, described in its brochure as a 'revival of craftsmanship, a reverence for beauty, above all, a personal commitment to the spirit embodied in a book rather than merely a commitment to the publishing business' (Collier, 1972: BRA 7). The Book Fair was meant to showcase some of the hundreds of small presses that had emerged over the preceding years, publishing often short runs of innovative fiction, practical, how-to paperbacks and other lifestyle books. 'If any East Coast publisher had showed up', Frederic Mitchell of Scrimshaw Press recalled to a *Publishers Weekly* correspondent, 'he would have flipped out. The atmosphere was unpetty and cooperative. It was something new in publishing and we all knew it. There was a sense that we had the double whammy on New York. We're not only managing to make a little money off our books, but we're having fun too' (Collier 1972: BRA 7).

The book fair provides a window into the publishing and bookselling industry emerging in the Bay Area in the early 1970s: formed in a uniquely organic professional and business spirit, the discourse of lifestyle was more than illustrated and argued in the pages of the materials it circulated, but performed and realized in the very organizational style of the network itself. Diehl (1973: 38) characterized the interests of many of these small publishers:

> Indian lore, Esalen-type therapeutics, ecological alarm, the occult explosion, sex experiments, the counterculture, and various forms of the New Life itself are what readers nationwide are buying. This frontierland of transplants has generated a contemporary mythology of its own, and with it, the re-examination of all our national values.

A publishing and bookselling tradition in the Bay area consisted of distributors and publishers like Bookpeople, Shambhala, and North Point Press, Chronicle, Ten Speed, Nolo, Sierra Club and others that came to define the literary and commercial world of countercultural publishing, while making steady advances into the mainstream of American book sales (See, 1992). One of the earliest and most significant breakthroughs came with the success of the *Whole Earth Catalog,* a jumbled compendium of ecologically inspired books and gadgets whose astronomical sales opened up the West coast publishing industry to the interests of the Eastern houses. The *Catalog*, which developed from a small circle of back-to-naturists working in a garage in Menlo Park, south of San Francisco, offered detailed commentary on dozens of items useful to the erstwhile commune dweller or similarly inclined lifestylist. Its cluttered pages, crudely pasted down with blocks of type and found images, literally immersed the reader, buzzing like an Eastern bazaar with myriad new ways of doing ordinary, taken-for-granted things from shoe repair to star-gazing, accompanied by informal product reviews of hardware, clothing and books (Binkley, 2003b). Yet in spite of all of its discord, the catalogue sought to provide a framework for a unified life, one attentive to the needs of the environment and ways of living holistically and authentically in a technologically advanced society. This life was advised and instructed in dozens of product reviews and articles mailed in from alternative lifestylists across the country. Perhaps no single moment better typifies the clash between the Western valorization of experiential lifestyle and the Eastern insistence on distanced, literary seriousness than the row over the awarding of the 1972 National Book Award for current affairs to the *Catalog,* which was met with surprise and indignation by many, and inspired the resignation of one of the jurors appointed to award the prize. Unswayed, editor Stuart Brand accepted the award with the hope that 'it encourage[d] still more self-initiated, amateur, youth-based, non-New York publishing' (Raymont, 1972a: 35; see also, Raymont, 1972b). The alarming success of the *Whole Earth Catalog*, purchased from local Bay area distributor Bookpeople by Random House and sold nationally, defined the model for West coast books: off-beat, grassrootsy and suggestive of new morally purposeful ways of life.

Bookpeople was founded by Don Gerrard in 1968 with a short list combining local authors and titles with national paperbacks, relying on his own mail-order catalogue 'with a funky, anti-New York stance' (Collier, 1972: BRA 7). Within a year and a half, Bookpeople mushroomed into a $2,000,000 business with twenty-five employees, and their list of mostly how-to titles, catalogues and manuals had drawn eager interest from the larger East coast firms. John Muir's *How to Keep Your Volkswagen Alive: A Step by Step Manual for the Complete Idiot* sold 125,000 copies; Jeanie Darlington's *Grow Your Own: An Encounter With Organic Gardening* sold 56,000 copies; and Alicia Bay Laurel's *Living On The Earth* sold 10,000 copies in its first four months, and, like the *Whole Earth Catalog*, was quickly picked up by Random House where it became a national bestseller (Collier, 1972: BRA 7).

Like the *Whole Earth Catalog*, *Living On The Earth*'s success grew from its insurrectionary entry onto the American book-publishing scene, which celebrated the immediacy of the lived moment over the distanced reflection manifested in traditional definitions of cultural sophistication. On Brand's recommendation, Bay Laurel (her real name is Kaufman, though she preferred to be named for her favourite tree) took her collection of folios to Don Gerrard, who had been looking for something that would follow the success of the *Whole Earth Catalog*, though most of what he had seen, he told *Publishers Weekly*, was too commercial. Twenty-one-year-old Alicia had been living at Wheeler Ranch, a commune in California where she had penned (quite literally) a manuscript in her own handwritten script. Without so much as a table of contents, the book offers page after page of instruction on the myriad problems that confront the commune dweller in the course of daily life: how to make a lantern for a candle from a tin can; how to build an ice chest; how to make you own baby food from organically grown fruits and vegetables; how to tie-dye; how to deal with troublesome neighbours (moths, rats, ticks); and how to cure a cold (*New York Times*, 1971: 34; Mungo, 1971: BR 6). The serendipitous ordering of all this advice is accented with Bay Laurel's own renderings: flowing, childish, Matisse-like line drawings, depicting every variety of subject matter to illustrate her instructions.

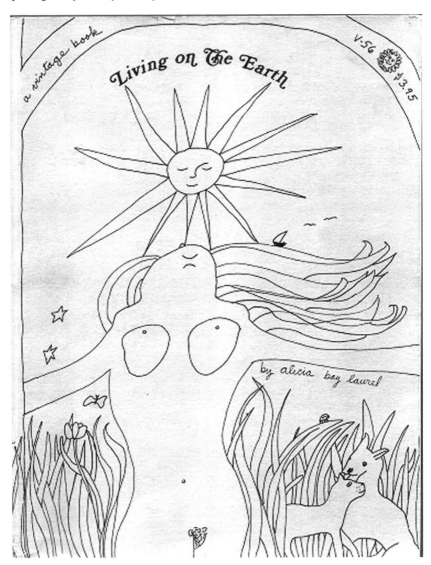

Figure 7.1 Cover of *Living on the Earth* by Alicia Bay Laurel
       (reprinted with permission)

Smiling moons look down on a sleeping-bagged couple snuggled in tall grass; naked gardeners tilling soil; a bearded figure strums a guitar. In her introduction, Bay Laurel explains the ordering of the book:

> This book is for people who would rather chop wood than work behind a desk so they can pay P.G. and E. It has no chapters, it just grew as I learned; you may find the index your only guide to this unmapped land. However, if you have a feeling for the flow of things, you will discover a path: from traveling the wilds to the first fence, simple housing, furnishing, houses, crafts, agriculture, food preparation, medicine – not unlike the development of our ancient ancestors. When we depend less on industrially produced consumer goods, we can live in quiet places. Our bodies become vigorous; we discover the serenity of living with the rhythms of the earth. We cease oppressing one another. (Bay Laurel, 1971: front matter).

'She came in with her book in a little blue suitcase', Gerrard recalls, 'We took it home and read it and flipped out'. Calling it a 'turn on book', Gerrard said that 'if you could impersonate the Little Prince as a chick, you'd have Alicia' (*New York Times*, 1971: 34). Originally published by Bookworks, the title was eventually picked up by Random House as a Vintage paperback, with a first printing of 100,000 copies. A two-page spread on *Living on the Earth* in *Publishers Weekly* mimicked the book's chirographic style: in meandering script, a reviewer lavished praise on the book's authenticity and simplicity: 'we decided that we couldn't tell you about it in stodgy type, because then you might not realize the rather startling statement this book makes about the making of books: It is still reasonable to simply write a book, print it, bind it and sell it. As someone once said, the only thing Gutenberg had over the scribes, after all, was the novelty of a justified line' (*Publishers Weekly*, 1971: 72-3).

Shambhala was another small press that earned its reputation through its dedication to New Age spirituality and a uniquely countercultural version of Eastern mysticism associated with many West coast houses. Started in 1968 by two Berkeley graduate students in the basement of a bookstore they owned and operated, Shambhala's mission was to be 'a house dedicated to exploring and mapping man's inner world and expressing creatively the potential of Man's evolution', a purpose that was realized quickly: after only three years of operation, Shambhala had over 30 titles in print including *Mandala*, the *Tassajara Bread Book* and *Meditation in Action*, an instructional manual on meditation and Eastern mysticism written by Chogyam Trungpa, a Tibetean Monk (Stutaford, 1972: 45). *Meditation in Action* was assembled in the basement of the bookstore in 1969, and by 1972 it had proven an indisputable hit for Shambhala, selling over 26,000 copies. But a more sensational experiment for Shambhala was the *Tassajara Bread Book*, a collection of recipes, sketches and philosophical ruminations on bread preparation written by Edward Espe Brown, a monk at a California Zen retreat called Tassajara (Brown, 1970; Hodgman, 2003).

Figure 7.2 Cover of *Tassajara Bread Book* by Edward Espe Brown
(reprinted with permission)

Written on a hundred dollar advance and printed in an initial edition of 3,000 copies, by the mid-1970s sales would reach 300,000 and ultimately pass 750,000, securing it an enduring legacy as a classic in cooking and bread baking instruction. The book's rustic, earth tone cover of coarse brown cardstock lent it the sense of rootsiness that was complemented by titles and chapter headings written in swirling calligraphic type, seemingly drawn with quill pen, and illustrations of scenes from the monastery and diagrams of bread baking technique drawn with casual but steady line contours. Woven throughout these instructions was a consistent reflection on mundane tasks as intrinsically meaningful, even in their minutiae: 'Bread makes itself' an opening statement relates, 'by your kindness, with your help, with imagination running through you, with dough under hand, you are breadmaking itself, which is why breadmaking is so fulfilling and rewarding' (Brown, 1970: front matter). Brown, who moved on to prominence as a chef at Greens, a restaurant owned by the San Francisco Zen Center, was to follow this success with two other titles: *Tassajara Cooking* and, much later, *The Tassajara Recipe Book*, all with Shambhala, and all to eager readers and enthusiastic reviews (Hodgman, 2003). By 1976, Shambhala had left Bookpeople and gone to Random House for distribution, and with 18 titles in 1977, the house was doing $800,000 in trade sales.

Body Work

A discourse on lifestyle as a realm of direct, de-distanciated experience took a special interest in the body as a source of pleasure and authentic self-realization – a quality that is developed in several instructional texts on massage, yoga, exercise, stretching, diet and health, loosely summarized under the heading of 'body work'. Perhaps the most influential anthology of writings on body work with a demonstrable link to the Bay Area counterculture appeared with Anne Kent Rush's *Getting Clear: Body Work for Women*, published by Bookworks in 1973, and distributed by Random House. In the early 1970s, Kent Rush was a writer, body therapist and socialite in the Bay Area Growth Movement, conducting workshops at the Esalen institute in Big Sur and at the Gestalt Institute in San Francisco. She traces her interests in body work to her experiences as a 21-year-old college student in Boston: 'Sitting in a chair feeling out of shape and tired', Kent Rush recalls, 'I began to let myself go into the way my body felt: flabby, numb, hungry, tired', although this changed with her discovery of Yoga: 'I felt whole' (1973: 3-4). Upon arrival in the Bay Area in 1969, she continued her interest in body work at the Free University in Berkeley. She began training in massage with an Esalen instructor in San Francisco, and later began teaching the Esalen massage technique. She emerged as one of the key practitioners of 'polarity therapy' in the Bay Area scene, a technique fashioned on Chinese acupuncture aimed at releasing emotional and physical tension in the body, which she combined with her training as a Reichian therapist.

Figure 7.3 Cover of *Getting Clear* by Anne Kent Rush
          (reprinted with permission)

In 1972, Kent West provided illustrations for *The Massage Book* by Esalen instructor George Downing, published in 1972 by Bookworks, a title that was to soar to over 2,000,000 sales in the next decade (Downing, 1972). On the success of this project, in May of that year she began work on a collection of body work therapies and techniques with a feminist slant – *Getting Clear: Body Work for Women* – which was also completed for Bookworks, in January of 1973. Gathered from dozens of interviews with female body work practitioners and therapists of different stripes, *Getting Clear* included 290 pages of material on every aspect of body work. Throughout, the collection inventories techniques and methods meant to cultivate a sense of wholeness within the body, to mend a gap instituted within Western cultural traditions between mind and body, and to release sensations, experiences and potentials that are necessarily suppressed in this unfortunate divorce of intellect and flesh. These techniques, in short, aimed to induce a relaxation or release of the self into the body, to allow one to feel one's embodiment in the present moment, and to remake patterns of everyday life around the powers and pleasures of the newly recovered unity of the mental and physical self. 'What I feel and the work I do are based on the premise that mind and body are one', Kent Rush writes. 'When I use the word "body" in this book, I am always referring to the whole person, including mental functions' (1973: 11).

The collection begins with an autobiographical section, 'Starting With Yourself', a collection of 'physical and mental self–awareness experiments' that span topics from 'Reclaiming your Genitals' to 'Pain', 'Food Awareness' and 'Centering, Breathing and Bellypower'. Other sections include 'Women with Women' – with sections on 'Closeness and Competition' and 'Touching and Talking' – 'Women with Men', 'Men and This Book' and 'Back to Yourself'. Throughout *Getting Clear,* exercises are provided to illustrate more general ideas and to provide direct practical ways of implementing ideas in practical techniques, generally centred around the relaxation of mental control over the body and its sensations. One exercise called 'Squeeze and Relax' instructs the reader to undertake a series of exercises on specific muscle groups:

> Squeeze and hold the area, then relax it... Tense, then relax the muscles of your scalp and forehead... Tense, and relax the muscles around your eyes. Tense and relax your neck ... Tighten the muscles of your thighs – and relax... When you reach your toes and have relaxed the muscles of your feet, tense all the muscles in your body and constrict yourself with all your effort. Intensify whatever position your body pulls into, and be aware if it seems to express some emotion. Now release the tension and relax your whole body. Let every muscle relax. Imagine your breathing can relax your muscles more and more with each exhalation, as though the tension could flow out of your body with your breath. Let your whole body sink more and more into the carpet. Let the floor support your weight. Think of the floorboards under you which are holding your weight. And think of the structure which holds up that floor, which is finally connected with the earth below. After you have gone through these steps you will be very relaxed. (Kent Rush, 1973: 20-21)

Relaxation here affirms the sensuality of the body as a daily practice, but it is anything but hedonistic in a narrow sense: it is a technique of bodily control and decontrol that invokes the authority of a non-traditional discourse on selfhood and lifestyle whose techniques stand in marked contrast with seductive messages of commercial media. Relaxation is a caring technique, aimed not at exciting a desire for remote objects and identities, but at establishing the self as an object of caring and cultivation.

Conclusion

An admittedly selective case study of a lifestyle print culture that developed in the Bay Area in the early 1970s reveals a specifically textual discourse on lifestyle that exercised a very different sort of persuasion over its audiences and practitioners than similar messages expressed in visual media. Taking up the case of one specific group of such cultural intermediaries, the unique properties of written texts are linked to specific effects on the constitution of identity and subjectivity. In much media theory, visual images call out to audiences in ways that effectively split them between real and imagined selves: borrowing from Louis Althusser's thesis on the interpellation of the subject in ideology, media theorists have studied advertisements for the way they interpellate not the real viewer herself, but the viewer's imaginary ideal of a desired self – a longed-for identity that sustains only within the moment of address itself, the 'hailing' of the ad. 'So advertisements appellate us as unique', Judith Williamson (1978: 52-3) writes, 'since the ad speaks to an imaginary individual which then becomes us. By buying a Pepsi you take place in an exchange, not only of money but of yourself for a Pepsi Person'. I have tried to offer an alternative view of this calling out, one fashioned more on Michel Foucault's view of the care of the self, wherein ethical advice and guidance are offered in a manner intended to consolidate rather than dissipate the self, by outlining a way of living that speaks to a unified ethical purpose.

As discussed, the fragmenting effect of visual media is offset, however tenuously, in other textual, discursive media. In the form of a lifestyle discourse, such media aim to restore, not immerse, the reflective self, focusing its attention on the authenticity of the self in a thematically unified way of living. The demand for more precise explication of its subject matter, to a thoughtful reflection and linear coherence that defines print discourse, contrasts with visual experiences which invite fantastic and imaginary investments in fleeting and changing representations.

But media by themselves tell only part of the story. In a study of some of the specific groups of cultural intermediaries who produced these discourses, I have drawn on a theoretical treatment of postmodernity which examines the specific professional and social groups most often associated with the dissemination of postmodern cultural effects, studies by Featherstone, Lash and Urry that examine the role of the new middle classes as the mediators of culture and everyday life. More specifically, postmodernization processes are read here as symbolic struggles between aesthetic distanciation practiced by the older fractions of the middle class, and the de-distanciated styles of newer fractions, styles that become increasingly hegemonic as postmodernization processes accelerate and expand. In short, I have argued that, where the old middle class highbrow pondered art, the new cultural intermediaries immersed themselves in it. Most importantly, in the lifestyle discourse of the 1970s, de-distanciation is not immediately linked with a hedonistic fragmentation and dispersal of identity, but with the cultivation of the self as an object of care. It is suggested here that hedonism, as a rejection of conventions dictating a distanced relationship to cultural content, to pleasure and to experience, is, as expressed in this particular lifestyle subculture, an implicitly ethical practice: it invokes powerful imperatives of self-development and self-care through ways of life that are unified around a sustained practical and philosophical project of self-authentication.

References

Amin, A. (ed.) (1994) *Post-Fordism: A Reader,* Cambridge: Blackwell.

Baudrillard, J. (1981) *For a Critique of the Political Economy of the Sign*, St. Louis, MO: Telos Press.

Baudrillard, J. (1975) *The Mirror of Production*, St. Louis, MO: Telos Press.

Bay Laurel, A. (1971) *Living on the Earth*, New York: Random House.

Bell, D. (1962) *The End of Ideology: on the Exhaustion of Political Ideas in the Fifties*, New York: Free Press.

Bell, D. (1973) *The Coming of the Post Industrial Society*, New York: Basic Books.

Bell, D. (1976) *The Cultural Contradictions of Capitalism*, New York: Basic Books.

Binkley, S. (2000a) telephone interview with Stewart Brand, June 24.

Binkley, S. (2000b) telephone interview with Dick Raymond, May 23.

Binkley, S. (2002) 'Consuming Aquarius: Markets and the Moral Boundaries of the New Class', PhD Dissertation, New York: New School University.

Binkley, S. (2003a) 'Cosmic Profit: Countercultural Commerce and the Problem of Trust in American Marketing', *Consumption, Markets and Culture*, Vol. 6(4), pp. 231-49.

Binkley, S. (2003b) 'The Seers of Menlo Park: The Discourse of Heroic Consumption in the *Whole Earth Catalog*', *Journal of Consumer Culture,* Vol. (3)3, pp. 283-313.

Binkley, S. (2004) telephone interview with Patricia Holt, January 29.

Bourdieu, P. (1984) *Distinction, A Social Critique of the Judgment of Taste.* trans. R. Nice, Cambridge: Harvard University Press.

Brand, S. (1972) *The Last Whole Earth Catalog*, Menlo Park: Portola Institute.

Braunstein, P. and W. Michael (2002) *Imagine Nation: the American Counterculture of the 1960s and 1970s*, London: Routledge.

Brennan, T. and M. Jay (eds) (1996) *Vision in Context: Historical and Contemporary Perspectives on Sight*, London: Routledge.

Bruce-Briggs P. (ed.) (1979) *The New Class?* New Brunswick, NJ: Transaction Books.

Brown, E. E. (1970) *The Tassajara Bread Book*, Boulder, CO: Shambhala.

Burris, V. (1986) 'The Discovery of the New Middle Class', *Theory and Society*, Vol. 15(3), pp. 317-351.

Carroll, P. (1982) *It Seemed Like Nothing Happened*, New York: Holt, Rinehart and Winston.

Clecack, P. (1983) *America's Quest for the Ideal Self*, New York: Oxford University Press.

Collier, D. (1972) 'For Fun and Profit in San Francisco', *New York Times*, February 13: BRA 7.

Debord, G. (1977) *Society of the Spectacle*, Detroit: Black and Red.

Diehl, D. (1973) 'Revitalizing the National Mainstream', *Publishers Weekly,* November 5, pp. 36-38.

Dietz, L. (1973) 'Price/Stern/Sloan', *Publishers Weekly,* October 3, pp. 42-43.

DiMaggio, P. (1991) 'Social Structure, Institutions and Cultural Goods: The Case of the United States', in P. Bourdieu and J. S. Coleman (eds) *Social Theory for a Changing Society*, New York: Russell Sage Foundation.

Downing, G. (1972) *The Massage Book*, San Francisco/New York: Bookworks/Random House.

Du Gay, P. (1996) *Consumption and Identity at Work*, London: Sage.

Eco, U. (1986) *Travels in Hyperreality*, trans. W. Weaver, San Diego: Harcourt Brace Jovanovich.

Ehrenreich, B. (1989) *Fear of Falling: The Inner Life of the Middle Class*, New York: Pantheon Books.

Ewen, S. (1988) *All Consuming Images*, New York: Basic Books.

Ewen, S. and E. Ewen. (1982) *Channels of Desire: Mass Images and the Shaping of America*, New York: McGraw-Hill.

Featherstone, M. (1991) *Consumer Culture and Postmodernism*, London: Sage.

Featherstone, M. (1987) 'Lifestyle and Consumer Culture', *Theory, Culture and Society*, Vol. 4(1), pp. 54-70.

Frank, T. (1997) *The Conquest of Cool: Business Culture, Counterculture and the Rise of Hip Consumerism*, Chicago: University of Chicago Press.

Foucault, M. (1986) *The History of Sexuality Vol. III: The Care of the Self*, trans. R. Hurley, New York: Vintage Books.

Giddens, A. (1991) *Modernity and Self-Identity: Self and Society in the Late Modern Age*, Stanford: Stanford University Press.

Goldman, R. and S. Papson (1996) *Sign Wars: the Cluttered Landscape of Advertising*, New York: Guilford Press.

Habermas, J. (1991) *The Structural Transformation of the Public Sphere: an Inquiry into a Category of Bourgeois Society*, trans. T. Burger and F. Lawrence, Cambridge, MA: MIT Press.

Hammond, J. (1986) 'Yuppies', *Public Opinion Quarterly,* Vol. 50(4), pp. 487-502.

Harvey, D. (1989) *The Condition of Postmodernity: an Enquiry into the Origins of Cultural Change*, Oxford: Blackwell.

Hodgman, A. (2003) 'Flour Power', *New York Times Magazine,* March 30, p. 32.

Holt, P. (1976) 'Viewing the West as a Book Market', *Publishers Weekly*, September 27, pp. 31-35.

Holt, P. (1977) 'Some New Directions in the Total Mix', *Publishers Weekly,* October 17, pp. 49-51.

Holt, O. (1978) 'The End of "Me-ism" in (Western) America', *Publishers Weekly*, November 18, p. 32.

Jameson, F. (1991) *Postmodernism, or, The Cultural Logic of Late Capitalism*, Durham: Duke University Press.

Kellner, D. (1992) 'Popular Culture and the Construction of Postmodern Identities', in S. Lash and J. Friedman (eds), *Modernity and Identity*, Oxford: Blackwell, pp. 141-177.

Kellner, D. (1995) *Media Culture: Cultural Studies, Identity, and Politics Between the Modern and the Postmodern*, London/New York: Routledge.

Kent Rush, A. (1973) *Getting Clear: Body Work for Women*, New York: Random House.

King, P. (1978) 'Publishers Look West for New Ideas', *Rockford Sunday Magazine,* June 25: B30.

Lash, S. (1990a) *Sociology of Postmodernism*, London: Routledge.

Lash, S. (1990b) 'Discourse or figure? Postmodernism as a "regime of signification"', in *Sociology of Postmodern*, London: Routledge.

Lash, S. and J. Urry (1987) *The End of Organized Capitalism*, Cambridge: Polity Press.

Lash, S. and J. Urry (1993) *Economies of Signs and Space*, London: Sage.

Leach, W. R. (1993) *Land of Desire: Merchants, Power and the Rise of a New American Culture*, New York: Pantheon Books.

Leiss, W., S. Kline and S. Jhally (1986) *Social Communication in Advertising: Persons, Products, and Images of Well-being*, Toronto, New York: Methuen.

Lury, C. (1996) *Consumer Culture*, New Brunswick: Rutgers University Press.

Lyotard, J. (1984) *The Postmodern Condition: a Report on Knowledge*, trans. G. Bennington and B. Massumi, Minneapolis: University of Minnesota Press.

Mirzoeff, N., (ed.) (1998) *Visual Culture Reader*, London, New York: Routledge.

Mirzoeff, N. (1999) *An Introduction to Visual Culture*, London: Routledge.

Mungo, R. (1971) 'Living on the Earth', *New York Times*, March 21: BR 6.

Murray, R. (1989) 'Fordism and Post-Fordism', in S. Hall and M. Jacques (eds) *New Times: the Changing Face of Politics in the 1990s*, London: Lawrence and Wishart.

McRobbie, A. (1998) *British Fashion Design: Rag Trade or Image Industry?* London: Routledge.

Nixon, S. and P. Du Gay (eds) (2002) 'Special Issue: Who Needs Cultural Intermediaries', *Cultural Studies*, Vol. 16(4).

Nixon, S. (2003) *Advertising Cultures: Gender, Commerce, Creativity*, London: Sage.

New York Times (1971) 'Her Hymn to Nature is a Guidebook for the Simplest of Lives', March 26, p. 34.

Pace, E. (1973) 'Publishing is Flowering on Coast', *New York Times*, June 19, p. 30.

Packard, V. (1957) *The Hidden Persuaders*, New York: D. McKay Co.

Publishers Weekly (1971) 'Bookmaking', April 14, pp. 72-3.

Raymont, H. (1972a) 'Juror Quits Book Panel Over "Whole Earth Catalog"', *New York Times*, April 5, p. 35.

Raymont, H. (1972b) 'Notes of Concern Mark Book Award Ceremony', *New York Times*, April 14, p. 21.

Reisman, D., N. Glazer and R. Denney (1950) *The Lonely Crowd: A Study of the Changing American Character*, New Haven: Yale University Press.

Schulman, B. (2001) *The Seventies*, New York: Free Press.

See, L. (1992) 'California Style', *Publishers Weekly*, October 12, pp. 32-34.

Shi, D. (1985) *The Simple Life: Plain Living and High Thinking in American Culture*, New York: Oxford University Press.

Slater, D. (1997) *Consumer Culture and Modernity*, Oxford: Polity Press.

Sontag, S. (1966) *Against Interpretation*, New York: Farrar, Straus and Giroux.

Stephens, M. (1998) *The Rise of the Image, the Fall of the Word*, New York: Oxford University Press.

Stuttaford, G. (1972) 'Northern California's Exploding Book Market', *Publishers Weekly*, October 9, pp. 39-46.

Vidich, A. (ed.) (1995) *The New Middle Classes*, New York: New York University Press.

Warner, W. L., M. Meeker and K. Eells (1949) *Social Class in America: The Evaluation of Status*, New York: Harper Torchbooks.

Welles, A. (1972) 'Steady Expansion in Southern California', *Publishers Weekly*, October 9, pp. 47-54.

Whyte, W. (1956) *The Organization Man*, New York: Simon and Schuster.

Williamson, J. (1978) *Decoding Advertisements: Ideology and Meaning in Advertising*, London: Boyars.

Wouters, C. (1986) 'Formalization and Informalization: Changing Tension Balances in Civilizing Processes', *Theory, Culture and Society,* Vol. 3(2), pp. 1-18.

Chapter 8

Depression and Recovery: Self-Help and America in the 1930s

Sue Currell

> The normal man is an individual who lives in society and whose mode of life is so adapted that ... society derives a certain advantage from his work ... from a psychological point of view he has enough energy and courage to meet the problems and difficulties as come along. (Adler, 1929:103)

> A style of life ... is built up through the striving for a particular goal of superiority. (Adler, 1929:117).

The production and maintenance of a 'normal' style of life, as pointed out by the American psychologist Alfred Adler in 1929, continues as a mainstream pursuit in lifestyle guides to this day. As Adler indicates above, embedded within this striving for 'normality' is another goal that problematizes the first; that is, the goal of also achieving superiority by adjustments in lifestyle. Self-help guides and mass-market success literature proliferated in the twentieth century precisely because they could appeal in this protean way to readers' insecurities and their pride. Yet these books relied on fixed definitions of normality, where the measurement of self-esteem, sanity, and social usefulness appeared possible because of the scientific application of social and psychological statistics that had been generated in the first few decades of the emerging social and psychological sciences.[1] These statistics made it appear possible to categorize and define 'normality' for the first time in history and made vagaries, such as 'keeping ahead of the crowd' and meeting problems with correct amounts of 'energy and courage', appear scientific and measurable. These sentiments and attitudes now appear to hold less meaning with the breakdown of such rigid certainties in post-modern, multicultural, society. Despite this, self-help has continued to thrive.

There are now vast offerings for those who seek lifestyle guidance. In any large bookstore there is an abundance of self-help books devoted to improving relationships, health, fitness, diet, beauty, family, children and fertility. According to these, self-help and self-improvement should begin before conception. Then there are others devoted to mental and educational improvements and accelerated learning techniques; a pseudo-scientific literature that treats the human as an underutilized machine, with titles such as *A User's Guide to the Brain* (Ratey, 2001), *The Owner's Manual to the Brain* (Howard, 2000), *How Intelligent Are*

You? Brain Building in Just 12 Weeks (Serobriakoff, 1970), *Speed Reading* (Buzan, 1984), and *Quantum Learning* (DePorter, 1992). These books offer strategies to 'unlock' the vast potential that appears to be trapped inside the individual. The genre has become so successful in recent years that there is even a how-to guide for how-to guides titled *Writing Successful Self-Help and How-To Books: Strategies for Developing a Bestselling Book* (Strine, 1997), a title which suggests that the true success from success literature is for the bestselling author. In response to the proliferation of success guides the anti-self-help book has also emerged to denounce the crassness of the formula in mirror-image satires of self-help: *How to Lose Friends and Alienate People* (Young, 2001), *Yoga for People who Can't Be Bothered to Do it* (Dyer, 2003), and *How to Be Idle* (Hodgkinson, 2005). Again, the success of these titles relies on a broad understanding and general acceptance of what they pitch themselves against.

Whatever name you give to lifestyle literature – success, self-improvement, self-help, how-to, adjustment, pop-psychology – from its origins it has never been a single genre but a fusion of various styles of instructional literature that have a long history, and yet which taps into the zeitgeist of the generation or group it addresses. With such a welter of old and new philosophies of living it is not easy to trace a lineal history of the self-help manual. It has many histories, despite the fact that such books have made an art of appearing ahistorical, if not universal. At the same time, certain recurrences offer clues to the history and success of success formulas. Such books frequently market the wisdom and veracity of the book upon the authority of the author (only these type of books add Dr or Ph.D. to the author's name) or alternatively employ a media celebrity whose authority on the issue needs no introduction. The book usually continues with an outline of 'the problem,' offers anecdote, science and biography as combined evidence, suggests a programme of progression (often in a recognizable five, seven, or twelve stepped phases) and the promise of a better (if not utopian) future. In short, they offer complete success through a new style of life, made available in a single cheap book.

What is interesting about this is that while the anecdotes and content of the books may have changed, the formula has remained consistent for the past eighty years. As I shall show in the following outline of self-help in the 1930s, there is something reassuringly and disturbingly historical about the persistence of self-help books. Reassuring because aspirations to improve and understand human happiness still underlies the quest for self-transformation, and disturbing because so much of that aspiration is rewarded with recycled ideas and assumptions that are generated out of truisms from unquestioned and unexamined sources. Further, the categories of 'normality' are based on a culturally specific drive for superiority and success that relegates difference to a problem.[2] By looking in more detail at the history of self-help publications this chapter will trace back to the source of some of self-help's truisms and show that, while it is more popular than ever, self-help contributes to a culture of conformity and self-surveillance that is often quite the opposite of the liberating promises touted on book covers.

Self-Help: A Brief History

Since the invention of text there has been a literature of self-improvement and instruction, guides for living written by the wise for the self-betterment of the not-so-wise. From Aristotle, philosophers have examined the nature and pursuit of human happiness. While indebted to a wide history of philosophical musings, the direction that these enquiries have taken in recent times relates specifically to the rise of a new empire that resulted from the colonization of America. To early religious settlers in search of new styles of living, the New World offered the chance to attain spiritual and social perfection. Many went in search of a new life free from tradition and persecution that necessitated developing new styles of living. While colonists brought their own rules for living with them to the New World, new rule books catering to this new lifestyle soon emerged alongside the old.[3]

As literacy rates grew, Americans turned increasingly to books for advice on how to behave and act successfully in new or challenging environments. For those in search of wealth and opportunity, John Cawelti notes, 'The manifest opportunities of a large and relatively empty continent and the openness of a rapidly growing and changing society impressed the idea of self-improvement on the [American] public imagination' (1965: 3). Independence from Europe magnified the possibilities and importance of self-reliance and the formation of new ideals of living that dismantled aristocratic elitism. The revolutionary and liberating possibility of self-making appeared greater in America than anywhere else, an idea that continues to function in the cultural imaginary. American culture and literature was formed on this bedrock of philosophies concerning self-help, self-reliance and the formation of new social structures requiring new social strictures: Thomas Jefferson, Benjamin Franklin, Ralph Waldo Emerson and Henry David Thoreau all contributed to a self-help and self-culture ideal that was uniquely American.[4]

Success literature generated by the changes in Western culture altered again with the period of rapid industrialization in the nineteenth century. Improvement manuals based on Christian ethics were replaced by self-help books that discussed success in terms of the marketplace, influenced by ideas of evolutionary progress based on Darwinian discoveries. Massive waves of immigration from Europe increased the importance of adapting and surviving, of judging the crowd and keeping above it, in a climate of capitalist acceleration and expansion. By the 1880s, religious and moral precepts that had underpinned many conduct and 'how-to' books were being replaced by scientific theories of human potential and self-making based on the new science of experimental psychology. Ideas about how to improve oneself were increasingly influenced by studies in intelligence and personality undertaken in laboratories to establish qualitative definitions.[5] Increasing literacy, print technology and a growing market led to the proliferation of popular philosophies in print. As America industrialized, self-help books became part of widening lifestyle choices as well as a way to deal with the disappointments of options that were closed by the changes.[6] The appearance of psychotherapy in the early twentieth century shifted the nature of these texts again, creating an adjustment literature that proffered help with the stresses and strains associated with the shift to modernity. Following the discovery of psychiatric conditions such as shell-shock in World War One, the goal of self-help consolidated into refitting the 'misfits' and alienated back into contemporary modern society.

With new understandings about the human mind, the management and control of lifestyle assumed a new importance to industry, and shifted again with changes in industrial organization introduced by the industrialist Henry Ford. In his essay 'Americanism and Fordism', written from prison in the early 1930s, Italian philosopher Antonio Gramsci pointed out how a worker's usefulness to the corporate economic order was premised on the utilization or control of his free time. Gramsci observed that inherent to Fordism was the organization of a planned economy whereby 'subaltern' forces, in this case the workers, were manipulated both in and out of work in order to effectively service the planned economy. Although overtly coercive incentives were necessary – either in the form of high wages or threats of unemployment – a vital factor in this planning entailed a psychological, sexual, and social conformity that dominated the workers' leisure time, which appeared to originate with the worker himself in the form of self-control but which in actuality was enacted by the industrial management. Gramsci (1971: 286) claimed that, in America, 'rationalization has determined the need to elaborate a new type of man suited to the new type of work and productive process', and that the concern of industrialists, particularly Ford, with the leisure time behavior of their workers, indicated new forms of regulation over the psycho-social body of the worker.

In particular, Gramsci's essay made explicit the way that sexual mores and 'the enormous diffusion' of psychoanalysis appeared as an expression of 'the increased moral coercion exercised by the apparatus of State and society on single individuals' employed in the pursuit of the rational planned society (p. 280). Even prior to the Depression, 'Americanism and Fordism' envisaged how Ford's example could become national policy at a time of crisis, 'if the private initiative of the industrialist proves insufficient or if a moral crisis breaks out among the working masses which is too profound and too widespread, as might happen as a result of a long and widespread crisis of unemployment.' (p. 304) Such a crisis was manifested in the Great Depression.

Self-Help in the Great Depression

Belief in success and progress through capitalist expansion and a laissez-faire marketplace came under severe strain during the 1930s, and many sought new systems of living that would replace the one that had apparently broken down. Adjusting Americans to new ways of living following this new 'culture shock' became of paramount importance, and the flurry of books on how to do this proliferated.

Many pathologized the problems of the national economy, and depicted economic breakdown in terms of a psychological illness from which the patient sought 'recovery'. To observers, the Depression was a 'sickness' of capitalism, in part caused by the acceleration of technological culture that had outstripped human ability. Social scientists had subscribed to this pessimistic view of human progress since the mid-twenties, and the Depression provided fitting evidence that they had been right all along. Having invented the term 'cultural lag' to describe this phenomenon in 1922, sociologist William Ogburn argued that it was probably America's greatest problem (President's Research Committee on Recent Social Trends, 1933: xiii). Balance between social and technological advancement was of paramount importance for the future survival of America and its people, he argued. Many concurred that fitting humans to their new physical and cultural environment, and equipping them with new abilities and skills, was vital for the future of American civilization:

> Members of a changing society must be prepared to readjust their ideas and their habits of life. They not only must be possessed of certain types of knowledge and skill which were common at the time when they went to school, but they must be trained in such a way as to make them adaptable to new conditions. (p. xviii)

Even Franklin D. Roosevelt (1933) pointed out that the sickness plaguing the economy was a problem of mass psychology. In his first inaugural address to the nation, he famously put it that 'This great Nation will endure as it has endured, will revive and will prosper. So, first of all, let me assert my firm belief that the only thing we have to fear is fear itself – nameless, unreasoning, unjustified terror which paralyzes needed efforts to convert retreat into advance.'

Books and articles that proliferated from the burgeoning 'mental hygiene' movement at this time confirmed the view of the Depression as a problem of mass psychology. For example, Austen Riggs's *Play: Recreation in a Balanced Life,* published in 1935, confirmed and elaborated on Roosevelt's message:

> Both the country as a whole and its citizens suffer from a typical fear neurosis. The disease is called Depression but is not just a matter of dollars, nor of over-production. It is chiefly a psychological disorder, a question of morale, of lost courage, of shaken faith. It must run its course, and there is much suffering entailed, even though the patient, in this case the nation, will surely survive. Months – perhaps years – are consumed in recovery. First there is paralysis – the weak, unfit organizations that flourished in the atmosphere of false prosperity perish. The patient's recovery depends upon remodeling his life, upon rebalancing his time budget as well as his financial budget and upon recasting his values. (Riggs, 1935: 3)

The impact of Freud's psychoanalytic theories on sociological thinking was still fairly new at this time, but the Depression had made the combination a crucial way of understanding what had happened to America. Most books and articles on the need for new lifestyles combined sociological and psychoanalytic theories as a way of explaining the condition of, and thereby curing, the ailing social patient.

Life Begins At Forty

In this context of heightened anxiety and increasing emphasis on the importance of lifestyle habits for the generation of well-being, a bestseller emerged that heralded a new philosophy of life, one that embraced and celebrated the new world prefigured by the disaster of the 1929 Crash. *Life Begins at Forty* offered a path to happiness based on self-cultivation in leisure and adjustment to modernity. The author, Columbia Professor Walter B. Pitkin, reassured the reader that the Depression was merely symptomatic of changes that were leading towards a better lifestyle, one where intelligence and improved social organization would lead to more leisure and self-cultivation; 'Yes, you are the luckiest of all,' he told them (1932a: 5). *Life Begins at Forty* offered advice for a new lifestyle that would fit in with the changes in industrial culture heralded by the Depression. More productive use of leisure would facilitate the end of the nation's most pressing problems of poverty, crime and bad-housing, he argued, as more people would be put into social work, education and welfare (1932a: 143). Like many others at the time, Pitkin argued that the 'New Leisure' of the thirties was a result of scientific improvements and machine-age abundance, and that Americans now needed to adjust their lifestyles to a permanent and effective use of that leisure to create a highly planned, rationalized social and economic order led by the 'keenest' minds (1932a: 159).[7]

Self-help and popular instruction manuals proliferated in the aftermath of the 1929 crash. The books aimed to psychologically adjust people to a new age and functioned as semi-scientific 'proper' leisure reading for the newly unemployed middle-class male. Pitkin was one of the more prolific writers of 'inspirational' or lifestyle literature during the late 1920s and the 1930s, as the following selection of titles shows: *The Twilight of the American Mind* (Pitkin, 1928); *The Art of Rapid Reading: A Book for People Who Want to Read Faster and More Accurately* (Pitkin, 1929); *The Psychology of Achievement* (Pitkin, 1930); *How We Learn: A Book for Young People with Emphasis Upon the Art of Efficient Reading* (Pitkin, 1931); *Life Begins At Forty* (Pitkin, 1932a); *The Consumer: His Nature and His Changing Habits* (Pitkin, 1932b); *A Short Introduction to the History of Human Stupidity* (Pitkin, 1932c); *More Power to You: A Working Technique for Making the Most of Human Energy* (Pitkin, 1933); *The Chance of a Lifetime: Marching Orders for the Lost Generation* (Pitkin, 1934); *Take It Easy: The Art of Relaxation* (Pitkin, 1935a); *Let's Get What We Want: A Primer in a Sadly Neglected Art* (Pitkin, 1935b); *Learning How to Learn* (Pitkin, 1935c); *Capitalism Carries On* (Pitkin, 1935d); and *Escape from Fear* (Pitkin, 1935e). His books, containing notions of cultural improvement, societal improvement, and self-improvement, also spawned an industry of imitators in the popular publishing market, books that also reached the top ten non-fiction bestseller list in the 1930s, such as Edmund Jacobson's *You Must Relax* (1934); Dale Carnegie's *How To Win Friends and Influence People* (1936); Dorothea Brande's *Wake Up and Live!* (1939), Lin Yutang's *The Importance of Living* (1937); and Marjorie Hillis's *Orchids on Your Budget* (1937) and *Live Alone and Like It* (1936). Many of these were bestsellers for several years and some, such as Carnegie's *How to Win Friends and Influence*

People, are still popular and in print (despite being a facsimile of the original, replete with dated examples and language). Such books became bestsellers at a time of concern over social and cultural decline, during a period of fear that the wheels of progress and advancement had come to a halt.

Historians of this literature have commented that the books at this time represent a shift towards a 'pleasure ethic' or an accommodation to unemployment, leisure and reduced incomes (Chenoweth, 1974; Recken, 1993). In many ways, however, the books exhibit the opposite, showing an intensified demand for more efficient use of energies and skills, arguing that 'recovery' was only possible by improving personal efficiency and streamlining oneself for new market conditions. Rather than relaxing and kicking back, then, the reader was to become more efficient at using their energies and their new-found leisure-time to become more productive citizens through leisure rather than work. Moreover, the writers directly connected the adjustments in lifestyles and habits to the recovery of the national economy.

Self-help books persistently indicated that, like the economy, the individual was not operating efficiently enough and that this was affecting his or her ability to succeed in the modern world. For example, in 1936 Columbia educator James Mursell argued that 'you, the average man of today', impresses most on the psychologist 'Your toleration in yourself of needless personal inefficiency in an age which requires efficiency'. 'Streamline Your Mind', his book commanded (1936: 9).[8]

The notion that you could channel mental energies for 'recovery' that would lead to economic security was expanded by success writer Napoleon Hill (1937), who argued that you could 'Think and Grow Rich', by controlling the way that the mind dealt with fear and thoughts of failure. Just as Roosevelt had attempted to revive confidence in the American market by suggesting that fear would hamper recovery, Hill's book suggested that fear and lack of persistence could be overcome by methods to control the subconscious will and the libido, using auto-suggestion and positive thinking. Not only was the reader promised success in this way, but, he argued, the system would lead to vast personal wealth. The book was (and still is) a hugely popular bestseller.

Like Pitkin, Hill wrote that the Depression was a blessing in disguise that gave everyone a 'new opportunity', and that capacity to transform tended to increase rather than decrease at forty (1937: 311, 281). These theories of rationalization and control over impulse and emotion offered an antidote to the weaknesses often revealed by psychoanalysis, and combined a bastardized Freudianism with New Thought and the popular philosophic theories of pragmatism, which demanded rigorous application of intellect over emotion and rationalization over impulse.[9] Various related systems to combat these common weaknesses and failures were promoted in Britain and America at this time, such as the 'New, Improved System – "Personology"' that was promised in the *Picture Post* in 1938 (Anon., 1938: 64).

Streamlining the self for the market and marketing techniques to enhance personal success became a popular antidote to the Depression in the thirties. Pitkin argued for self-adjustment and recovery through self-analysis, commanding

Americans to remarket themselves as a business proposition: 'You should begin by analyzing yourself as a human product in the market for a buyer ready to pay a right price for the proper commodity ... Do try to sell yourselves as a better product' (Pitkin, 1938). In *Life Begins at Forty* he celebrated this streamlining of the self as a future prospect: 'You will remodel your frames and your temperaments with cunningly concocted foods and pills' (1932a: 5). This remodeling was about more than streamlining or improving individuals: Pitkin argued for a total reorganization of the capitalist system that would put an end to the chaos of uncontrolled human development, where improvements in education and intelligence via personal engineering would result in 'a new class society where the skilled and the experienced tinker with the clumsy, the young, the senile, the malicious and the pathological precisely as mechanics now tinker with automobiles' (Pitkin 1935d: 108). The new division of labour that Pitkin proposed involved fewer people working fewer hours in jobs tailored to their personality, gender, age and education. Offering a model of 'recovery' that was both political and personal, Pitkin's books proposed a new social order where 'downtrodden' Americans could reassert their 'natural' vigour and authority over their mental and social inferiors and take the lead again. Offering the chance to see the fantastical as normal in his chapter titled 'The New World,' he wrote that

> Between now and 1975, superior people will grow steadily less and less
> dependent upon low-grade workers. Drudgery disappears from farm and
> field, from mill and factory, from school and home. Super-power wipes
> out most of it; the rest will soon be erased by scientific organizing, by
> teamwork, and by inventions. Already we begin to drive out the stupid,
> the unskilled, and the misplaced alien, not with whips and scorn but
> through the kindlier method of firing him for keeps (Pitkin, 1932a:140).

To Pitkin, the outcome of his programme was the ascendancy of an elite who lived rationally and without want. Those who failed to keep up, who hampered or lagged behind these developments, were expelled to foreign territories outside of the US and left to fend for themselves. Pitkin's success in selling this formula made him a household name in the 1930s, with frequent appearances and commentary in popular magazines and several popular radio shows.

The Globalization of American Self-Help

The appearance of such self-help literature during the Depression is perhaps unsurprising to us in an era of what sociologist Frank Furedi (2004) has called 'therapy culture'. Clearly the Great Depression was a time of severe stress and anxiety for many, and it would be easy to dismiss the phenomenon as historically and culturally specific and irrelevant to our own times. Yet these books symbolize the emergence and dominance of a cultural phenomenon that in many ways characterizes the twentieth century: the emergence of a dominant new philosophy in the West, based less on the precepts of mainstream Christianity and the protestant work ethic, than the new philosophy of 'tailored' or 'Taylored' lifestyles, that function to sustain new economic markets. To Furedi, the increasing dominance of therapy culture also indicates the emergence of a culture of increased social control and conformity, a breakdown of community along with increasing political domination of the private sphere.

While it is easy to dismiss the popularity of self-help literature as a cheap psychological prop during hard times, its function in relation to economic and social changes and its continuing longevity makes it more significant than may first appear. When the Depression went away the ideas and the popularity of pop-psychology remained and grew; the phrase 'Life Begins at Forty' quickly gained global currency despite the fact that the originator of the book was soon forgotten. The phrase has worldwide common usage in many languages. Few in the West have not heard it used and recycled in a variety of formats. Within a year of publication the book became a bestseller and the phrase became a household catchphrase. By 1935, the spin surrounding the phrase had led to a popular song recorded by 'Red Hot Mama' Sophie Tucker, and a Hollywood comedy starring Will Rogers. In 1942, Twentieth Century Fox released *Life Begins at Eight-Thirty*. 1959 saw the release of Ronnie Diamond's song 'Life Begins at 4 O'Clock'. In 1965, *Life Begins at Fifty* appeared, written by Walter Pitkin's son, Walter Pitkin Jr. *New Life Begins at Forty*, written by Ron Peterson, emerged in 1967. In 1978, *Life Begins at Forty* became a long-running British television comedy series. John Lennon wrote a song with the title shortly before he died. The catchphrase currently appears as the title of a novel by Dimitru Crac and an album by the band Lemonhead. It reappears in a variety of journalistic reports and advertising spinoffs: self-help websites introduce men's health products with 'Life begins at 40. Well, so they say'; 'Life begins at 33.8' for graduating Ph.D.s; 'Life begins at 60' or any other age that is appropriate to the article; 'Life Begins at 240 mph' for the *Yankee Lady Corvette Gazette*; and *Life Begins at 80* for Eric Shackle in his recent ebook. The phrase spins off into the comic 'Life Begins at Death', or the serious 'Life begins at Conception' (for pro-life campaigners).

The term has come to signify a juncture in life, the possibility of self-transformation, survival against the odds, and the chance to shake off old habits and to begin again. The phrase, in many ways, summarizes a twentieth-century optimist philosophy that replaced religious belief in an afterlife, signifying that life can be better on Earth through changes made to the physical and psychological self. On the other hand, the internationalization of the phrase also hints at the global dominance of American-style philosophies that emerged during its period of industrialization whereby the promotion of the 'American way of life' became part of the drive to dominate the global marketplace. Ironically, this emerged most forcefully when the very foundations of that system appeared under greatest strain.

American-style self-help can now be found far beyond the boundaries of the United States. The usefulness of self-help to the global economy in creating workers whose lifestyles and habits become those from which 'society derives a certain advantage' continues to be illustrated by the increasing adoption of American self-help manuals by those outside of the West. Since the growth of IT industries in India, for example, the *Hindustan Times* notes that self-help and motivational literature has undergone a boom period. Commenting that there is 'a marked preference for books written by foreign authors' such as Dale Carnegie or Napoleon Hill (both originally published in the 1930s), 'the prospects for self-help books never looked brighter' ('Young Professionals go Gaga over Self-Help', 2004.) This globalization of self-help indicates how the formation of lifestyle philosophies continues to underpin American economic dominance, confirming Gramsci's point that a sudden diffusion of psychoanalysis is driven by the demand for psychological conformity to changing economic systems, even in a post-Fordist, global economy.

Despite this, self-help has been relegated as trashy ephemera unworthy of consideration, a neglect that has severed the connection to past traditions in American utopian thought and political philosophy. The popularity of self-help books is sustained by an apparently apolitical, ahistorical neutrality, seeming to appear subconsciously to fill the gaps left by misdirected political and social policies that have isolated individuals from one another and created feelings of helplessness and inadequacy. Reading self-help is seen as private act of building self-esteem in a complex world of struggle and disappointment, and not as something connected to wider social and political developments. Yet the business of self-help is more Manichean, less responsive to than symptomatic of the changes in modern structures of existence. For one thing, self-help is a consciously marketed programme of mass publishing aimed at increasing the mass consumption of books. Self-improvement literature operates as a huge self-generating business, creating a protean product for a mass market that always needs new formulas and can always find new problems – or rehash the old. In the 1930s, however, Walter Pitkin became the 'high priest of this new literary science', a savvy pulp writer employed in the 'Word Business', as he called it (Barzini, 1977:151; Pitkin, 1944: 170).

With the market primed, self-help transformed alongside further developments in psychology. The popularization of therapy and Freudian theory came to transplant the rationalization demanded by pragmatism, Taylorism and Fordism. Despite these changes what remained was the appeal of self-transformation, where the metamorphosis of the mind and body has become an even stronger obsession in the early part of the twenty-first century, where the personal drive to self-improve, streamline and transform is manifested in the mass-market publishing phenomenon of self-help and lifestyle guides. In most large bookshops the vast shelf space now taken over by self-help and self-improvement literature is testament to the fact that many still believe that life can begin again at any age, that we can renew our minds and bodies, and that through this autogenesis we will become happy. Despite over a century of diets, training, body conditioning and life coaching, formulas for success still do not saturate the market. In fact, each new formula for living renews the quest for self-renewal and revives the optimist drive for happy living. Each year life can begin again, and again, and again. The formula is a mass-marketing dream: the more that are published, the more people want to buy.

Seventy years after the bestsellers by Pitkin, Hill and Carnegie were written, self-help literature continues to peddle the idea of achieving normality based on lifestyle choices that have been generated in the context of an imperializing and global American marketplace, where a culturally and historically specific 'normality' may be achieved through changed styles of life. In fact, technological changes have expanded this already popular market for adjustment and survival, and websites continue the tradition of offering self-improvement through software designed to train you to be smarter, happier and more intelligent. Self-help books vastly outsell volumes of poetry, and fifty years after Pitkin's death the streamlined ideal is manifested in commonplace techniques of body morphing such as plastic surgery, obsessive dieting and exercise. Additionally, accelerated learning techniques demand a greater speed up than ever with the arrival of the computer and Internet (see, for example, http://www.selfgrowth.com). Creating individuals who can perform well in this global marketplace may not be the obvious or explicit aim of such self-help books and advice, but as individuals increasingly turn to American-style therapeutic cures containing such historically-specific ideas of 'normality' and lifestyle, it is useful to consider how these books have functioned in the past, how they may indicate limits to, rather than improvements in human happiness, and what may happen as newly industrialized societies experience the uncertainties and economic disruptions of American capital.

Notes

1   For a discussion of this, see Coon (1993: 761). For a history of experimental psychology, see Boring (1957). The history of psychological testing, the creation of IQ, and the use of statistics to create the 'normal' or 'average' person is discussed in Blum (1978) and, for further discussion of related issues, see also Gould (1981). For a study of Francis Galton and the development of the science of statistics, see Mackenzie (1981) and Sokal (1990).

2   In this chapter I do not have space to address important issues of difference, especially that concerning the gendering of self-help literature, or its contemporary reception. For discussions of this aspect of self-help, see DeFranscisco (1995: 107-10), Ebben (1995), Gauntlett (2002) and Rapping (1996).

3   For a history of conduct books and advice manuals in America, see Newton (1994) and Schlesinger (1947); see also Anker (1980).

4   For a discussion of these changes and developments in American success literature, see Cawelti (1965), Chenoweth (1974), Huber (1971), Rischin (1965) and Weiss (1969).

5   See, for example, Allport and Allport (1921). These studies ushered in an era of popular self-evaluation in the form of magazine personality tests.

6   Because of the space available in this chapter, I have not addressed the complex transatlantic crossings in self-help traditions. For example, Emerson's philosophies were popularized by William Ellery Channing, who influenced the British author Samuel Smiles to write *Self-Help* in 1859, and whose work was consequently popularized back in America and influenced another generation of self-help writers in the late nineteenth century. For a brief discussion of this, see Jarvis (1997), Richards (1982) and Tyrrell (1970). I also have not addressed here the tradition of self-help or self-culture ideal by working men in the nineteenth century, as manifested in mutual societies and working men's clubs. These tended to be financial groups that offered insurance against the vicissitudes of the capitalist market, though did encompass

education for improvement. For a discussion of these, see Gosden (1973) and Hopkins (1995).

7   For further discussion of the new leisure of the Great Depression, see Currell (2005).

8   For a history of the scientific management movement, see Haber (1964).

9   Cawelti discusses the influence of John Dewey's pragmatist philosophy on the re-evaluation of success and democracy in the period in chapter eight of *Apostles of the Self-Made Man*. Pitkin was undoubtedly influenced by Dewey's ideas concerning a scientifically organized rational community that could direct human energies in to the benefit of society as a whole. For a discussion of Dewey and his ideas of self-making and community, see Cawelti (1965: 245).

References

Adler, A. (1929) *The Science of Living*, New York: Garden City Publishing Company.

Allport F.H. and G.W. Allport (1921) 'Personality Traits: Their Classification and Measurement', *Journal of Abnormal and Social Psychology*, Vol. 16, pp. 6-40.

Anker, R. (1980) 'Popular Religion and Theories of Self-Help' in T.M. Inge (ed.) *Handbook of American Popular Culture*, Westport, CT: Greenwood.

Anon. (1938) '7 Weeks to Conquer the Weaknesses that are Holding You Back From Success', *Picture Post*, December 31, p. 64

Barzini, L. (1977/1985) *O America, When You and I Were Young*, New York: Penguin Books.

Blum, J. M. (1978) *Pseudoscience and Mental Ability: The Origins and Fallacies of the IQ Controversy*, New York: Monthly Review Press.

Boring, E. G. (1957) *A History of Experimental Psychology*, 2nd edition, New York: Appleton, Century, Crofts.

Brande, D. (1939) *Wake Up and Live!* New York: Pocket Books.

Buzan, T. (1984) *Speed Reading*, New York: E.P. Dutton.

Carnegie, D. (1936) *How to Win Friends and Influence People*, New York: Simon and Schuster.

Cawelti, J. (1965) *Apostles of the Self-Made Man*, Chicago : University of Chicago Press.

Chenoweth, L. (1974) *The American Dream of Success: The Search for the Self in the 20th Century*, North Scituate, MA : Duxbury.

Coon, D. (1993) 'Standardizing the Subject: Experimental Psychologists, Introspection, and the Quest for a Technoscientific Ideal', *Technology and Culture*, vol. 34(4), pp. 757-83.

Currell, S. (2005) *The March of Spare Time: The Problem and Promise of Leisure in the Great Depression*, Philadelphia: University of Pennsylvania Press.

DeFranscisco, V. (1995) 'Helping Ourselves: An Introduction', *Women's Studies in Communication*, vol. 18, pp. 107-10.

DePorter, B (1992) *Quantum Learning: Unleashing the Genius in You*, New York: Dell.

Dyer, G. (2003) *Yoga for People Who Can't be Bothered to Do It*, New York: Pantheon.

Ebben, M. (1995) 'Off the Shelf Salvation: A Feminist Critique of Self-Help', *Women's Studies in Communication*, vol. 18, pp. 111-122.

Furedi, F. (2004) *Therapy Culture: Cultivating Vulnerability in an Uncertain Age*, London: Routledge.

Gauntlett, D. (2002) *Media, Gender and Identity: An Introduction*, London: Routledge.

Gosden, J.H. (1973) *Self-Help: Voluntary Associations in the Nineteenth Century*, London: B. T. Batsford.

Gould, S. J. (1981) *The Mismeasure of Man*, London: Penguin.

Gramsci, A. (1971) Americanism and Fordism, in Q. Hoare (ed. and trans.) *Selections From the Prison Notebooks*, London: Lawrence and Wishart.

Haber, S. (1964) *Efficiency and Uplift: Scientific Management in the Progressive Era, 1890-1920*, Chicago: University of Chicago Press.

Hill, N. (1937) *Think and Grow Rich*, Cleveland, OH.: The Ralston Publishing Company.

Hillis, M. (1936) *Live Alone and Like It*, New York: The Bobbs-Merrill Company.

Hillis, M. (1937) *Orchids on Your Budget*, New York: The Bobbs-Merrill Company.

Hodgkinson, T. (2005) *How To Be Idle*, New York: HarperCollins.

Hopkins, E. (1995) *Working-Class Self-Help in Nineteenth Century England*, London: University College London Press.

Howard, P.J. (2000) *The Owner's Manual for the Brain: Everyday Applications from Mind-Brain Research*, Austin, TX: Bard Press.

Huber, R. (1971). *The American Idea of Success*, New York: McGraw-Hill.

Jacobson, E. (1934) *You Must Relax*, New York: McGraw-Hill.

Jarvis, A. (1997) *Samuel Smiles and the Construction of Victorian Values*, Stroud: Sutton Publishing.

Mackenzie, D.A. (1981) *Statistics in Great Britain*, Edinburgh: Edinburgh University Press.

Mursell, J.L. (1936) *Streamline Your Mind*, Philadelphia: J.B. Lippincott Company.

Newton, S.E. (1994) *Learning to Behave: A Guide to American Conduct Books Before 1900*, Westport, CT: Greenwood Press.

Peterson, R. (1967) *New Life Begins at Forty*, New York: Trident Press.

Pitkin, W. B. (1928) *The Twilight of the American Mind*, New York: Simon and Schuster.

Pitkin, W.B. (1929) *The Art of Rapid Reading: a Book for People who Want to Read Faster and More Accurately*, New York: McGraw-Hill.

Pitkin, W.B. (1930) *The Psychology of Achievement*, New York: Simon and Schuster.

Pitkin, W.B. (1931) *How We Learn: A Book for Young People with Emphasis on the Art of Efficient Reading*, New York: McGraw-Hill.

Pitkin, W.B. (1932a) *Life Begins at Forty*, New York: McGraw-Hill.

Pitkin, W.B. (1932b) *The Consumer: His Nature and His Changing Habits*, New York: McGraw-Hill.

Pitkin, W.B. (1932c) *A Short Introduction to the History of Human Stupidity*, New York: Simon and Schuster.

Pitkin, W.B. (1933) *More Power to You: A Working Technique for Making the Most of Human Energy*, New York: Simon and Schuster.

Pitkin, W.B. (1934) *The Chance of a Lifetime: Marching Orders for the Lost Generation*, New York: Simon and Schuster.

Pitkin, W.B. (1935a) *Take it Easy: the Art of Relaxation*, New York: Simon and Schuster.

Pitkin, W.B. (1935b) *Let's Get What We Want: a Primer in a Sadly Neglected Art*, New York: Simon and Schuster.

Pitkin, W.B. (1935c) *Learning How to Learn*, New York: McGraw-Hill.

Pitkin, W.B. (1935d) *Capitalism Carries On*, New York: McGraw-Hill.

Pitkin, W.B. (1935e) *Escape From Fear*, New York: Doubleday, Doran and Co.

Pitkin, W.B. (1938) 'After-Forty Chances', *Literary Digest*, Vol. 125.

Pitkin, W.B. (1944) *On My Own*, New York: Charles Scribner's.

Pitkin W. Jr, (1965) *Life Begins at Fifty*, New York: Simon and Schuster.

Presidents Research Committee on Social Trends. (1933) *Recent Social Trends in the United States: Report of the President's Research Committee on Social Trends, Vol.1*, New York: McGraw-Hill.

Rapping, E. (1996) *The Culture of Recovery: Making Sense of the Self-Help Movement in Women's Lives*, Boston: Beacon Press.

Ratey, J. (2001) *A User's Guide to the Brain: Perception, Attention, and the Four Theaters of the Brain*, New York: Vintage.

Recken, S. (1993) 'Fitting In: The Redefinition of Success in the 1930s', *Journal of Popular Culture*, vol. 27, pp. 205-22.

Richards, J. (1982) 'Spreading the Gospel of Self-Help: G.A. Henty and Samuel Smiles', *Journal of Popular Culture*, vol. 16, pp. 52-65.

Riggs, A. F. (1935) *Play: Recreation in a Balanced Life*, New York: Doubleday, Doran & Co.

Rischin, M. (1965) *The American Gospel of Success*, Chicago : Quadrangle Books.

Roosevelt, F. D. (1933) First Inaugural Address, March 4 1933, http://feri.org/archives/speeches

Schlesinger, A.M. (1947) *Learning How to Behave: A Historical Study of American Etiquette Books*, New York: The Macmillan Company.

Serobriakoff, V. (1970) *How Intelligent Are You?*, London: New English Library.

Simmonds, W. (1992) *Women and Self-Help Culture: Reading Between the Lines*, Brunswick, NJ: Rutgers University Press.

Simmonds, W. (1996) 'All Consuming Selves: Self-Help Literature and Women's Identities', in D. Grodin and T. Lindlof (eds) *Constructing the Self in the Mediated World*, London: Sage.

Sokal, M.M. (1990) 'James McKeen Cattell and Mental Anthropometry: Nineteenth-Century Science and Reform and The Origins of Psychological Testing', in M.M. Sokal (ed.), *Psychological Testing and American Society 1890-1930*, New Brunswick, NJ: Rutgers University Press.

Stine, J. (1997) *Writing Successful Self-Help and How-to Books*, New York: Wiley.

Tyrrell, A. (1970) 'Class Consciousness in Early Victorian Britain: Samuel Smiles, Leeds Politics and the Self-Help Creed', *Journal of British Studies*, vol. 9, p. 102-25.

Weiss, R. (1969) *The American Myth of Success*, New York: Basic Books.

'Young Professionals go Gaga over Self-Help', *HindustanTimes.com* (August 25, 2004), online at http://hindustanitimes.com

Young, T. (2001) *How To Lose Friends and Alienate People*, London: Little, Brown.

Yutang, L. (1937) *The Importance of Living*, New York: John Day.

Chapter 9

Pushing Pneus: Michelin's Advertising of Lifestyle in Pre-World War I France

Stephen L. Harp

For much of the twentieth century, commentators and historians portrayed France and much of Europe as 'backward' or 'behind' American economic development. Particularly in the world of advertising, the United States has been held up as a model for the French, both by inter-war advertisers and more recently by historians (Chessel, 1998; de Grazia, 1989). This chapter is a case study designed to qualify such generalizations. By focusing on the Michelin tyre company's attempts to create demand for its products in the Belle Epoque, this chapter offers an alternative view. Instead of assuming a linear development of advertising, in which the Americans advanced and the French followed, we need to recognize that the creation of lifestyle-oriented advertising, held up as one of the most important innovations in American advertising by the 1920s, may not have originated in the United States.

In his pathbreaking study of inter-war American advertising, Roland Marchand (1985) maintained that the primary innovation of the 1920s was above all the focus on selling lifestyles rather than products. Whereas nineteenth-century postcards and posters featured either products, the factories where they were produced, or pictures of the manufacturers, in the 1920s the ever-larger advertising firms sold lifestyles rather than products. Increasingly, advertisements were informing viewers how they would be seen and what their new identities might be, rather than laying out the virtues of the product itself. French advertising agencies, well aware of American norms, are supposed to have increasingly adopted this form of advertising in the inter-war years (Chessel, 1998).

The problem is that such an approach basically neglects pre-World War I poster art as it emerged in France. Beginning in the late 1860s, Jules Chéret created boldly coloured poster advertising a product or a business. By the 1880s, posters, though advertisements, were recognized as a legitimate art form in France, as witnessed by the admission of Chéret's work at the Universal Exposition of 1889 and the government's award of the Légion d'honneur to Chéret (Weill, 1985: 24-28). In the 1890s, he pioneered the beautiful, vibrantly coloured posters generally associated with poster art in turn-of-the-century France, for which Henri de Toulouse-Lautrec and, to a lesser extent, Edouard Manet are sometimes known (p. 31-53). Although newspapers continued to consume the largest chunk of advertising expenditure in France, posters became increasingly important, particularly within large cities and especially in Paris (Levin 1993: 82-108; Martin 1992: 109-20). Moreover, posters were short on words and long on images. They portrayed lifestyles as much as they did products, sending messages about what consuming a certain product or service might promise. The Folies Bergères and the Moulin Rouge posters, while promoting the nightclubs, promised a veritable way of life; men could reinforce their class and gender identities by watching poorer, scantily-clad women perform. Michelin posters, while offering tyres, also offered women and reaffirmation of social class for wealthy white men. Postcards, seemingly taking a cue from posters, similarly offered up lifestyles over products.

This chapter will focus on poster and other representations of Bibendum (the Michelin Man) as he revealed and generally reinforced gender, racial, and class hierarchies in early twentieth-century France. While like those of any cultural artifact, representations of him can be extremely ambiguous and even contradictory, but a few features remained almost entirely consistent. Bibendum was a white, upper-class, French man, often a veritable man about town [*mondain*], who could advise and dominate fellow men, 'conquer' women, and control racial inferiors. He embodied, in several important respects, strong assumptions in pre-war France about what well-off men should be. He offered a 'lifestyle' that every man should want, a 'lifestyle' that every man who could afford Michelin tyres might have.

André Michelin (the older brother charged with advertising, while Edouard ran the firm in Clermont-Ferrand) contracted Marius Rossillon, who signed his name O'Galop, to draw a poster that became the first representation of Bibendum in 1898. Both the company and popular historians have told and retold the history of this poster. As the legend goes, in 1894, the two Michelin brothers attended the Universal and Colonial Exposition in Lyon. At the Michelin booth, an employee had stacked two tall piles of tyres at the entry. Edouard is reputed to have said to his older brother André that one pile looked like a man. In early 1898, André met with O'Galop, who showed André some of his work. André was quite interested in one design that O'Galop had originally done for a brewery in Munich. It featured a large man who was supposed to be Gambrinus, the legendary king who invented brewing. The large king held a beer stein while announcing that '*Nunc est bibendum*', ('now it is time to drink' in Latin). The expression was one that the epicurean Horace had placed in the words of Marc Antony during the battle of Actium, in 31 B.C. André, remembering his brother's comment about the man made of tyres and himself long accustomed to referring to how the pneumatic tyre could swallow (*avaler*) or drink (*boire*) the obstacle (*l'obstacle*), had O'Galop redraw the poster to substitute the man of tyres for Gambrinus. The man did not, however, have a name. In July of 1898, at the time of the Paris-Amsterdam-Paris race, the driver Léon Théry, who did not know Latin, yelled to André, 'voilà Bibendum, vive Bibendum' thus equating the man in the poster not only with André, but naming the man of tyres in the poster 'Bibendum' ('Samedi de Michelin', 1920: back cover; Arren, 1914: 298-300; Darmon, 1997: 22-23; Lottman, 1998: 63-68; Miquel, 1962: 379).

O'Galop's poster itself tells us much about the marketing of tyres in turn-of-the-century France and about the social divisions within France. First, Bibendum's size is remarkable; he is bigger, much bigger than his competing tyre men Continental and

Dunlop. Obviously, he still has air in his tyres whereas his competitors have developed small holes, leading to their deflated, flaccid state. It is important to keep in mind that at the time weight was a sign of wealth, and French newspapers also carried legions of advertisements for various potions men could take to become larger, both in the sense of muscular development but also in terms of overall size. We should not anachronistically project the current preoccupation with flat stomachs into turn-of-the-century France. Thus, Bibendum represents upper social strata and upper-middle-class men in particular, the only people wealthy enough to buy both abundant rich food and automobile tyres. It goes without saying that Bibendum appears as a man dominating other men, and not as a woman.

Bibendum originates from the aristocracy or upper-middle class. The pince-nez is an obvious sign, as are the rings on his fingers and his overall size. Most telling, however, is the glass of champagne. At a time when middle-class reformers worked to promote temperance among the working classes, champagne was becoming an ever more important symbol of status among middle classes who associated the drink with the aristocracy and bourgeoisie (Guy, 1999: 211-39). Bibendum is not drinking red wine, itself a symbol of France but available to all classes in some form, though the spilled glass on the right indicates that perhaps the head of Continental to his left had been drinking red wine. As interesting are the contents of Bibendum's glass, which are shards of glass and nails in this first poster, though horseshoes with the nails still attached are featured in later editions of the poster. These are the pieces of glass and nails quite prevalent on French roads, harmless for horse-drawn traffic, but perilous for cyclists and particularly automobilists, given the speed of the latter. At any rate, the nails and glass are termed 'obstacles', supposedly because André Michelin had earlier noted how well Michelin pneumatic tyres could '*boit l'obstacle* [drink the obstacle]' (Darmon, 1997: 22-23). But André Michelin was not alone. The importance of surmounting 'obstacles' of the road is a constant theme in the *Revue du Touring Club de France*, the forceful non-profit advocate for the bicycle and then the automobile. Use of the term 'obstacle' reinforced a link between automobiles and horses, but of elite horsemanship in particular. 'Obstacle' was and is the word used in the French steeplechase. The '*course d'obstacles*' consisted of the hedges, barriers, and pools of water over which showmen of horses needed to jump. The aristocratic connotations are obvious. Of course, hierarchies of class involve differentiation as part of identity. André Michelin's account of the naming of Bibendum is here telling because it points out the social differentiation between many car owners and race drivers; it was because Théry did not know Latin, that learned language of the educated bourgeoisie, that he considered Bibendum the name of the man rather than understanding its accurate Latin meaning.

Later adornments gave Bibendum a certain social standing. Although in the first poster of 1898 Bibendum had not yet acquired his cigar – that ultimate symbol of the well-off man in early twentieth-century France – O'Galop added one to Bibendum's hand in later re-editions of the poster. In fact, through the 1920s, the vast majority of portrayals of Bibendum included a cigar. As is so often the case, a symbol of class cannot always be separated from one of gender; the cigar simultaneously reinforced Bibendum's masculine image at a time when only the 'New Woman' smoked, and when she – like George Sand back in the 1840s – was berated for such masculine behaviour. Moreover, Bibendum's occasional appearance in a fur coat placed him squarely among France's wealthy.

Michelin also worked to associate the company and Bibendum with royalty and the international aristocracy. Given the appeal of many royal and aristocratic trappings for wealthy bourgeois in nineteenth-century Europe, the strategy is not surprising, though it does reflect Michelin's assumptions about the desires of its potential clients. Michelin regularly made the claim that the company produced the highest quality tyres in Europe, playing on the French bourgeoisie's association of early French industrial goods with artisanal *articles de luxe*. Before World War I, even the automotive and tyre industries were organized as large combinations of smaller workshops, so the claim of 'artisanal production' was not farfetched. In one poster done by O'Galop for the British subsidiary in 1905, 'Sir Bibendum' holds a jousting stick topped with a glass of champagne filled with 'obstacles' in one hand. In the other he holds a shield, which features his four symbols: a glass of champagne with 'obstacles', his pince-nez, cigars, and the cross-section of a tyre pressured but not punctured by a nail. The caption, a paraphrase from Tennyson, read 'My strength is as the strength of ten/ Because my *rubber*'s pure ["rubber" emphasized with blue rather than red print in the original]' (Poster Collection, Michelin archives; Darmon, 1997: 40).

The company also frequently pointed out in 'Lundis', brochures, and on postcards that 'the Michelin tyre is not only the king of tyres, it is also the tyre of kings'. Like Louis XIV, Michelin proclaimed that there were no longer any Pyrenees when the Spanish king bought Michelin tyres ('Le Lundi de Michelin', 1905a: 7) and that even the German emperor had bought a set of Michelins ('Le Lundi de Michelin', 1905b: 8). One brochure featured a picture of King Edward VII in his car and reminded the reader that the kings of Britain, Belgium, and Italy, as well as the Czar, equipped their cars with Michelin tyres (Michelin, 1904: 27). Even the nobility, notably the French automobile manufacturer the Marquis de Dion, as well as the Russian Prince Wladimir Orloff, used Michelin tyres ('Lundi de Michelin', 1912: 5). Buying Michelin tyres, whose slightly higher prices reinforced an image of quality, could confer status.

As historians have recently begun to focus on class not as a strictly social category in the Marxist sense but as a cultural category, we have increasingly considered class through the eyes of the people who made class distinctions to describe the society in which they lived (Kocka, 1995: 783-806; Bonnell and Hunt, 1999: introduction). Companies participated in the process. On the one hand, it was obvious to all that only the wealthy could afford an automobile in pre-war France, and Michelin clearly wanted to capture that lucrative market. By appealing to bourgeois who could afford to buy tyres with advertising that appealed to their sensibilities, and thus set them apart from their social inferiors, Michelin might sell them tyres. Like other products, Michelin tyres could help to establish or confirm social identity. On the other hand, as was clear in so many of the company's actions as well as its pronouncements, Michelin wanted above all to increase the eventual market in tyres, hence the advertisements devoted to cyclists, who not only bought tyres in the short term but were also likely users of the automobile in the longer term. Here too, however, distinctions made between social groups in pre-war France could be useful for sales. As long as the middle and eventually the lower middle classes were not actually insulted, these groups could, by buying Michelin tyres for their automobiles or even their bicycles, attain the much-vaunted 'quality' of a 'French product', a preoccupation among nineteenth-century bourgeois consumers in France that Michelin brilliantly exploited (Walton, 1992; Auslander, 1996).

The presentation of Bibendum was not, however, the only way that one might use images of class difference in order to sell a product. 'Nectar' (as in the nectar of the fruit of the grape), the icon that wine distributor Nicolas began to use in 1922, provides a startling contrast, showing not a different notion of class but a different way of reinforcing class difference. The Nicolas business, which had expanded rapidly in the nineteenth and early twentieth centuries, consisted of opening shops where fine wines might be bought, thus avoiding the buyers' need to work directly with vintners at a time of growing wine consumption. One of the primary advantages of buying wine at Nicolas was that the distributor then delivered the purchases. Nectar, who was supposedly modelled after an actual Nicolas employee by the artist Dransy, embodied the wine deliverer. He generally carried more than a dozen bottles in each hand, sometimes white wines in one hand, red in the other. Whereas Bibendum was young, strong, and healthy with a chest shaped like a barrel, Nectar was older, seemed overburdened, and had a narrow chest. Whereas Bibendum was pure white, Nectar – who much more closely resembled an actual man – wore the typical blue of a working-class man. Both men drank heavily. But whereas Bibendum, with his constant thirst, suffered no ill-effects, Nectar had a red face with a large red nose (Weill, 1986). In buying Michelin tyres, one might fashion oneself as a strong, rich, bourgeois superman of sorts, resembling Bibendum; in buying wine chez Nicolas, one might assert superiority differently, contrasting one's own privileged position with that of the lowly deliverer. In both cases, class was clearly operative within the marketing strategy, but it worked in very different ways. Both figures, nevertheless, reinforced the notion that there were real differences between the classes in the minds of contemporaries, even though an absolutely accurate recreation of those social categories has proven so elusive for historians.

Bibendum was not only well-off; he was a well-off Frenchman. Perhaps the least obvious quality in O'Galop's first poster is Bibendum's nationality. In the poster, Bibendum is holding a glass of champagne, a product assumed in France to be exclusive to France. The stein of beer in O'Galop's original design would no doubt have seemed inappropriate for a French audience. Bibendum is above all French, whereas his primary competitors in the sales of pneumatic (as opposed to solid rubber) tyres were Dunlop and Continental. On the left of the poster is a caricature of Harvey du Cros, head of Dunlop (called 'pneu y' in later editions) and on the right a caricature of the head of Continental, 'pneu x'. Upon close inspection, the 'x' looks remarkably like a German iron cross. Although in various national markets Bibendum later found himself transformed into an Englishman, a German, an Italian, and so on, he was primarily French.

Later pre-war appearances of Bibendum confirmed his nationality and tightened the link between Bibendum and France. Often referred to as *'notre Bibendum national* [our national Bibendum]', Bibendum could drink all of his competitors under the table. In one newspaper advertisement, Bibendum drank his glass of obstacles, winning the Gordon-Bennett in 1905, while his competitors 'pneu x' and 'pneu y' lie flat on the ground exhausted and deflated. 'Pneu y' is literally under the small table next to a Bibendum holding a champagne bottle in one hand, drinking from the other, and leaning back grandly in his chair ('Bibendum à la Coupe Gordon Bennett', 1905: 2). Advertisements featured dialogues between Frenchmen and foreigners, who had heavy accents. O'Galop drew a postcard in which a German and a British man approach a French officer on a bike. Both say they are introducing him to a 'very French tyre'. The German says, making all of the supposed errors in French typical for a German, *'Che vous brésente oun bneumatique pien vrançais!'* The British man counters that *'je présentais vô oune tyre tôt à fait française'*, himself making the presumably classic errors of an English speaker. The French soldier, recognizing the foreignness of these supposedly French tyres, opts for a Michelin tyre (Postcard Collection, Michelin archives).

Interestingly, even in pre-war advertisements in Britain, Germany, and Italy, Michelin did not hide or understate Bibendum's French nationality. A postcard representing a pyramid constructed of Bibendum's racing trophies and Bibendum as the sphinx overlooking Napoleon's troops during the Egyptian campaign appeared in German as well as in French (Postcard Collection, Michelin archives). A drawing for the Italian subsidiary featured Bibendum having a drink with Napoleon himself (Darmon, 1997: 88). Napoleon simply did not bring back moments of German and Italian grandeur, embodying instead the grandeur of France at the expense of those two nations. A poster from early 1914 designed for the British market read 'Michelin Tyres: A Link with France giving Safety, Economy, Comfort, and Speed' and featured a drawing of a channel tunnel constructed of huge Michelin tyres through which automobiles could come from France to England (Darmon, 1997: 95). Despite the Entente, it is difficult to imagine potential British clients becoming excited over a tunnel that allowed French products and French people to invade the British market. Bibendum's assertion of his French origins seems a rather bold assertion of the place of both Bibendum and France within Europe. International advertising took for granted that Michelin tyres could be seen as a superior product, a sort of manufactured French luxury item.

Despite the initial grey and eventual carbon black of tyres, Bibendum began as and remained a white man, making him a representative of the civilized, progressive West in the face of Africa and the East. In O'Galop's original poster of 1898, Bibendum was white, standing against a black background. It is noteworthy that Bibendum remained white with only a few rare exceptions, even when portrayed outside Europe. Bibendum became a white European in a world dominated by European empires.

In the late nineteenth century, companies selling early branded products frequently used racial images of the 'Orient' or Africa to advertise their goods. By the early twentieth century, this 'commodity racism' was a well-established motif in

European advertising, and its existence helps to explain the tenacity of European assumptions of superiority among groups of people who never read even the popular works of Social Darwinists. As recent research has suggested, the notion of racial superiority in Europe was not just constructed and reinforced by racial theorists, politicians, educators, but also by manufacturers who used those racial images in the attempt to sell their products. Michelin fit squarely into this tradition (McClintock, 1995).

In a poster with five scenes from 1913, entitled '*A travers les âges*', O'Galop told the life of Bibendum. Bibendum emerged from the clouds to the cry 'Noël, Noël, the birth of Bibendum', thus replacing the Old Testament Bibendum of the Ten Commandments with Jesus Christ. Because, once again, Bibendum's appetite was 'incontinent' [in the French sense of having unbounded appetites], all of the negroes [*nègres*] spread out in hoards in the virgin forests and set about to gather and coagulate precious rubber. The white brothers snatched up, for a king's ransom, these large masses and hurried to carry them into numerous factories (Poster Collection, Michelin archives). Of course, one might claim that because the portrayals were meant to be humorous, there was no harm done; no one could possibly have believed them, and that these images did little to reinforce European images of white and other. It is nevertheless noteworthy that there was not a comparable self-deprecating humour that placed non-western over western. Moreover, only a few years after Leopold II of Belgium's abusive control of Congolese rubber gatherers became common knowledge at least among the political elite of Europe, even the reference to blacks profiteering from white manufacturers could not have been funny unless, on some level, the reader assumed without question that Europeans were superior to Africans, minimizing suffering in the Congo.

Even technical innovations could be explained with recourse to non-western peoples, here again with a mixing of various people and regions that revealed little knowledge of the world outside Europe. For drivers who found Michelin's introduction of the 'lever' – a tool for removing tyres from rims – a potentially insulting invention given drivers' presumed skill in changing tyres, Bibendum responds that one 'should think of our overseas clientele, of our friends the colonies, of those who, in Brazil, in the Sudan, in Australia, as in Canada, only want to drive on Michelins. Do you think that these distant friends run into a nice tyre dealer every ten kilometres who is ready to give them lessons in mounting tyres? Their mechanics are negroes [*nègres*] or coolies'. It was for them that the instruments were developed: 'Today, they … repeat the following, "Is good, massa Bibendum, is good way to mount big tyres without pinching [them] or pinching fingers. No longer get … kicks in butt. Now have fun all the time! [*Y en a bon, moussu Bibendum, y en a moyen de monter gros pneus sans pincer, ni pincer doigts. N'y en a plus recevoir … coups pied derrière. Même chose rigoler tout le temps!*]"' ('Le Lundi de Michelin', 1913: 5). Michelin reminds the reader that the fine invention of the levers, supposedly developed for the less capable coolies and blacks, will ease the task for European men as well. In the process, the advertisement strongly reinforced the stereotypical black man's inferiority; he could not even speak proper French. Not surprisingly, the drawing at the top of the 'Lundi' shows Bibendum with a colonial hat sitting in a rocking chair. To his right is a black man changing a tyre, and to his left an Asian (presumably Indochinese) man, both of whom are characteristically smaller than him.

Stereotypical Africans also appeared riding bicycles on a pre-war Michelin postcard drawn by 'Gaugé'. An extremely skinny black man with huge lips and oversized hands, wearing a top hat and a ring in his nose, describes why he has Michelin tyres and his wife does not. She, a fat woman with big pants to cover her huge hips, sits passively on tyres called '*Noyau-de-Pêche*'. The man says '*Li, rembourrée, monter pneu Noyau-de-Pêche! – Moi, pas rembourré, monter bon pneu Michelin*' [Her, well-padded, mount Hard-As-Rock/ Me, not well-padded, mount good Michelin tyre] (Postcard Collection, Michelin archives).

Michelin advertisements consistently portrayed black people, both men and women, with big lips and hands. Important distinctions did exist, however, between images of men and women. The men were consistently skinny and the women were fat. Both wore few clothes. The portrayal of blacks in Michelin ads was inextricably tied to cultural notions of superiority and inferiority. For a West that usually associated clothing with civilization and even class status with more as well as better clothing, nakedness represented inferiority. From the point of view of Europeans, whereas the ideal woman needed a small waist – even when big breasts and hips were desirable – the black woman was supposedly huge, despite the paucity of foodstuffs in Africa when compared to those available to the wealthy in Western Europe. Moreover, in the West, a civilization where men were dominant, for women to be huge and men skinny also implied the inferiority of Africans. Male Africans' consistently smaller size further tamed them, as Bibendum towered over them or rode on their backs.

Michelin was not unique in its portrayal of Africans. Turn-of-the-century advertisements frequently offered caricatures of Africans. Advertisements for La Végétaline, a sort of shortening with coconut oil, featured a poorly dressed black boy with big lips and pants rolled up to his knees, a bandaged leg and one shoe missing, offering up some *végétaline* to a French chef, dressed of course entirely in white, shaped like a pear, and standing with his legs apart, thus in a more dominant pose. The relationship of server to served is unmistakable ('La Végétaline', Collection Bibliothèque Forney; Ghozland, 1984: plate 90). Similarly, a poster from 1893 advertising 'Old Jamaïca Goodson Rhum' featured two strangely dressed black men. Though one is better dressed than the other, his colour combination signifies his inability to properly dress himself. He is hitting a thinner black man with torn pants over the head with Old Jamaica Rum, so that the man drops his own generic rum. Both have the trademark large mouths and lips ('Old Jamaïca', Collection Bibliothèque Forney). A whole range of European companies peddling food and beauty products, especially soap, used stereotypes of Africans and other non-western people (McClintock, 1995; Richards, 1990). In the process, they propagated racial notions made ever more credible by force of constant repetition, reflecting and helping to create European cultures that consistently placed Europeans at the top of a presumed racial hierarchy.

With a few rare exceptions among the hundreds of thousands of representations of the figure, Michelin always portrayed Bibendum as a man. In the original poster by O'Galop, Bibendum is clearly masculine, and one might read sexuality into his virility, but no women are present in the poster itself. When women are present in later posters, Bibendum is overwhelmingly dominant in his stance and particularly his size. In several cases, his relationship with a woman – who is always pretty – is vague, though Bibendum regularly towers over women who literally stand between his legs. In one poster from 1916, Bibendum holds a woman in a diaphanous gown in the palm of his hand as she shows a bicycle tyre. Does Bibendum have a lady friend or does the man purchasing the tyre get the woman? There is no indication that she is actually going to ride a bicycle, though the poster does not exclude that possibility; she is merely holding the tyre (Poster Collection, Michelin archives). There may not be a sexual relationship here, but there is clearly a difference of power when the size of the man, Bibendum, is grossly exaggerated vis-à-vis the size of the woman. Bibendum is obviously in control. Other pre-war posters and designs are frequently more suggestive of sexual relations. In a poster by Louis Hindre from 1911, Bibendum has picked up a young woman whose mate – he looks far too young to be her father and she seems to be dressed as a married woman though she is not wearing a ring – cannot adequately chase them because the tyres are peeling off of his bicycle. With a cosy house in the background, the maid and child look on helplessly as the woman herself waves to the stranded partner. They ride through a veritable field of 'obstacles', a field of melons in cloches, the glass protectors of the individual fruits. The man without Michelin tyres does not stand a chance (Poster Collection, Michelin archives).

In the domain of racing, Bibendum's amorous exploits are even more pronounced. After equipping victorious cars in five international races in 1907, Michelin boasted in *L'Auto* of the 'conquests of Bibendum'. Playing on the feminine gender of the word '*coupe*' so that each of the women signifies a '*coupe*', Bibendum has taken and leads around five women, '*la Sicilienne*', '*la Russe*', '*l'Allemande*', '*la Normande*' and '*la Milanaise*'. Although as barrel-chested as ever, Bibendum is here rather more graceful looking, prancing with his 'conquests' in tow. A week later, in the same newspaper, Bibendum returns from his two wins at Brescia. Bibendum is entering France through customs at Modane. The official asks whether he does not have anything to declare and Bibendum replies, 'Oh yes, two delightful women from Milan that I picked up at the circuit of Brescia'. With a blonde on one side and a brunette on the other, the placement of his hands and their placement and appearance are unambiguous in showing the relationship between Bibendum and the two Milanese women. Bibendum, the Frenchman, has thus made 'conquests' in several senses: he is a Frenchman triumphing at home and abroad; he is virile, more so obviously than other men; and he has 'picked up [*enlevé*]', and 'made conquests' of women, who can simultaneously represent both the races themselves and the nationalities through terms like '*la Russe*', '*l'Allemande*', and so on. Bibendum is thus doing what a successful wealthy French man, a veritable *mondain*, presumably should be doing: dominating men of other nationalities and taking their women. However willing the women may appear, the terms 'conquest' and '*enlever*', give away the assumed dynamics between the sexes (*L'Auto*, 16 September, 1907: 8).

Michelin advertisements using gender thus served, as in the case of race, to reflect contemporary French assumptions about the social hierarchy of France in the Belle Epoque. Men controlled women just as men controlled automobiles and supposedly inferior peoples. While some images, such as that of Bibendum riding off with another man's mate, might be seen as a spoof on some social conservatives' claims about the deleterious moral effects of the bicycle (Thompson, 1997: 175-215), the company did not go so far as to feature women actually riding bicycles alone or driving a car. In general, advertisements confirmed certain fundamental notions about the 'essential' differences between men and women, making what were actually social differences seem like physiological ones, thereby injecting the idea of gender into these new products, reflecting broader cultural notions at the time and reformulating them along the way. The perception of a threat to established gender roles of 'modern' or 'new' women who cycled or drove after the war (just as they smoked or wore more 'masculine' clothing or hairstyles) resulted at least in part from the way that those would-be gender-neutral objects became gendered before the war. Michelin, like other companies, thus took an important, though easily overlooked, role in defining the places of women and men in French society.

In the end, pictorial representations of Bibendum offered much, much more than a product; in fact, the product takes a backseat in the 'Michelin man's' drive to offer up a whole way of life. Well-off, white French men – the primary market for automobiles and their tyres before World War I – could establish or reaffirm identities by purchasing tyres. Admittedly, Michelin was in the avant-garde of advertising before the First World War, but it was by no means the only company to use poster art and other representations that represented lifestyles as much as products (Guy, 2003). The fact is that historians have not yet systematically examined pre-war advertising or tied it to longstanding generalizations made about interwar French advertising. Combined with the importance of early French department stores' efforts to create demand and with French and other Europeans' use of world's fairs to sell lifestyles as well as mere products, the example of Michelin poster art and other pictorial representations makes it unclear that Americans led the French in first selling lifestyles and not just products.

References

Arren, J. (1914) *Sa Majesté la Publicité*, Tours: Mame.

Auslander, L. (1996) *Taste and Power: Furnishing Modern France*, Berkeley: University of California Press.

'Bibendum à la Coupe Gordon Bennett' (1905) *L'Auto*, 31 July, p. 2.

Bonnell, V. and Hunt, L. (eds) (1999) *Beyond the Cultural Turn: New Directions in the Study of Society and Culture*, Berkeley: University of California Press.

Bourdieu, P. (1984) *Distinction*, trans. R. Nice, Cambridge, MA: Harvard University Press.

Chessel, M.-E. (1998) *La Publicité: Naissance d'une Profession, 1900-1940*, Paris: CNRS.

Darmon, O. (1997) *Le Grand Siècle de Bibendum*, Paris: Hoebeke.

De Grazia, V. (1989) 'The Arts of Purchase: How American Publicity Subverted the American Poster, 1920-1940', in B. Kruger and P. Marini (eds) *Remaking History*, Seattle: Bay Press.

Dumond, L. (1996) 'L'Industrie Française du Caoutchouc, 1828-1938: Analyse d'un Secteur de Production', Doctorat Nouveau Régime, Université de Paris VII.

Ghozland, F. (1984) *Un Siècle de Réclames Alimentaires*, Tournai: Milan.

Guy, K. (1999) 'Oiling the Wheels of Social Life: Myths and Marketing in Champagne during the Belle Epoque', *French Historical Studies*, Vol. 22 (2), pp. 211-39.

Guy, K. (2003) *When Champagne Became French: Wine and the Making of a National Identity*, Baltimore: Johns Hopkins University Press.

Kocka, J. (1995) 'The Middle Classes in Europe', *Journal of Modern History*, Vol. 67, pp. 783-806.

'Le Lundi de Michelin' (1905a) *L'Auto*, 23 October, p. 7.

'Le Lundi de Michelin' (1905b) *L'Auto*, 9 October, p. 8.

'Le Lundi de Michelin' (1913) *Le Journal*, 13 January, p. 5.

Levin, M. (1993) 'Democratic Vistas – Democratic Media: Defining a Role for Printed Images in Industrializing France', *French Historical Studies*, Vol. 18(1), pp. 82-108.

Lottman, H. (1998) *Michelin, 100 Ans d'Aventure*, Paris: Flammarion.

'Lundi de Michelin' (1912) *Le Journal*, 25 November, p. 5.

McClintock, A. (1995) *Imperial Leather: Race, Gender, and Sexuality in the Colonial Contest*, New York: Routledge.

Marchand, R. (1985) *Advertising the American Dream: Making Way for Modernity, 1920-1940*, Berkeley: University of California Press.

Martin, M. (1992) *Trois Siècles de Publicité en France*, Paris: Odile Jacob.

Michelin (1904) *Le Pneumatique et l'Automobile, 1894-1914: Influence du Perfectionnement du Pneumatique sur leDéveloppement de l'Industrie Automobile*, Clermont-Ferrand: Michelin.

Miquel, R. (1962) *Dynastie Michelin*, Paris: La Table Ronde.

Perrot, P. (1994) *Fashioning the Bourgeoisie: A History of Clothing in the Nineteenth Century*, trans. R. Bienvenu, Princeton: Princeton University Press.

Richards, T. (1990) *The Commodity Culture of Victorian Britain: Advertising and Spectacle, 1851-1914*, London: Verso.

Said, E. (1978) *Orientalism*, New York: Pantheon.

'Samedi de Michelin' (1920), *L'Illustration*, June 4, back cover.

Schneider, W. (1982) *An Empire for the Masses: The French Popular Image of Africa, 1870-1900*, Westport, Conn.: Greenwood.

Segal, A. (1995) 'The Republic of Goods: Advertising and National Identity in France, 1875-1914', Ph.D. dissertation, UCLA.

Thompson, C. (1997) 'The Third Republic on Wheels: A Social, Cultural, and Political History of Bicycling in France from the Nineteenth Century to World War II', Ph.D. dissertation, New York University.

Walton, W. (1992) *France at the Crystal Palace: Bourgeois Taste and Artisan Manufacture in the Nineteenth Century*, Berkeley: University of California Press.

Weill, A. (1986) *Nectar comme Nicolas*, Paris: Herscher.

Weill, A. (1985) *The Poster: A Worldwide Survey and History*, Boston: G.K. Hall.

Chapter 10

Creating 'Modern Tendencies': The Symbolic Economics of Furnishing

Tracey Potts

We seem to be witnessing the democratization of interior design. If the current British lifestyle media is to be believed, now is the time that 'everyone can be a designer' (Milne, 2005: 19). Magazines such as *Elle Decoration* regularly alert our attentions to the existence of 'beautiful buys for every budget' (Ogundehin, 2005a: 29); daytime and primetime TV programmes offer design advice and education, again, apparently regardless of financial constraints. From the *60 Minute Makeover* to more ambitious *Grand Designs*, in the UK so-called 'good design' has perhaps never been so accessible or so ubiquitous, permeating every aspect of our daily lives (Attfield, 2000). The acceptance of modern design in the home was less straightforward than this may suggest however. The established narrative tells a tale featuring, at the beginning of the twentieth century, knowing designer-makers, reluctant consumers and clever marketing ploys. The concerted efforts of design industries are held largely responsible for educating the British consumer out of a nineteenth-century taste for what Baudrillard terms 'monumental' furniture (1996: 17) and into a design orientation towards the home. Consumers, so the argument runs, were literally taught how to see and appreciate the new forms of the machined object through enticing display and aesthetic re-education.

This chapter offers an adjunct to this accepted account of the creation of 'modern tendencies'[1] via an exploration of the archive records of prominent British furniture retailer Heal and Son Ltd in London's Tottenham Court Road, refracted through the work of Pierre Bourdieu. Spanning over a century, the Heal's archive is revealing of some of the techniques and mechanisms through which shifts in bourgeois domestic taste were orchestrated.[2] As it stands there is an over-reliance on the retraining of eyes and minds operating in accounts of furniture consumption and design reform. Choices and tastes, as a result, are deemed little more than the outcome of dazzling display, appeals to fantasy and deference to tastemakers. The result is a neglect of the production of furniture and domestic objects as what Pierre Bourdieu would term *symbolic goods*, that is, objects endowed with precise, albeit euphemized, capital value. What encouraged specifically middle-class consumers to transfer their investment towards the modern, I argue, was the promise of symbolic revenue for their efforts. The conjuring of symbolic capital simultaneously functioned to serve as a new means of securing social distinction. The surreptitious manufacture and distribution of the currency of this emerging form of value ensured that any apparent democracy of furnishing (mass manufactured furniture implied mass consumption) was circumvented.

The importance of noting the distinction between an explicit education in design, on the one hand, and a process of inculcation into a system of value, on the other, should not be underestimated. Beverley Skeggs (2004) has recently outlined the dominance of symbolic economies as new sites of social inequality and discrimination. Residual class prejudice parades itself in the guise of a disdain – at its mildest – for the tasteless amongst us. Symbolic poverty – an individualized and moral failure of lifestyle – vies with economic hardship as a means of discriminating against the have-nots. Unmasking the mechanisms of symbolic capital manufacture therefore becomes especially crucial in challenging and dislodging the hegemony of certain forms of design discourse in the space of the home. The current dominance of the idea of the home as 'the plastic expression of the personality' (Benjamin, 2002: 20) renders domestic space readable in relation to identity. Our homes betray us; our design successes – and failures – communicate facts pertaining to elements of our innermost thoughts, beliefs and selves. Given the perceived free availability of design principles it follows that we can be held to account for what our homes say about us. The era of design democratization is simultaneously that of harsh and unsparing judgment. The illusion of a flat and open field of choices and decisions legitimizes violent adjudications about one another's lifestyles and living arrangements.

Reconstructing early scenes of symbolic capital creation is intended, therefore, to reverse what have become naturalized and congealed attitudes and dispositions. Turning nature into history becomes a crucial element in exposing the hidden class transactions that stratify past and present schemes of inhabiting.

Totalities and Documents

The story of modern furnishing viewed as macrology tells of a progressive movement toward design as an organizing feature of the domestic interior. In separate accounts, for instance, Walter Benjamin and Jean Baudrillard identify the emergence of a designer's disposition as a dominant European attitude toward dwelling with the incursion of mass production technologies. If the nineteenth century was the era of 'monumental' furnishings replete with 'moral theatricality' (Baudrillard, 1996: 17) inhabited by a figure known to Benjamin as 'furnished man' (1999: 5), then the twentieth century witnessed a tectonic shift that unseated the bourgeois individual from the snug depths of his armchair. The materials of industrialized manufacturing processes (glass and metal), characterized by Benjamin as being quite literally less accommodating than those of the preceding era (velour and plush), inaugurate the 'liquidation of the interior' (2002: 20) and establish the preconditions for a design orientation toward the home. For Baudrillard, the process is more enigmatic and the monumental age is simply superseded by that of a technologically informed interior design ethos. 'The sociology of furnishing' gives way to a modernist scheme of domestic orientation organized by the inhabitant-turned-designer as 'active engineer of atmosphere' (1996: 25).

The patent expansion and professionalization of channels of interior design advice can only serve to confirm this view of the modern attitude to the home as the scene less of dwelling than of designing. The notion of interior space as a 'blank canvas' for the expression and performance of something that has become known as 'lifestyle' is without doubt a current commonplace of both professional and popular discourses around home decoration. Contemporary domestic living arrangements insofar as they are projected by an aspirational lifestyle media, lend clear support to both Benjamin's and Baudrillard's view; the stylist's stance is everywhere in evidence, from the pages of *Good Homes, Elle Decoration* and *Grand Designs* to entire TV channels offering round the clock interior design advice.

Such evolutionary narratives – the era when wardrobes ruled the earth appears to either die out or else is struck by the meteor of technology – are contradicted, however, by the authorized biography of furnishing which identifies an initial, some would say protracted, reluctance on the part of the British public to accept the machined forms of 'the modernist paradigm' (Putnam, 2002: 81) into their homes (Kirkham, 1992; Sparke, 1992; Woodham 1997). As Jonathan Woodham (1997) notes, an ideological battle between subscribers to an Arts and Crafts belief in mutual respect for materials and the labour of the artisan, on the one hand, and modernizers investing in the technological progress and scientific rationalism brought by the machine, on the other, dominated the British furniture industry for many years. The sluggish acceptance of what are legible today as design principles has been attributed to the successful initiatives of the design reform movements as well as to the triumph of something called 'good design'. The British homemaker, it is argued, was subject to a sustained re-education calculated to engineer an appreciation of the new furniture that evolved in the direction of design progress. Taught by producers how to appreciate the new forms of the 'serial object' (Baudrillard, 1996: 16), the consuming public is given the aesthetic means to discern 'good' from 'bad' design. Early twentieth-century designer-makers are thus seen to navigate the furniture industry out of the 'confusions' brought about by mass manufacturing processes and back onto the course of so-called 'sound' or 'basic' design principles (Agius, 1978; Cooper, 1987; Goodden, 1984; Lucie-Smith, 1979).

A sociological approach tells a different story. For Bourdieu, the age of mass production witnesses the emergence of new economies. A market in 'cultural goods' can be seen to form, specifically, a trade conducted in the currency of symbolic capital, which can be seen to aid the restructuring of middle-class consumer taste:

> 'Symbolic capital' is to be understood as economic or political capital that is disavowed, misrecognized and thereby recognized, hence legitimate, a 'credit' which, under certain conditions, and always in the long run, guarantees 'economic' profits. (1993: 75)

The coinage of symbolic capital disguises itself as something other than money. It may present itself as "'prestige" or "authority"' (*ibid.*) or as a diffuse air of knowingness around cultural goods and practices and is, therefore, necessarily *charismatic* in appearance (one of Bourdieu's favourite words which refers to the sleight of hand which denies the social genesis of knowledges, dispositions and aesthetic and cultural codes). Accordingly, in producing belief and believers in the virtues of modern furniture, retailers and other agents can be seen to be, surreptitiously, mobilizing and transferring capital funds between objects, and not simply conjuring a revaluation of appearances. The twentieth-century bourgeois homemaker was, then, to be re-educated not only into a change of *aesthetic* preference – the machined for the chiselled – but also into an exchange of *currencies*, relinquishing the conspicuous display of economic advantage and investment for the deferred and quiet rewards of symbolic revenue. The capital gains of embracing modern machined forms – formalist appreciations of which being one source of symbolic capital – can, then, be seen to assist in the aesthetic retraining of the consumer. Consumers, rather than being the passive, pliable, even fickle characters implied by accounts favouring the hypnotic, bewildering quality of display or else the hegemonic power of a taste dictatorship, are here figured as agents, who, once admitted into the gentlemen's club that constitutes the market in symbolic goods, are consummate players in the game of amassing profits.

This game becomes apparent in the history of furnishing viewed as micrology; a privileged insight can be gained into the creation of a symbolic economics of furniture consumption by alighting on details from the Heal's archive. Of especial interest, in addition to the many fascinating essays, pamphlets and catalogues, is the establishment of an art gallery on the uppermost floor of the furniture showroom in 1915. According to the authorized biography of Heal's, the Mansard Gallery solved a problem of how to fill a hitherto unused area as well as performing a vital role in tempting customers to walk throughout the entire space of the store (Goodden, 1984: 60). However, while the exhibition as a marketing tool has been noted for its influence upon the way consumers learned to view the commodity (Benjamin, 2002; Simmel, 1997), and by extension the world, less has been said about its role in the creation of value. Seen in terms of Bourdieu's ideas around the art business and the class of practices that collect around the business of art, exhibitions become the site of capital generation and exchange. The gallery in the shop is, then, far more than a mere visual technology of persuasion; the Mansard Gallery becomes one point in a field of cultural production responsible for the generation and distribution of symbolic, and eventually economic, wealth.

Eyes, Minds and Design Reform

The techniques by which furniture producers sought to engineer a shift in aesthetic preference have been bracketed as successful programmes of 'didactic display' (Clarke, 2001: 24), 'systematized advice' (Putnam, 2002: 86) and 'design propaganda' (Sparke, 1992: 65). In short, consumers were *taught* to move progressively toward an 'acceptance of the machine as a positive and creative force' (Habegger and Osman, 1997: 8). Professional bodies such as the Design and Industries Association, established in 1915 as a direct response to the successes of the German organization *Deutscher Werkbund*, made it their business to promote so-called good design practice, organizing exhibitions, lecture programmes, discussion groups and publishing magazines such as *Design in Industry* and *Design Today* (Sparke, 1992: 64). The origins of design reform can be traced much earlier, though, and in essence accompany the rise of mass production techniques. The perceived threats of unrestricted industrialization comprised the object of the Arts and Crafts movement's aesthetic theories, which advocated a highly politicized philosophy of furniture making based on a belief in respect for materials and production techniques. Henry Cole's Museum of Decorative Arts represented a further mid-nineteenth-century attempt to utilize a design collection as a means of improving design standards in the face of a perceived degeneration of public taste brought about by machine processes. Art Manufacturing sought to improve matters by infusing manufactured object with 'art' content (Sparke, 1992: 64). The Modern Movement, on the other hand, drawing on the aesthetic vocabulary of the architect, promoted the simpler outlines of machined objects as the more rational, progressive and even spiritual choice. Regardless of ethos, however, producers of furniture used a vast range of promotional and pedagogical tools to market their wares and established themselves as early channels for domestic design advice.

This explicit 'teaching' by design professionals combined, it is argued, with less obvious, even surreptitious, marketing techniques that were becoming a discernible feature of the twentieth-century retail landscape (Dant, 1999). Viewed as totality the histories of interior and of consumption converge in their explanations regarding our transformation as modern shoppers and, indeed, subjects. The reorganization of domestic living arrangements and schemes of inhabiting follow patterns that have been identified as features of twentieth-century consumption habits. Changes in public taste and purchasing patterns that mark the twentieth century as a 'consumer society' tend to be attributed to the development and elaboration of a repertoire of visual and psychological techniques (Bowlby, 2000; Dant, 1999; Simmel, 1997). Seductive arrangements of objects, appeals to eyes and (unconscious) minds, divert aesthetic preference in new directions. Governed by the spectacle and by desire we learn to shop differently, investing our purchases with social aspiration and utopian possibility (Dant, 1999). The ingenuities of a new profession of merchandisers renders even the mundane attractive; even buckets and brooms become irresistible, and we are dazzled into acts of expenditure often despite ourselves (Bowlby, 2000).

Exhibitions, shop window displays, catalogues and pamphlets thus mobilized conscious and unconscious forces to comprise a 'frontal assault' on the home (Putnam, 2002: 82) by the burgeoning design industries, which is said to have steered the British domestic interior into the modern age. However, while it clear that the consumer was subjected to a formidable marketing offensive, archive sources show more of 'a process of familiarization which may or may not have been accompanied by specific teaching' (Bourdieu, 1993: 108) to be at work in rerouting public tastes. In the case of the bourgeois consumer, retailers such as Heal's needed to take account of the *capital* investments embedded in the craft object – in skilled and time-consuming labour, in quality materials – in attempting to persuade customers to redirect their tastes toward objects that were identifiable products of the machine age. Furniture manufacturers who aimed their products toward a middle-class clientele needed to reconcile a number of antagonistic forces in order to secure their market. On the one hand, in order to remain economically viable, producers necessarily embraced new mass production techniques; on the other, they risked losing a clientele who were heavily invested in craft ideologies as a source of value. Staging the evacuation of 'the old furniture' in favour of the 'serially produced' (Baudrillard, 1996), then, was a serious, *capital* undertaking and cannot be explained away by sole appeal to clever marketing ploys, education programmes, or in Baudrillard's figuration, to a shift in the sign value of things. As Judy Attfield points out, the significance of material objects cannot be reduced to their position in a field of representation and their concomitant value taken to be semiotic. Modern design is 'part of an *economic* system' (2000:16; my emphasis) and is therefore a good deal more than the sum of its visual and textual mediations.

Details from Heal's marketing and publicity materials reveal something of the process whereby consumers were persuaded to switch allegiances toward serial objects. Specifically, process of capital transfer can be discerned whereby new currencies were conjured as compensation for surrendering old investments. The manufacture of serial objects as 'cultural goods', as design objects or icons for example, is crucial to the consideration of taste formation. What follows, then, is an exposition of the key moves that enable the emergence of symbolic forms of revenue. To this end, three related manoeuvres are isolated as of particular significance: the denial of commerce and the 'economy' and the emergence of 'disinterested' criteria for the appreciation of objects; the cultivation of a consumer 'nobility' or connoisseurship; and, finally, the singularization (Kopytoff, 1986) and diversion (Appadurai, 1986) of objects via what is determined as a 'field of restricted production', that is, a purified realm 'independent' of the monetary economy (Bourdieu, 1993: 78).

Joyous Adventures and Vulgar Commerce: an Economic World Denied

The production of mass manufactured objects as 'cultural goods' can be seen to rely upon the institution of autonomous criteria – a 'pure' aesthetic for instance – as the basis for value. Made possible by the dissolution of aristocratic and ecclesiastical authority and the subsequent competition for cultural legitimacy, the emergence of notions of disinterest in the form, say, of an autonomous art market, by the end of the nineteenth century, offer fertile grounds for new sources of value to take root. The aesthetic, paradoxically the product of the 'evolution of an impersonal market', elevates itself above the market conditions that enable its independent existence and thus constitutes the prime site of a new economy 'based on the disavowal of the "economic"' (Bourdieu, 1993: 74). Aesthetic considerations become the prime location of symbolic capital generation and the art-object, enjoying its newfound independence from relations of tutelage and patronage, takes on the appearance of existing for its own sake (*l'art pour l'art*).

The notion of pure aesthetics is founded upon, first and foremost, a denial of the world of commerce and the 'laws of competition' that are seen to govern the economic field. Determined as vulgar, sordid, crass (to mention a few adjectives that serve as indelible markers of the commercial sphere), 'the field of large scale production' constitutes the ground above which the artistic realm, in Bourdieu's formulation 'the field of restricted production' (1993: 78), floats, in illusory transcendence of the conditions that lend it possibility. Bourdieu explains how this move inaugurates symbolic capital as precisely a currency that denies itself:

> Even if these struggles never clearly set the 'commercial' against the 'non-commercial', 'disinterestedness' against 'cynicism', they almost always involve recognition of the ultimate values of 'disinterestedness' through the denunciation of the mercenary compromises or calculating manoeuvres of the adversary, so that disavowal of the 'economy' is placed at the very heart of the field, as the principle governing its functioning and transformation.
> (p. 79)

Symbolic value is, thus, a form of value that feigns disinterest or disdain toward questions of value and is further determined as a form of double bluff, as 'above' issues of capital gain.

Not surprisingly, the 'disinterested' ground of the aesthetic serves as the basis for the transformation of schemes of furniture consumption. Mass produced or serial furniture becomes marketed, in the case of Heal's, as aesthetically distinct regardless of production cost. The Heal's brochure 'Reasonable Furniture' (1921), for instance, disarticulates production costs and market value from cultural value and puts in place new distinctions between the cheap and the reasonable. *Reasonable furniture* is 'reasonable in price' unlike that which becomes determined as 'furniture substitute' (Heal and Son Ltd, 1921: 1). Decreed 'flimsy', constructed from 'faulty materials' and '"blown together"', furniture substitute is manufactured in bad faith, it is '"made to sell"' rather than 'to use' (*ibid.*); the opponent is at once cast outside of the game as 'calculating' and 'mercenary' and used to establish the brand identity of Heal's as trustworthy and honest. In an audacious reversal of accepted equations of value, furniture substitute is deemed costly, ultimately offering the consumer false economy: 'Most people would agree that such stuff is dear at any price; they seldom realise that a great deal of it is not only relatively but are actually higher in price than honest furniture of simple type' (*ibid.*).

The true cost of furniture substitute is hidden. Honest furniture, on the other hand, whilst 'planned for convenience and durability', combines the 'frank and straightforward' economies offered by the machine 'with an eye to good proportion and pleasant outline' (*ibid.*). In contrast to the untrustworthy mass produced object – which goes so far to disguise itself through the application, post-production, of machine-made ornament – honest furniture reveals its inherent beauty for all to see, its materials left untreated so as to display literally its plain unvarnished truth: 'Stain and polish often hide a multitude of faults both of material and construction; unpolished furniture must be of picked material and clean workmanship if it is to pass the scrutiny of even an inexperienced eye' (p. 2).

Grounded in commonsense notions of quality and pleasantness, Heal's designs thus promote themselves as examples of the 'honest' and the 'sincere' and in doing so achieve the separation of aesthetic and commercial concerns so necessary to the cultivation of symbolic capital. At the same time, a new orthodoxy is attempted; modernist 'fitness for purpose' is established as a rational aesthetic – the shop contains 'all that is most modern within the bounds of sanity and good humour' (Heal and Son Ltd, 1927: 8) – and thus granted a legitimacy that is hard to resist.

With the divorce of the aesthetic from commerce, shopping at Heal's is reconfigured, fundamentally, as an adventure, as an aesthetic encounter. 'Good taste' is uncoupled from expense – Heals' designs are 'within reach of the most modest [of] purse[s]' (Heal and Son Ltd, 1922: 4) – and the shop becomes the location for *disinterested* conversations about 'modern decorative schemes' (Heal and Son Ltd 1917: 2), for opportunities to view 'delightful things of use and beauty ... the dominant note being that of courageous good taste and gay adventure' (Heal and Son Ltd, 1922: 4) Crucially, the shop *becomes a gallery*, transmuted into the scene of an 'aesthetic conversation' (Heal and Son Ltd 1909: 1):

> If you are already acquainted with Heal's you will know that you are welcome to visit their shop at any time without being expected to buy. If you are not, may we say that *it is, in effect, a permanent – and constantly changing – exhibition* of present-day furniture and furnishings in which you can rely upon finding fresh objects of interest whenever you like to come. (Heal and Son Ltd, 1919a: 10)

Heal's thus markets itself via what Bourdieu (1993: 81) terms 'euphemized publicity' as opposed to vulgar advertising which is marked as beneath contempt in brochures such as 'The Elysian' (Heal and Son, 1927). In this instance, a semi-comic narrative is elaborated around a fictitious Oxbridge student (figured as the ideal owner of the illustrious Elysian lounge chair) for whom 'Advertisements are taboo' and 'garbage which no undergraduate will so far debauch his intelligence as to read' (p. 1). The reader is then issued with an open invitation to visit the store at his or her convenience, to converse 'with plenty who will take pleasure in showing you the latest and most amusing things, and who can even discuss them intelligently if you are so minded' (p. 8). The pamphlet thus invites the consumer to consider or interpellate him/herself, likewise, as inhabiting the higher plains of the intellectual, as above the obvious appeal of advertising.

The invitation is the technique *par excellence* of euphemized publicity, mirroring perceived cultural or 'society' events exemplified by the 'private view' of the art world. Borrowing from such spheres of public culture allows producers to further conceal what is actually going on; the invitation to browse without obligation to buy functions as disguised means of attraction that works via flattery: consumers are implicitly construed as *worthy* of invitation to a place that orchestrates itself in terms of exclusivity and privilege. The appearance of disinterest is, simultaneously, the outcome of a temporal delay intrinsic to the game of symbolic capital manufacture. The 'gift' of an invitation to a retail space, that markets itself as above commercial interest, to participate in adventures and to view 'the latest and most amusing things', is illusory to say the very least (*ibid.*). If in the 'economic economy' of the large-scale field of production exchanges is explicit and direct, the symbolic economy conceals its own logic of exchange by feigning a disregard for any return. As Bourdieu notes, the restricted field affects a relation of altruism towards its products in a twin gesture of philanthropy and purified interest – say, the love of art – and disdain for profits and forms of 'vulgar' accumulation:

> Investments are recompensed only if they are in a sense thrown away, like a gift, which can only achieve the most precious return gift, recognition (reconnaissance), so long as it is experienced as a one-way transaction; and, as with the gift, which it converts into pure generosity by masking the expected return-gift which the synchronisation of barter reveals, it is the intervening time which provides a screen and disguises the profit awaiting the most disinterested investors. (1993: 101)

What appears as largesse – the opportunity to experience pure delight – amounts more to a 'long' retail game whereby profits are realized further down the line. The time lag between investment and return distracts from the fact of the exchange operation and is crucial to the illusion of disinterest. 'Symbolic goods', Bourdieu argues, 'are a two-faced reality, a commodity and a symbolic object' (p. 113); to function as effective symbolic objects they necessarily have to hide their economic features. If the delay between perusal and purchase is insufficient, if delight is cut short, then the scene of symbolic capital production is exposed and negated. A detail in the Heal's archive betrays the necessity of concealing the economic facts in order to maintain the illusion of disinterest:

> A customer wrote to us complaining that the buying of some of our furniture, to which he had looked forward as a joyous adventure, had (through some lack of understanding on the part of one of our assistants), become "a sordid and merely commercial transaction". On this occasion we had failed, and we admit it frankly. But this complaint was also a tribute – a tribute to the sort of pleasant experience to which this customer had learnt to look forward at *The Sign of the Fourposter*. (Heal and Son Ltd, 1916: 1)

Deployed as an exception that proves the rule, this complaint is cunningly recuperated as a complement. The incompetent assistant, nevertheless, unwittingly blurts out the economic truth at the heart of the joyous adventure; a trade is being conducted even if money changes hands furtively and beneath the surface of polite, euphemized transactions. That the customer was irate enough to write is revealing, further, of the fact of his investment in the illusion and gives some clue as to the emergence of consumer interest in the potential profits of a symbolic economy.

Cultivating the Cultivated: Collusions and Connoisseurs

In order to function as a genuine currency, the production of symbolic capital necessarily involves the simultaneous production of a class of investors capable not only of subscribing to its funds but also of ensuring its continued circulation and renewal. If the process by which the denial of the economy is achieved is a required secret then so is the process by which a consummate consumer is created. To become legal tender (symbolic capital, like symbolic violence, loses its purchase when exposed for what it is), the scene of cultural acquisition must remain concealed. Given Bourdieu's point that cultural goods 'are bound to precede their market' (1993: 120), the means of their appropriation lags behind their issue. Codes and dispositions for the appreciation of such things must therefore be produced, so to speak, after the fact.

The creation of a class of consumers who are positioned and who come to position themselves as *connoisseurs* can be seen to be the result of a diffuse education which is the outcome of a collusion between highly interested producers and consumers. The exhibition pamphlet 'The Shop of Adventure' (Heal and Son Ltd, 1922) offers a useful case in point in that it constitutes both a form of 'euphemized' publicity and a surreptitious lesson in modernist aesthetics. Designed to pave a route between store and exhibition stand, the leaflet gives careful guidance in how to view the items on show: not as 'exceptional' pieces – the accepted logic of the furniture exhibition until well into the twentieth century (Aslin, 1962) – and certainly not as 'flash in the pan of special advertisements' (Heal and Son Ltd, 1922: 2). Continuity is thus established between exhibition and retail space which is intended to draw the exhibition-goer into the store, a subsidiary but by no means insignificant effect of which being that an 'exhibitionary attitude' is effectively carried back into the store. Importantly, the reader/visitor is interpellated not as future customer but as adventurer, art historian and philosopher, a fellow traveller in the aesthetic journey that is seen to distinguish Heals from other furniture makers and sellers: an avant-garde yet conservative voyage combining a taste for 'ceaseless experiment' and 'respect for the finest traditions of the past' (*ibid.*). That this subject-position, a fully-fledged connoisseur of modernist forms, precedes its occupant – its hail has yet to be answered – is, however, betrayed not only by the leaflet's very existence but also by its concluding assurances: 'It is not so dangerous: no one will pounce upon you from behind a pillar and ask you to stand and deliver, i.e. insist on your buying. You may simply go to look, and attendance will be yours only if and when you need it' (p. 8). The consumer-adventurer is revealed potentially to be a rather timid travelling companion, possibly lagging behind the producer as he strikes out in new uncharted directions. This likely gap in sensibility – essentially a mismatch between the habitus of the producer and the consumer – exposes something of the temporal logic of the concealed system of education in the field of symbolic goods.

The direct opposite of a 'following', where trends are set so that consumers can follow in their wake (a movement associated more with the field of large scale production), the temporality of the production of symbolic capital is deceptively belated and retroactive. As is the case with many articles from Heal's promotional literatures, the producer necessarily gives the impression of preaching to the converted and thus takes the risk of stating the obvious. The 'Plea for Simplicity in Cottage Furniture' admits in arguing for simplicity in cottage decor, for instance, 'On the face of it this seems to be a point that hardly needs pleading – so sane and right does it appear' (Heal and Son Ltd, 1919b: 1). That this point *fails to go without saying*, however, demonstrates that the preacher is in fact addressing *an about-to-be-converted audience as if they're already converted*. The positioning of one's potential following as if they are, instead, peers is a not only a powerful technique of persuasion but it is also a necessary sleight of hand in order to ensure the production of symbolic value which after all must remain enigmatic in character. The soon-to-be-cultivated must be addressed as if they are *already in the know*, thus allowing the scene of knowledge acquisition to remain well and truly hidden and hence to circulate in entirely charismatic form.

The manufacture of belief in symbolic goods proceeds as if their value is intrinsic, regardless of subscription, when in actuality symbolic value is a scene under construction awaiting the arrival of investors for its completion. A select audience is invited to view a select collection of objects, chosen – rather, *curated* – 'according to a clearly defined standard of good taste' (Heal and Son Ltd, 1922: 4). In gathering at the appointed meeting-place – pamphlets sets up a future indeterminate 'rendezvous' at the store – the appointed audience thus completes a circuit of mutual appreciation: the retailer congratulates the customer for possessing the good taste to shop in his store and the shopper confirms the retailers belief in his/her perceived good taste by confirming the retailers' good taste. The producer of symbolic value necessarily acts as if that particular form of value already exists in order to produce a set of believers capable of investing in and maintaining its codes. However, it is only when the belief in the symbolic value of, say, aesthetic form or 'fitness for purpose' is met by an appropriate class of believers that symbolic capital generation can be said to begin. The circuit of capital flow comes together only at the last minute, when the adventurer turns up to the appointed assignation and in doing so reciprocates the producer's confidence with the return investment of recognition, appreciation and belief in the universe that effectively is the product of their shared but seemingly 'objective connivance' (Bourdieu, 1993: 83).

The apparent courage of the producer is subsequently undermined with this realization in that he/she is less single-mindedly striking out in the direction of excellence as arbiter and ambassador of 'good design' than organizing a more or less self-fulfilling prophecy. Viewed sociologically, the success of Ambrose Heal and his store becomes less a matter of the designer's boldness (Agius, 1978: 109) and 'sharp eyed confidence' (Sir Hugh Casson, cited in Goodden, 1984: 1) than of an accrued capital of consecration resulting from his position in the field of cultural production. If it needs acknowledging that the cultivated must be cultivated then it also follows that the cultivators themselves need cultivating: as Bourdieu puts it, 'what creates the authority with which authors authorize?' (1993: 76). Without becoming overly distracted by the question of 'who creates the creator?' (*ibid.*), the circuit of recognition and belief, of mutual admiration, that operates between producer and consumer needs to be extended to include producers themselves. The value of the gift in question – *is the invitation worth the return gift of acceptance?* – is further dependent upon the perceived worth of whoever is seen to be behind the gesture.

Consecrations and Diversions

The formation of something that becomes known charismatically as a 'reputation' can be seen to rest upon the degree of regard granted by other players in the field. If the cultural businessman's trade is revealed to be reliant on upon a power of consecration – a capacity to bless, recommend and endow objects with a value beyond their immediate production cost – then 'the more consecrated he personally is, the more strongly he consecrates the work' (Bourdieu, 1993: 77). The blessings and praise of fellow producers and consecrators serve to increase the value of the blessings that any producer might bestow upon cultural goods. In the case of Heal's the recognitions of peer designers and opinion makers constitute crucial elements in the establishment of the store's standing as 'design pioneer' (Pevsner, 1987; Sparke, 1999). Furniture maker and designer Gordon Russell, for example, praised Heal as 'the only man in the retail trade of that time who had any real interest in and knowledge of design', while Nikolaus Pevsner extolled his 'good progressive furniture ... living amongst such objects we breathe a fresher air' (both cited in Cooper, 1987: 237). Furthermore, such endorsements served not only to nurture reputations but simultaneously to provide powerful sources of euphemized marketing. In 1898, for example, noted interiors journalist Gleeson White, then editor of the influential Arts and Crafts magazine *The Studio*, contributed a booklet entitled 'A Note on Simplicity of Design in Furniture for Bedrooms with Special Reference to Some Recently Produced by Messrs Heal and Son'(Heal and Son Ltd, 1926). Sir Lawrence Weaver, president of the Design and Industries Association, and typographer Joseph Thorp also wrote essays applauding the Heal style. Thorp writes of his first visit to the shop in 'An Aesthetic Conversation':

> I drifted in search of a convenient upholsterer, and I found an artist-craftsman with a business-like air and method, and came gradually to distinguish a definite artistic purpose in the work of this house. (Heal and Son Ltd, 1909: 1)

Likewise, Weaver muses: 'we talked of other things than prices and merchandise' detailing the contours of a conversation spanning the designer's relation to tradition and the meaning of the 1925 Paris Exhibition of Decorative Arts to Britain (Heal and Son Ltd 1926).

Ambrose Heal's reputation as an artist-craftsman was augmented by frequent exhibitions of his furniture. The 1923 British Industrial Art exhibition, for example, as with the Paris Exhibition, functioned to advertise and display but also to consecrate objects as *works*, as art-objects. The exhibition thus forms a crucial element in the exponential circuit of consecration. With reputation secured, Heal established his own art institution within his shop: the Mansard Gallery, drawing energy from the wider institutional sphere of the art world, served as an autonomous source of sanctification, praise and hence symbolic capital.

The exhibition has been singled out as an especially powerful technique of persuasion and soon functioned as a mainstay of the furniture retailer's promotional repertoire. At the quality end of the British furniture industry, West End firms competed for custom using increasingly expansive showrooms and galleries. Waring & Gillow, for example, instated permanent exhibition galleries dedicated to the display of reproduction furniture in 1903, while Whiteley's pioneered window displays of complete room settings as early as 1882 (Agius, 1978: 156-7). Heal's, meanwhile, showed designs in the Mansard Gallery from 1917, and in a fully furnished flat adjoined to the roof terrace which provided a convenient display area for garden furniture. Designed both to inform and seduce (Goodden, 1984: 56), the room setting provides a stage for the imagination and certainly, with its 'exterior' winter garden complete with fountain. It can clearly be viewed as an instance of what Benjamin refers to as 'the phantasmagoria of the interior' (2002: 22).

Aside from enlivening 'dead' retail space, and retuning the senses of consumers to allow desire the upper hand, the gallery constitutes the engine room of symbolic capital production and as such performs a magical action upon both the objects and consumers that pass through its milieu. Ostensibly a refuge to indulge in the illusion of further freedom from obligation, the Mansard Gallery appears to be a gallery within a gallery (the shop has already been subject to a transmutation from commercial to art space). The apparent extravagance of retail floor space given over to aesthetic adventuring seems less so once refracted through Bourdieu's eyes: the institution of a gallery in a shop becomes a matter of a restricted field of production being established in the large-scale or commercial field, albeit one disguised through a prior euphemization. The effects of this arrangement are at once to install a distinction between 'interchangeable products reducible to commodity value' associated with the field of large-scale cultural production and 'unique products of "creative genius"' associated with the restricted field (Bourdieu, 1993: 114). In other words, a division between the art object and the commodity is attempted allowing for cultural value to circulate independent of commercial value. An explicit exhibition as opposed to display space, the Mansard Gallery produces what Kopytoff (1986) has termed the 'singularization' of objects presented within its setting. Briefly, singularization describes the process whereby things become removed or diverted from the commodity sphere, treated as sacred (Appadurai, 1986), beyond price, and outside of the system of economic exchange. The exemplary singular object is the artwork and yet, as Kopytoff notes, the worlds of art and money

> cannot be kept separate for long; for one thing, museums must insure their holdings. So museums and art dealers will name prices, be accused of the sin of transforming art into a commodity, and in response, defend themselves by blaming each other for creating and maintaining the commodity market. (1986: 83)

The resulting tension – the pricelessness of a Picasso is effected through reference to its exorbitant cost – renders the singular object deeply paradoxical in its composition: 'singularity ... is confirmed ... by intermittent forays into the commodity sphere, quickly followed by re-entries into the closed sphere of singular "art"' (*ibid.*). By exhibiting rather than merely displaying furniture, the Mansard Gallery draws commodities into the orbit of the art world and temporarily out of the commodity sphere. Housed in space governed by aesthetics rather than economics, Heal's furnishings take on features associated more with painting and sculpture; items bear the maker's signature,[3] for example, or are framed in art or burgeoning design discourses, emphasizing form and line.

The diversion of objects through gallery space and their subsequent elevation from the realm of the commodity – inaugurating, Bourdieu would say, their entry into the field of symbolic value – is not the only mechanism of capital generation in the gallery, however. The diversion of consumers out of the commodity sphere is equally important in the production of a cultivated habitus and thereby is productive of cultural capital in its embodied state (Skeggs, 1997). In ascending the stairs to the exhibition – of 'French Art 1914-1919' (Heal and Son Ltd, 1919c) which included works by Matisse, Modigliani and Picasso, or of 'Modern Tendencies' (Heal and Son Ltd, 1930), for example – consumers were effectively leaving behind the realm of the commodity and entering the purified domain of art. Having sloughed off the remaining vestiges of the commercial, the consumer becomes instead a visitor or the recipient of an invitation to a private view or a connoisseur of modernist form and hence further 'integrated into the producer's field' (Bourdieu, 1993: 116). Here, in the elevated realm of art, the visitor/connoisseur is set apart from those referred by W. H Cowlishaw in 1917 as 'dizzy shoppers' (Goodden, 1984: 39) and left to contemplate the quiet and restful forms of purified aesthetic objects.

Conclusion, or, Economies With a Difference

If initially the production of machine-made furnishings threatened to empty objects of their value, potentially negating their value as ciphers for social distinction through a process of asset stripping, this threat was soon assuaged through the creation and circulation of emergent forms of capital investment. The mobilization of a newly minted means of appreciating – in both its aesthetic and 'financial' senses – the value of things as cultural goods served to erect a secret source of revenue that flowed between members of what amounted to an exclusive club. The surreptitious methods by which symbolic economic value can be seen to be manufactured and circulated undermines the appearance of democracy that runs through marketing campaigns designed to appeal to 'various purses'.[4] If the 'economic' economic field seemed to be flattening out, the invention of new obstacles, invisible to those not in the know, in the form of exclusive discourses and codes by which to appreciate what were ostensibly mass manufactured objects, ensured that social distinction was maintained. To borrow the title of Heal's utility era range of furniture (circa 1933), an 'economy with a difference' was created at the very moment that social divisions appeared to be dissolving, at least with regard to their material reflection in the domestic interior.

Looking back, revisiting early sites of symbolic capital manufacture via archive records, enables a reconsideration of the birth of the designer's disposition as a modern domestic attitude. In exposing the capital interests at stake in effecting a shift of taste in the direction of the serial object, the class dimensions of the story of furnishing can be discerned.[5] Instead of heralding a democratic revolution in the home – where we all get to be 'stylish' regardless of 'budget' – the circulation of the mass manufactured object within a separate and masked symbolic economy has allowed new forms of discrimination to emerge. A recent British edition of *Elle Decoration* opened with a declaration from designer Karl Lagerfeld: 'people with bad taste aren't poor, they just have bad taste' (Ogundehin, 2005b: 13). With discount outlets like TK Maxx selling 'Barcelona' chairs and with 'bargain' chandeliers on offer in Matalan, there is no longer an ethical obligation to regard any connection between economic resources and so-called 'lifestyle'. As a result, it is entirely legitimate to expose the taste of others to unveiled contempt; *there's no excuse*, 'your next stop doesn't have to be some D-list celebrity designed hideosity from Sofas-R-Us! Look around. There are some brilliant buys out there' (*ibid.*). The same lifestyle media that furnishes us with visions to aspire to simultaneously pathologizes 'disordered' modes of inhabiting as individualized and moral failure (Bauman, 2000): cluttered, over-decorated homes 'behaving badly', to borrow the title of a current daytime TV programme, are the faults of their owners, manifestations of psychopathologies or domestic depravities. As Skeggs (2004: 14) notes:

> Making legitimate (making things valid) places the thing (be it persons or object) that is being valued in the realm of dominant categorizations. As it is inscribed with value it becomes part of the symbolic economy. The moral evaluation of cultural characteristics is central to the workings and transmission of power.

The moral evaluation of interior décor is inescapable at present. Those who find themselves outside of the trade in symbolic meaning find themselves accused of aesthetic crimes and misdemeanours against which they have no defence (Bourdieu, 1999). Given the necessarily inequitable distribution of the coinage of symbolic currencies ('scarce instruments of appropriation' (Bourdieu, 1993: 120) ensure the capital value of symbolic goods,) offenders are unlikely to be granted the means of securing their freedom. We might not, today as in Heal's heyday, 'have to spend a lot of money to have lovely things' (Ogundehin, 2005b: 16) but while the economy which lends value to loveliness remains hidden and charismatic the real costs are unappreciable.

Notes

1   Phrase taken from a series of furniture exhibitions staged by Heal's, which ran from 1930.

2   The archive allows for a reconstruction of a field of intended consumers in much the same way that a literary text, narratologically speaking, allows for a reconstruction of the figure of the ideal reader. The actual patterns of consumption that such marketing ploys helped to bring about must remain the subject of a further study.

3   The 'signed edition series' of furniture was marketed in the 1930s.

4   Invitations to exhibitions and private views staged at Heal's were distributed to the existing clientele or to a target audience, for instance, of 'telephone owners' living in properties with a rental value of over £50 (Gooden 1984: 80), which automatically predetermined the social class of future customers.

5   This is not to suggest an uninterrupted history stretching from the archive to the present. The divorce of the aesthetic and the economic is a messy one as a recent Ikea advertising campaign testifies. Briefly, a 'designer' – stereotypically rendered as precious and even pretentious – is depicted as being outraged that Ikea designs (formally similar to his own) are so cheap. The central message – good design doesn't have to be expensive – is evidently one that needs reiterating from time to time.

References

Agius, P. (1978) *British Furniture 1880-1915*, London: Antique Collectors Club.

Appadurai, A. (1986) *The Social Life of Things: Commodities in Cultural Perspective*, Cambridge: Cambridge University Press.

Aslin, E. (1962) *Nineteenth Century English Furniture*, London: Faber and Faber.

Attfield J. (2000) *Wild Things: The Material Culture of Everyday Life*, Oxford: Berg.

Baren, M. (1996) *How It All Began: Up the High Street*, Oxford: Past Times.

Baudrillard, J. (1996) *The System of Objects*, London: Verso.

Bauman, Z. (2000) *Liquid Modernity*, Cambridge: Polity.

Benjamin, W. (1999) *Selected Writings, Vol. 2 1927-1934*, Cambridge, MA, and London: The Belknap Press of Harvard University Press.

Benjamin, W. (2002) *The Arcades Project*, Cambridge, MA., and London: The Belknap Press of Harvard University Press.

Bourdieu, P. (1993) *The Field of Cultural Production: Essays on Art and Literature*, Cambridge: Polity.

Bourdieu, P. (1999) *The Weight of the World: Social Suffering in Contemporary Society*, Cambridge: Polity.

Bowlby R. (2000) *Carried Away: The Invention of Modern Shopping*, London: Faber and Faber.

Clarke, A. J. (2001) 'The Aesthetics of Social Aspiration', in D. Miller (ed.) *Home Possessions: Material Culture Behind Closed Doors*, Oxford: Berg.

Cooper J. (1987) *Victorian and Edwardian Furniture and interiors: From the Gothic Revival to Art Nouveau*, London: Thames and Hudson.

Dant, T. (1999) *Material Culture in the Social World*, Buckingham: Open University Press.

Goodden, S. (1984) *At the Sign of the Fourposter: A History of Heal's*, London: Lund Humphries.

Habegger, J. and J. Osman (1997) *Sourcebook of Modern Furniture*, New York: W.W. Norton and Co.

Heal and Son Ltd (1898) 'A Note on Simplicity of Design in Furniture for Bedrooms with Special Reference to Some Recently Produced by Messrs Heal and Son' (promotional material).

Heal and Son Ltd (1909) 'An Aesthetic Conversation' (promotional material).

Heal and Son Ltd (1916) 'Fourposter Sheet No. 5: the First Week in February' (promotional material).

Heal and Son Ltd (1917) 'Invitation to the Mansard Flat' (promotional material).

Heal and Son Ltd (1919a) 'The Joyous Adventure' (promotional material).

Heal and Son Ltd (1919b) 'A Plea for Simplicity in Cottage Furniture' (promotional material).

Heal and Son Ltd. (1919c) 'French Art 1914-1919' (exhibition poster).

Heal and Son Ltd. (1921) 'Reasonable Furniture' (promotional material).

Heal and Son Ltd. (1922) 'The Shop of Adventure' (promotional material).

Heal and Son Ltd. (1926) 'A Few Notes on Architects and Furniture by Sir Lawrence Weaver: but really an advertisement of Heal and Son' (promotional material).

Heal and Son Ltd. (1927) 'The Elysian' (promotional material).

Heal and Son Ltd. (1930) 'Modern Tendencies' (promotional material).

Heal and Son Ltd. (1933) 'Economy with a Difference' (promotional material).

Kirkham, P. (1992) 'Furniture History', in H. Conway (ed.) *Design History: A Student's Handbook*, London: Routledge.

Kopytoff, I. (1986), 'The Cultural Biography of Things: Commoditisation as Process', in A. Appadurai (ed.) *The Social Life of Things: Commodities in Cultural Perspective*, Cambridge: Cambridge University Press.

Lucie-Smith, E. (1979) *Furniture: A Concise History*. London: Thames and Hudson.

Milne, L. (2005) '20:20: Twenty Things We Find Seriously Tempting', *Grand Designs*, January, pp. 19-24.

Ogundehin, M. (2005a) 'Savvy Shopping, How to Save and When to Splurge: Beautiful Buys for Every Budget', *Elle Decoration*, April, pp. 22-34.

Ogundehin, M. (2005b) 'Editorial comment', *Elle Decoration*, January, pp. 13-16.

Pevsner, N. (1987) *Pioneers of Modern Design from William Morris to Walter Gropius*, Harmondsworth: Penguin.

Putnam, T. (2002) 'The Art of Home-making and the Design Industries', in C. Painter (ed.) *Contemporary Art and the Home*, Oxford: Berg.

Simmel, G. (1997) 'Berlin Trade Exhibition', in D. Frisby and M. Featherstone (eds) *Simmel on Culture: Selected Writings*, London: Sage.

Skeggs, B. (1997) *Formations of Class and Gender: Becoming Respectable*, London: Sage.

Skeggs, B. (2004) *Class, Self, Culture*, London: Routledge.

Sparke, P. (1992) *An Introduction to Design and Culture in the Twentieth Century*, London: Routledge.

Sparke, P. (1999) *A Century of Design: Design Pioneers of the 20th Century*, London: Mitchell Beasley.

Woodham, J. (1997) *Twentieth Century Design*, Oxford: Oxford University Press.

Index

acupuncture 123
Adler, A. 131
advertising 3
   lifestyle-orientated 16
   Michelin in pre-World War One
      France 16, 17, 145-54
aestheticization 1
African American 55
Althusser, L. 126
altruism 164
Americanism and Fordism
   (Gramsci) 134
Anderson, E. 61
anti-monotony 28
Aristotle 133
art of living 96
autonomy 96

Bach, J.S. 76
Baker, E. 64
B.A.S.E jumping 89
Baudrillard, J. 157, 158
Bauman, Z. 90
Bay Laurel, A. 120, 121
Beeton, I. 20
Belle Epoque 153
Benjamin, W. 157, 158
Bennett, T. and Woollacott, J. 100
Bergman, D. 97
Berkman, D. 55
Bibendum (Michelin Man)
   use in advertising 146-54
black
   consumer market 60-2
   middle class 54-68
   racial solidarity 65
Black Bourgeoisie 67
Bocock, R. 1, 70
body work
   lifestyle print culture 123-6

Bonham-Carter, Lady V. 34-5
Bonner, F. 4
Bourdieu, P. 6, 9, 10, 15, 42, 43, 90,
   103, 111, 156, 162, 163
   new petite bourgeoisie 92, 96, 99,
      101
bourgeoisie 55
Bowdler, T. 76
Bradbury, R. 75
Brooks Brothers 73, 74
Broyer, G. and Midol, N. 104
Brunsdon, C. 4

Cadillac 65, 66
capitalism 64
   sickness 135
Capper, W.B. 45
Catalog (1972 National Book
   Award) 118-19
censorship 75, 76
Chaney, D. 1, 43
Chéret, J. 145
Chicago 57
Chicago Defender 58
civil rights 14
   movement 55
Clair, R. 76
Clark, E. 104
class and taste 9-13
class distinctions 7
class identities
   reformulation 23
class mobility 16
clothing
   identity 74
Cohen, L. 64
Cold War culture
   USA 70-85
commodity fetishism 108
conformity 54

crisis of masculinity 79
  Playboy 78-84
consumer culture 1, 8
consuming personality 12
consumption 4, 7, 63, 64, 65, 82
  Playboy 73-85
  revolutions 5
convenience foods 29
cookery
  advertising and healthy eating 30,
    31, 32
  economy 32
  Good Housekeeping and the value
    of cooking 28-33
  health 30, 31
  and middle-class femininity 24-7
  science and technology 33-5
Corrigan, P. 7
countercultural lifestyle 15
Cousteau, J. 98
Cowlishaw, W.H. 169
Cox, H. 78
Crac, D. 139
Crawford, Sir W. 34
Crisis 59
cultural capital 9, 10, 35, 41, 44
cultural intermediaries 12, 91
cultural policy
  history 3
cultural reproduction 11

David, E. 46
Dedman, J. 73
department store
  golden age 9
design
  regime of value 17
  symbolic capital 157, 158, 159,
    161, 163, 165, 168, 170
  symbolic economics of furnishing
    156-70
detraditionalization 4
DeVault, M. 28
Dheil, D. 117, 118
Diamond, R. 139
diet 31

differentiation 7
DiMaggio, P. 113
Distinction (Bourdieu) 90
Diving Equipment Manufacturers
  Association (DEMA) 95
domestic modernity 2
domesticity 81
  gendering 12
Driver, C. 44

Ebony magazine 5, 14, 54-68
  advertising 58-60, 63
  black consumer market 60-2
  criticisms 67
  defining a lifestyle 62-4, 66, 68
  equality and status 65-7
economic determinism 109
economy 28
education 3, 95
education system 10
Ehrenreich, B. 79, 102
Elizabeth I 6
Elle Decoration 156
Emerson, R.W. 133
emulation 6, 9
English Folk Cookery Association
  50
Englishness 14
Europe 46
exhibitionary complex 17

Featherstone, M. 1, 10, 20, 71, 85,
  90, 126
Felski, R. 23, 35
Feminine Mystique (Friedan) 85
femininity 81, 82
Finkelstein, J. 43
Fisher, R. 84
Fordism 140
Foucault, M. 13
France
  new middle classes 11
Frankfurt School 108
Franklin, B. 76, 77, 133
Frazier, E.F. 55
Friedan, B. 81, 85

Furedi, F. 138, 139
furnishing
   aesthetic considerations 161, 162, 163
   art manufacturing 160
   collusions and connoisseurs 165-7
   consecrations and diversions 167-9
   design reform 159-61
   didactic display 159
   furniture substitute 162
   Heal and Son Ltd. 156, 159, 160, 162, 163, 165, 167, 169, 170
   symbolic economics 156-70
   totalities and documents 157-9
furnishings
   economies with a difference 169-70

gastronomy 41
Gebhard, P. 74
germ theory 30
Giddens, A. 1, 2, 4, 16
Giles, J. 27, 34
Gloucestershire 51
Glucksmann, M. 24
Good Food Guide 42, 44-8
   categories of judgement 45, 46
   criticism of British food 45
   shortcomings 47
Good Food Register 48-51
   focus on unprivileged rural women 49
Good Housekeeping 13
   British inter-war cooking and domestic feminities 20-36
   economy 32
   health and hygiene 30, 31
   labour-saving technologies 33
   science and cookery 33-5
   value of good cooking 28-33
Good Housekeeping Institute 26
Gramsci, A. 134, 140
Great Britain
   Good Housekeeping inter-war cooking and domestic femininities 21-36

inter-war transformation of middle classes 21, 22
Great Depression 16, 54, 57, 66
   self-help 134-5, 138
Great Exhibition (1851) 3
Gunn, S. 12

Haldane, J.S. 94
Hass, H. 97
hedonism 74, 88, 113, 114
Hefner, H. 73, 76, 77, 78, 82
Highgate 42
Hindre, L. 153
historical contexts 5-9
Hollows, J. 82
home products
   growth 7, 8
Humble, N. 24
Hunstrete House Restaurant 42

identity 108, 126
   clothing 74
   consumption practices 70
individual authenticity 16
individuality 1, 96
intellectual freedom 72
interior design 156-70
   see also furnishing

Jameson, F. 108
Jefferson, T. 133
Johnson, J.H.
   Ebony magazine 54-68
   Negro Digest 58
   professional background 56-7

Kent Rush, A. 124, 125
Kinsey Report 74, 75
Kopytoff, I. 168

Lagerfeld, K. 170
Lash, S. 90, 110, 113, 126
leisure business 88-105
   lifestyle sports 89-93
   postwar boom 95
leisure-work 8

Life Begins at Forty (Pitkin) 136-8
Life magazine 55, 59, 68, 83
lifestyle
    class and taste 9-13
    mediating 4-5
lifestyle print culture 108-27
    Bay Area 118-23
    body work 123-6
    East coast chauvinism 117
    lifestyle de-distanciation 110-15,
        127
    New Age spirituality 121
    new cultural intermediaries 110-
        15
    West Coast publishing 115-26
lifestyle sports 89-93
    fathoming the Phenomenon 93-6
    identity politics 89
lifestylization 7, 17, 27
Light, A. 22
literature
    pseudo-scientific 131
London 6
Los Angeles 97
Los Angeles Times 117
luxury
    democratisation 9

McCracken, G. 6
Maffesoli, M. 90
Manet, E. 145
Mansard Gallery 159, 167, 168
manufacturers
    marketing 7, 8
Marchand, R. 145
Marling, K.A. 71
Martens, L. and Warde, A. 47
masculinity and consumerism
    1960s scuba phenomenon 101-4
massage technique 123
material success 77
matriarchy 80
May, E.T. 80
media
    lifestyle 1, 4, 5, 20, 156
Mennell, S. 28, 29, 44

Michelin
    advertising in pre-World War
        One France 16, 17, 145-54
    role of Bibendum (Michelin Man)
        16, 17, 146-54
Michelin, A. 146, 147
Middle Ages 13
middle class
    black 54-68
middle-class femininity
    cookery 24-7
Midol, N. and Broyer, G. 104
mobility 12
modern femininity 22, 27
modern tendencies
    creating 156-70
modernity 70
Monroe, M. 75
Mort, F. 2, 96

National Association for the
    Advancement of Colored People
    (NAACP) 60
Negro Digest 58, 67
new nihilism 77
Newsweek 60
nobility 6
non-work time 3

Ogburn, W. 135
Opportunity 59

Pan-Africanism 63
Pevsner, N. 167
Picasso, P. 80, 169
Pilgrim, J. 83
Pitkin, W.B. 136-8, 140
Pittsburgh Courier 58
Playboy 5, 15, 103, 104
    censorship 75, 76
    conformity and problem of
        gender 78-84
    consumption 73-8
    lifestyle 73-8
    playmates 82-3
    politics 70-85

rejection of family 80-1
sexuality 73-8
womanization of America 81
politics 108
post-Fordism 1, 2, 3
post-modernity 70, 73
Postgate, R. 42
Good Food Guide 42, 44-8
postmodernity 73
postmodernization 12

Random House 119
Readers' Digest 58, 60
representation 108
restaurant guide 41-52
class and gender 43
good food 42
Hotel Magnifique experience 45, 48
pursuit of satisfaction 44
as romance 51-2
Richards, T. 3
Roosevelt, F.D. 135
Ross, A. 72
Rossillon, M.(O'Galop) 146, 149, 150, 152
Russell, G. 167

San Francisco Zen Center 123
Savage, W.G. 30
scuba diving 15
1960s 88-105
advertising 100, 101
ethic of fun 101, 104
fathoming the Phenomenon 93-6
James Bond 99
masculinity and consumerism 101-4
media promotion 97-101
television action series 99
scuba-diving boom 104-5
self-authentication 127
self-esteem 131
self-help
1930s America 131-41
brief history 133-4

Christian ethics 133
globalization of American 138-41
Great Depression 134-5
Life begins at Forty 136-8
mental hygiene movement 135
self-identity 5
self-improvement 10
self-realization 123
sex 16
sexuality
new and old middle-class 75, 77
Playboy 73-8
Shepherd's Bush 42
Simmel, G. 8
Skeggs, B. 157, 170
Skin Diver magazine 103
Slater, D. 2, 71
social groupings 6
Sontag, S. 111
Soviet Union 71, 72
spirituality 16
Supreme Life 56, 57, 58
symbolic capital 157, 158, 161, 163, 165, 168, 170

Tassajara Bread Book 121
taste
formation 11, 15, 17
practices 10
Taylor, P. 24
Taylorism 140
television
DIY shows 4
therapy culture 138
Thomas, D. 78
Thoreau, H.D. 133
Thorp, J. 167
Time 60
totalitarianism 72
Toulouse-Lautrec, H. 145
traditionalism 42

United Kingdom (UK)
food 14
United States of America (USA) 14, 46, 55, 81

1930S self-help books 131-41
black middle class 54-68
Cold War culture 70-85
consumer-oriented economy 91
Great Depression 16
middle class expansion 92
new middle classes 15
University of California 95
Urban League 56
urban living 8
Urry, J. 126

Veblen, T. 8
Vickers, Y. 78
visual media 108, 109, 111

Walton, I. 76
Warde, A. 1, 28

and Martens, L. 47
Weaver, Sir L. 167
Weber, M. 6
Wedgwood, J. 7
Welles, O. 77
Wheaton, B. 89
White, F. 29, 44
   Arts and Crafts Movement ideals
      49
   Good Food Register 48-51
Wilinsky, B. 75
Williams, R. 93
Williamson, J.126
Woollacott, J. and Bennett, T. 99
Wylie, P. 81

Yaeger, P. 46